# TRANSLATING Coaching
## Codes of Practice

Other books in the Series:

*Much Ado About COACHING* (Rydwairay)

# TRANSLATING Coaching Codes of Practice

*Insights from the leading edges
of everyday practitioners*

### EDITED BY

## Yvonne Thackray

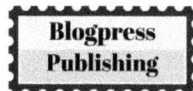

**Blogpress
Publishing**

Most of the material in this book first appeared on the World Wide Web in 2014-2016 on www.the-goodcoach.com

First Printing: 2016

ISBN: 978-0-9954895-1-6

Published by Blogpress Publishing: London

Special discounts are available on quantity purchases by corporations, associations, educators, and others. For details, contact the publisher at www.blogpresspublishing.org

# CONTENTS

## Chapter 3: Practitioners' next steps: Refining their practice/approach

**PART 2: CUTTING EDGE PERFORMANCE IN PRACTITIONER DELIVERY**

## Chapter 4: Creating engagement between the coach and the clients

## Chapter 5: Creating and maintaining that quality of attention

## Chapter 6: Perspectives on measuring coaching impact

## Chapter 7: Practitioner's self-reporting coaching impact from their front line

## PART 3: IDENTIFYING THE COMPETITIVE EDGES IN THE MARKET

## Chapter 8: Identifying the competitive edges – The reality of practice

## Chapter 9: Identifying the competitive edges – Coaching as a "profession"

## PART 4: EXTENDING THE FRONTIERS OF KNOWLEDGE THROUGH EACH PRACTITIONER'S PRACTICE

## Chapter 10: Moving forward, what next

# PREFACE

## WHERE IT BEGAN:

After publishing the first book, *Much Ado About Coaching* (2014), we intuitively knew that we were doing something different. For a start we weren't telling people what needed to be done, rather we were interested in sharing our experiences of what was working in practice through our writing. We were looking to inspire others to reflect on our collective learning experiences. We wanted to consider the insights that were relevant to others and help them find their own ways to apply them in their day-to-day. What's more we were breaking the rules and disrupting the norms that exist both in our field of coaching and publishing.

We were doing something that was quite leading edge too – we just needed to be able to articulate what that was! We needed to break down what it was we were doing. Everyone had a learning mind set. We all felt comfortable working with someone else from the group who supported us through the writing process. We were all excited in being able to share how our coaching experiences shaped us personally and professionally on a regular basis. On top of that there was something in our approach that supported each of us to stay open and honest about our practice. It required us to step back and do some further investigation to check whether we were on the right path. Hence it was necessary for us to expand our reach, gain new insights and perspectives, draw on each other's experience, and give each other room to continually develop our own practice. You might call that practitioner research, or even peer-to-peer coaching.

## WHERE WE ARE NOW:

Fast forward two years, and we're very excited to celebrate our second book, *Translating Coaching Codes of Practice: Insights from the leading edges of everyday practitioners*. A 'growing' collection of coaching knowledge from the leading edges of everyday practitioners who were answering a rather challenging question, "*How do you validate your own coaching practice?"* Now let me be clear this wasn't the lead-in question that we put forward to our practitioners – we'd scare a lot of them away rather than attract them! Coaches are still not well practiced at reporting their own practice and so we took a coaching approach (coaching coaches even) by asking them either what was currently important to them in their practice or what their top three coaching experiences were. It also became apparent that practitioners have very few opportunities to talk about these positive experiences. With every conversation we had we saw how they 'lit up' and became more engaged and animated as they got a chance to relive and share those moments with someone else. And then, when they translated those experiences and wrote them into their blog-article that gets published, another blog-article appears, and then another.

*Translating Coaching Codes of Practice* is an edited volume from a series of blogs first published on *the good coach*. Over fifteen established practitioners share their insights and experiences of how they translate these questions through their practice, and an exercise we think could be of value to coaches generally. Each coach works in a different context and in different locations around the world. Each share their leading edges of how they are making it work for them. Working with them led us to our most important insight, even confirmation, to date (particularly amongst *the good coach* blogitorial team): **the leading edges in practice come from every day practitioners**.

*"Why? What's the evidence?"* we hear you asking. Let us share how we arrived to this point:

- **In the market:** They have all been working and applying their coaching approach in contexts that best fit their practice, and they have developed their credibility and a reputation for delivering a professionally tailored learning space that meets the objectives of other stakeholders involved.

- **As a practitioner:** They are all passionate, and work hard at giving that quality of attention. This leads to engaging conversations that support their clients in strategically meeting their endeavours and continuously reaching their evolving potential.

- **Articulating practice via blogs:** They have willingly (and possibly even unknowingly) begun to translate and share their codes of practice that are unique to them. These practices are typically hard for another individual to fully replicate. Everyone has their own words infused with their own personal meaning to talk about what it is they are doing. Being able to talk about their approach, describing those behaviours and interactions in their own way, they bring alive the words and action in the context and environment they're each working in.

Moreover, the practice of writing a series of blogs and articles presented another opportunity to report on their experiences (some even call this their real Continuing Professional Development). These opportunities may be based around some immediate situation(s) or may be the result of an accumulation of learning experiences over a period of time (a month, six months, a year, even a lifetime). More often than not it's a combination of the two. Periodically sharing snapshots of the breadth and depth of their coaching from their environments, they are also disclosing their own personal development through their professional practice as well as demonstrating tenets of good research into where real knowledge lives about what works.

Connecting lived experience with, and where appropriate, to a broad array of currently available knowledge from the wider context, practitioners draw from both of these to make sense of and inform the space they work in with others. The breadth of their knowledge base is also compelling because it suggests that the current places for finding relevant coaching knowledge is too limited and narrow for the realities which practitioners actually operate in. Furthermore, it healthily demonstrates how practitioners are themselves life-long learners. This should in turn inform the coaching field that life-long learning is fundamental in any of the studies and research involved as we don't yet have a final solution.

Encouraging and nurturing this type of articulation and reporting of practice, which is then published through various platforms and made available to others in coaching, is raising the level of quality and rigor. Additionally, it reveals how each coach has found ways to move beyond the conventional codes of practice that can be viewed as being too vague and out of touch with people's reality. Experienced practitioners have a much more sophisticated approach of ensuring how they are 'fit for purpose' with their market. As one of the contributor's and reviewer's said, "*It's a high quality pick 'n mix where each time you dip into the book you'll look forward to coming back for more insights!*"

And so, the first three parts of *Translating Coaching Codes of Practice* presents:

Part 1: Leading edges in practitioner learning and development

Part 2: Cutting edge performance in practitioner delivery

Part 3: Identifying the competitive edges in the market

## WHERE NEXT

Our approach is not to rush to a 'final solution'; rather we're more interested in finding those patterns that may eventually lead to similarities that have evolved from the realities of the diverse practice that already exists. We can also learn how to move forward from other disciplines, and they may act both as a cautionary tale and an example of technological ingenuity, about the learning still to come about in coaching.

For example, from the field of biosciences the Human Genome Project (HGP): an ambitious international effort to sequence the three billion nucleotides within thirteen years that would revolutionise health and welfare benefits. It started with a simple premise known as the Central Dogma coined by Francis Crick, "*DNA makes RNA makes protein makes us*". However, it became clear through the research that protein constituted less than 2 percent of the DNA. The remaining 98 percent was referred to as 'junk' and as Rose and Rose (2014) pointed out, "*the term [junk], however, proved to be seriously misleading, with painful consequences for the hope of the HGP as 'the book of life'...But at the time when the HGP was being contemplated, it was the genes, not the junk, which offered clinical hope and raised the possibility of future patents*[1]."

---

[1] Hilary Rose and Steven Rose. *Genes, Cells and Brains: The Promethean Promises of the New Biology.* (Verso Publishing, 2014) pg 32

The term junk suggests that there was a lot of material non-relevant, however as studies progressed this turned out to be a long way from being junk. "*The revelation of the complexity of the human genome came as a surprise, at least in part due to the sequencers' failure to recognise the significance of the fact that the genome is the product of 3.5 billion years of evolutionary history[1]."* A lot has been discovered, but it has not produced that immediate personalised medicine based on genetic information (gene therapy).

There are a lot of parallels, even cautionary tales and lessons we can learn from the HGP and usefully bring into coaching – starting with evolutionary history; being curious about diversity rather than setting arbitrary boundaries (or what scientists unfortunately referred to as 'junk'); and the robustness of coaching approaches that may eventually hold the legal designation of a 'professional' that includes independent and objective validation. In this multidimensional and multifaceted world that coaching currently occupies, the good coach chooses to adopt an approach to ownership that is in-line with best practice for achieving real independence.

And so, in *Part 4: Extending the frontiers of knowledge through practitioners' practice,* the final section in *Translating Coaching Codes of Practice,* we offer some practical and pragmatic perspectives about sharing practitioner experience that we think will continue shaping the perceptions and insights of our field. We suggest using an open approach towards practitioner research, and in parallel building up a quality body of practitioner knowledge that truly represents the leading edges of everyday practitioners. That is where the real knowledge lives. We just have to keep finding ways to get to it.

Y.T. (May 2016)

---

[1] Ditto, pg 44

# ACKNOWLEDGEMENTS

*"Never doubt that a small group of thoughtful, committed
people can change the world.
Indeed, it is the only thing that ever has."*

*– Anon*

Our starting point.

I would like to thank everyone who has supported and participated in the editorial process to make this book possible. In this second book, I would like to thank the foresight and patience of Sue Young and Jeremy Ridge who were able to keep up with me and ensure that *Translating Coaching Codes of Practice* continues in the same vein and strength as *Much Ado About Coaching* and now with greater depth and breadth. I would like to thank again my original fearless 'just do it' fellow co-editors Charlotte Rydlund and Nicholas Wai, and obi-Sven Wilson who have continued to support our endeavours in the second book. Without any of these individuals neither of these books would have been possible. I'd also like to thank Light Hurley for being a formidable proof reader and Sven Wilson with Luciana Mazzocco for producing our stunning front cover.

This also wouldn't have been possible without our fellow authors and practitioners entrusting us with their words and believing that we can altogether leverage our collective intelligence and make a difference. Thank you to all our contributors for making a contribution to this book – Aurora Aritao, Charlotte Rydlund, Doug Montgomery, Eamon O'Brien, Isobel Gray, Jeremy Ridge, Kim Stephenson, Laura Bradshaw-Heap, Laurent Terseur, Lilian Abrams, Liz Pick, Lucille Maddalena, Lynne Hindmarch, Martina Weinberger, Morton Patterson, Nicholas Wai, R. Ramamurthy Krishna and Sue Young.

Finally I'd like to thank my greatest supporters, inspirations, and motivators. My husband, James Thackray, who has been my role model and always shown me that there are multiple ways of working towards living one's potential. He has listened endlessly to my witterings and he repeatedly scoured each draft with undue patience. And to my parents for giving me the greatest opportunities in life and showing how to live with them with compassion and humility.

I end with a quote from Margaret Mead; a choice inspired by a good friend, colleague and peer blogitor, Jeremy Ridge:

> *"Laughter is man's most distinctive emotional expression. Man shares the capacity for love and hate, anger and fear, loyalty and grief, with other living creatures. But humour, which has an intellectual as well as an emotional element belongs to man."*
>
> *– Margaret Mead (1979)*

# PART 1

## *Leading edges in practitioner learning and development*

# CHAPTER 1

# TRACING THE BOUNDARIES OF COACHING IN THE WIDER CONTEXT

## Coming out with all the benefits the coach gets from coaching

*Jeremy Ridge*

**t's a secret** in the industry that coaching does not just benefit the coachee. Coaching also benefits the coach themselves. The discipline of coaching might be considered more valuable if there was more attention drawn to what the coach can learn and gain by working with another person as a coach.

A straight model of coaching lays it on that coaching is just a sort of professional transaction. It implies the delivery of a service by the professional and an addressment of the requirements and needs of the client and the sponsors.

The coach's reward is typically seen as a financial re–imbursement for their time... an investment in the learning that enables them to deliver the service required.

The coach is not generally seen to meet any other needs of their own.

Having had the chance to study this wide field over several decades, I think the evidence is moving inexorably towards how coaches can only really deliver quality coaching by being a **full** person in the presence of the coachee (it's more than simply having a 'coaching presence').

After all

- Coaches are as involved in the dialogue as the coachee.

- Coaches can get a very important range of other benefits from this process.

- Coaches can learn something themselves!

Of course, this isn't simple. However, it is important to get the issue out into the open as it deserves more attention.

Personally, I have never met a single person who hasn't had the capability to amaze me. Getting a sense of a coachee's life and work experience, how they go about those things, enriches me every time. The wide range of personality out there means there is always a new perspective and a fresh energy to revitalize my own.

So, what are these other benefits?

## LEARNING ABOUT OTHER PEOPLE

The central issue here is like dark matter because it concerns learning about *a normal, healthy person*. Not a preconception, or a statistic, but a unique person with their own problems, goals and peculiarities. In short, someone that you meet every day!

Coaching is aimed at working with people who have an established and healthy approach to their life and work. Coachees are people. People at the seat of their own learning. Quite often coachees are so fully engaged in their busy lives that the coaching is an excuse for them to get some space and time away from it all and make sense of it.

## Our greatest learning challenge

There isn't really much established about a normal healthy life and its quirks. Given the possible differences between healthy normal lives, that isn't surprising. However, there is an abundance of extensive studies and generalizations on the problems of people, where there is an emphasis of difficulty rather than opportunity, and where obstacles overcome the natural ability people have to learn and grow.

Strangely enough, some difficulties of this sort can also make it easier to study. Patterns of behaviour are, by their very identity as patterns, established and consistent. Therein lies the problem. A healthy life should bring choice. We can choose how to behave. We can choose how to perceive things – *for example, is the bottle half full or half empty?* – and these decisions have important implications.

Most of the models that still inform coaching come from very different circumstances. Sometimes these sources offer valuable insights, but sometimes there are important gaps:

- At one end we have psychotherapy and counselling. These methods are designed to deal with the issues that can get stuck in a person's attitude towards their situation. It requires special care to unpack the significance that come with these difficulties.

All too often the learning is just practice... but without the insight to direct it.

- On the other, more structured, end, there is the emergence of 'cognitive behaviour therapy'. CBT is a straight rational approach, an analytical process for people with 'negative' patterns that upset normal healthy life, as we currently view them.

There is something of a telling emphasis in this approach though as every other person is labelled 'troubled' rather than healthy.

- And lastly we have psychology. Though, encouragingly, positive psychology has started to admit there are healthy people around who, rather than being considered automatically troubled, are acknowledged to need something different. However, this view in psychology is in its infancy.

Psychology wants to remain a traditional science – if it is too complex there would be real difficulty studying it. Generalities are easier to study for the scientist because they admit of patterns that are to be repeated and known. They are a way to interpret information and categorise personality. However, this potentially excludes the unique, of which every healthy human being is. In short, generalities can also be seen to be limits.

It is therefore easier to put immense effort and study into cases where people have a difficulty rather than an opportunity. If it was so simple, we probably wouldn't still be using the term 'coaching'!

For example, there is a term called 'adult learning' – or even andragogy – which is the filing system used for a huge amount of work on how normal healthy adults best go about learning.

But this theme is still a bit disjointed and abstract with the insights available.

Really, we learn about what and who another person is through our interactions and experiences of health and personality, and by sharing that with each other.

## GROWING AS A PERSON ... ENHANCING THE COACH'S OWN 'SELF'

Another huge benefit from coaching is getting to know what others can do to enhance your own 'self'. If coaching is just seen as a conversational exercise based around asking questions, rather than in the way it can transform the coach, then we are avoiding getting to the heart of how it works. We are ignoring one side to the relationship of coaching, without which even the coachee's side of the relationship cannot be understood.

When working with normal healthy people, our coaching circumstances are still very different from other sources of insight that focus more on the limited patterns of behaviour a person can have.

As one person said to me, recently:

> *"Jeremy, I don't want the nodding donkey approach, here. I want to know what you would do in my situation. I am quite capable of making my own mind up about what I will do, but I want you to show me you understand the situation / opportunities I have, and give me a fresh perspective about them. I don't want lots of theory and questions. Let's talk in my language and terms about it. I assume you have done your homework; I will add to it, and then let's have a real conversation – like being with the sort of ideal colleague."*

The main route to this discovery is finding the part of myself that the coachee feels comfortable with in their world.

This enables a coachee to build a space in the relationship, to progressively explore and find new experience and understanding about their world as it comes through to them. This requires developing awareness and appreciation of whole worlds of experience.

It often feels like a privilege to have the chance to exercise awareness in other people's worlds, and this adds to my own self.

Getting to this point is what coaching is about, yet it is so difficult to talk about.

One thing I am certain of though is that coaching is not mentoring, as I am not an established expert in the world on agenda – rather a fresh and independent person!

## LEARNING HOW TO FIND THE MOST EFFECTIVE BEHAVIOURS IN BEING YOURSELF!

Peer coaching (otherwise known as action learning etc.) is about highlighting how people without special training seem to be able to produce 'coaching' type outcomes.

Ordinary people can bring the sorts of special relationship skills as a matter of everyday learning and with an appreciation of others in dialogue. This to mutual benefit.

Can the coach be 'separate' from their coachee – or do they need to be fully involved depending on the person they are?

This question presents quite a challenge to coaching. Imagine if this caught on; what might happen to coaching in the future? A challenge lies here for all the moral high ground that coaches like.

So there are lots of obstacles in finding the right sort of self to be in the situation. There are matters of trust to be established. The coach does not merely utter the words 'trust me' and believe trust is then established.

I meet people with lots of normal healthy feelings – a vast variety of them – which are as different from emotions as night and day, and which is why some of the other areas of knowledge about people still lag behind.

Even the most confident and capable people are vulnerable. Even they can have feelings about this. How to ensure these feelings are received in a healthy manner is also a side still to emerge.

## WHAT'S NEXT?

For a coach to suggest there is nothing of their 'self' in the room, even when they are supposed to be straight with the client, is impossible. Whether we like it or not we are all present.

We look at a person. Words follow. Even in looking at another person there is already an explosion of inferences. I don't know how much longer we can ignore the personal chemistry that is unique to each person, each coach, each relationship, in any situation.

The presence of 'self' is vital to the kind of connection and conversation that coaching relies on. Unless I admit I am also another human being in the room, finding how to empathise with and appreciate another's feelings, I soon see my energy toward progress weaken.

We should be coming out and sharing all the benefits coaches gain from coaching. Are we really doing our job as coaches if it is only for the financial gain? For some, coaching will only be the lens through which they operate – they have no other way of knowing whether it has been of value. They often have difficulty explaining outputs from coaching, unless it is through money, as long–term consequence.

After each and every coaching session, I am a different person – a result of the new insights and experience of another person's world. That is an important gain for me.

What I ask is this:

*"Does this happen for you?"*

# What is coaching?

*Yvonne Thackray*

The moment has finally arrived. Those words roll off their tongue, *"So, tell me, what do you do for a living?"* With a sharp intake of breath and a sigh, the person in front musters their bravado and sureness: *"I'm an executive coach."* Blankness, followed by realization. How should the questioner respond? Some politely roll their eyes and shake their head in condolence. Others simply correct the executive coach standing in front of them and say: *"Oh, you're a life coach. Well that's just like counselling really…"* before moving onto another topic. Some genuinely do not know and ask, *"What is coaching?"* A minority quietly break out into a knowing smile, relax, and begin talking about their own experiences of coaching.

*Welcome to the confusing world of the newly emerging field called executive coaching.*

## WHAT'S IN A NAME THAT WE CALL A COACH? THE SEMANTIC HISTORY OF COACHING

A black box surrounds coaching. Originally the word 'coach' was that of an object. In those days it was used to describe a carriage or 'kocsi' in Kocs, a place near Buda in Hungary. However, the word has since undergone transformation. Its more current representation is of a skilful expert who works alongside management in 'unlocking a person's potential [and] maximising their own performance'. The noun 'coach' stems from the Latin *curro*, 'to run, to travel, to hurry, to speed, to move, to proceed, to traverse.'

Placing coaching in its historical context, Stec (2012: 232) identifies four distinct but overlapping phases, which are also complicated by the issue of payment and professionalism:

1. A technology that was a medium of transportation (fifteenth century to present day);

2. An object capable of conferring status (eighteenth century);

3. A character in sport (nineteenth century to present day); and

4. A management concept (late twentieth century).

The coach, in the context of carrying people from one place to another, has moved from horse–pulled coaches to describing how much an individual is willing to pay for space and comfort on modern transportations. During the eighteenth and nineteenth centuries, prestige was associated with the passenger (typically aristocrats), and the coach driver; who was capable of driving the horse and carriage with impressive speed, skill and responsibility. Coach drivers were admired for their impressive performance. Gentlemen (amateurs) 'sought coaching' to drive a team of horses which would pull the coach. This process would include rules of dress i.e. wearing the appropriate attire and the time before requesting coaching.

Within the eighteenth century, references to a sport coach became firmly associated with athletic competitions via rowing. These coaches were members of the working class, much like the earlier coach drivers.

This was also a revival period for the cult of sport, take for example Pierre de Coubertin and the Olympic games, in which the athlete symbolised "*the key figure of ancient somatic idealism*" and "*demonstrated an epochal change of emphasis in practice behaviour*" (Sioterdijk 2013: 27). In addition, educational reforms in 1870, particularly in England, increased the number of children (1.25–5 million) attending school. This in turn required access to more sport coaches (retired professionals) because sports were an integral part of the curricula for achieving social control (Stec 2012).

The coach (as both object and technology) represents two things. The coach is both a contraption that carried its passenger from place to place and also something that needed to be controlled and skilfully steered by the coach driver who needed to understand the assemblage (a team of horses, the carriage and its suspension, road conditions, acceptable comfort levels to the passengers versus speed). Accepting that technology (the coach) comes before him, the driver only becomes foregrounded after he has demonstrated his capabilities. In sports, the coach who was previously a professional or had credible experience in that game is now being paid to 'coach' others, from their experience, to improve their athletes' performance in preparation for competitions and to watch from the side lines[1].

In the eighteenth and nineteenth century, professional sport began to seem tainted because it was viewed equivalently with prostitution, since professional sportsmen used their body to earn money (Stec 2012). Furthermore there was a mixing of class. Regardless of the values being promoted in sports, aristocrats were not particularly interested in competing with others, though it was important to maintain "*the rules ... the de facto removal of the labouring class from eligibility*" (Harper and Hammond 1977: 124 cited by Stec 2012). Against the changing national landscape and the clashes of class and language, coaches persevered. Today, coaches are integral to individual and team sports.

Moving into the twentieth century, sports coaches continued to thrive. With a change in management techniques (post Taylorism and post Fordism) and an increase in leisure time and an affinity to sports, managers turned to books published by sports coach for inspiration.

---

[1] We should caution though that not every professional sportsman can be a coach either.

This is also why business writers and executive coaches frequently draw upon the experiences of athletic team coaches in 'bringing the best out of the individual and team' to describe what they do in workplace coaching.

## THE REALITY...

Retrospectively, it's a lot easier to broadly offer reasons why the field began: executive coaching emerged as a response to changes in modern working life in contemporary society.

For the recipients of workplace coaching, managers and leaders (also broadly referred to as executives) are typically under greater pressure to deliver results working in or leading a 'lean' team within a matrix organisational structure. At the same time these same managers and leaders are resolving complex challenges as a consequence of the rapid advancements in technology, innovating sustainable solutions that are important to maintain customers, and growing their market against fierce competition locally and globally. Changes in organisational structures, like the matrix structure (where employees are grouped by both function and product), and the working of project teams virtually and face to face with peers around the world, has changed working practices. Rather than a 'command and control' management approach we now see a risk taking and problem solving style that places more emphasis and accountability on individual and team autonomy. Furthermore, peripheral employees have been shifted in many organisations away from long–term employment to frequent short–term contracts.

And so, here are my top three reasons why executive coaching emerged:

1.  Executive coaching emerged as a response to changes in modern working life within a contemporary setting.

2.  Executive coaching creates the conditions for executives to work through the various degrees of complexities, often with less experienced/available resources, to be even more productive and still remain competitive in the market with their self–identity intact.

3. Executive coaching provides the space for executives to reflexively and meaningfully organise their thoughts and potential actions. It is a place for continuous self–improvement in order to adapt to the volatility of markets.

## EXPLAINING WHAT COACHING IS

That's a much harder question to answer beyond the simple model of coaching! Unfortunately, no one size fits all. There is no universalist paradigm. This is because individuals are unique. Coaches need to continually create and sustain appropriate conditions within which their clients can work through personal challenges.

Let me describe and share some examples of clients I've coached around some form of work–related issue:

- A Chinese lady (in her late forties) who worked as a senior HR manager and who was based in Beijing in English for an international medical and healthcare organisation.

- A retired Singaporean gentleman (in his late fifties), who formally served in the national army and then worked overseas in the technology industry, later repatriating to his homeland to start an entrepreneurial enterprise around sustainability.

- A Serbian gentleman (in his mid thirties) who formally worked in sales and training for a local engineering company before becoming a co–entrepreneur for potable water business, and who later lived through the political upheavals and changes of former Yugoslavia.

- An African–American lady (in her mid twenties), working as an entrepreneur fashion designer in bridal and special occasion dresses based in New York, with a concern to developing her online web presence.

In the face of so many unique needs, motivations and readiness, how do we explain to the 99.99994% what it is that we do as an executive coach?

How do we explain to the 99.99994% that coaching is like a conversation, but one which helps to sharpen both the competitive and collaborative edge of the individual in their working environment, impacting on both their professional and personal lives?

## HOW TO PROGRESS IT FORWARD

The market of today is a more sophisticated consumer of executive coaching. It wants to see progress. A current challenge in the field of coaching is about who 'owns' the definition of coaching and, consequently from which, how an expert body of knowledge will stem from this definition.

It is clear that each coaching practitioner comes from a diverse social and cultural background with a unique learning approach. Let our first steps towards understanding what it is we each do and how we apply our unique coaching approach in the various markets we operate in by simply sharing them as blogs, for example (like I and many others do at the good coach).

I've blogged about my practice of coaching for almost three years whilst writing over 30 pieces. I've continually investigating and connecting coaching to the broader disciplines (the social sciences, philosophy, politics, psychology, economics, consultancy, technology) and the market to really understand what coaching is. Every conversation I have on coaching helps me to understand a little more of and make sense of it. Altogether, they all inform and help me make more sense of my coaching approach and a better appreciation of the field of coaching. And perhaps, along with other like–minded practitioners, we can better demonstrate and validate the practice of coaching together.

# Great leadership and great coaching have a lot in common!

## *Jeremy Ridge*

L eadership has always been something we know is important. We are still working at this idea of how coaching fits into the picture. I would like to put forward a view that we are discovering that there may be more in common between the two ideas. That great leadership and great coaching are both increasingly concerned with getting the best out of others and have a lot in common in general.

What comes to mind when you think of leadership? Is it where the leader is visibly the leader? Climbing out of the trenches to lead the troop? Or in front of the press – making a statement about how something important is going to be handled. Or on the sports field, taking charge and telling the team what to do?

I am fascinated by the gradually evolving image of 'it' that people have. I have seen its image go through important transitions in how leadership works, for example:

- It is something you are either born with or not.

- It is something that depends on whether you have been born in the right social class.

- It is something that depends on whether you have had the right class of education – been to the 'right school or university' or not.

In more recent times:

- It is something that is granted by appointment (i.e. giving someone a title means automatically that whatever they do is leadership – whether they know what they are doing or not).

- There is only ever one leader. It doesn't make sense to have more than one after all.

- Leadership is about being able to take something important away from people unless they comply. Leadership requires 'power'.

The increasing challenges to these sorts of views, of the most effective forms of leadership, seem to coincide with the sudden surge of interest in this idea of coaching. It is about getting the best out of other people; even the really challenging thought that people can actually 'learn' leadership (though we still tend to refer to it as leadership 'development'.) In this case it's not mystical any longer!

The really exciting opportunity that seems to be emerging is the rather amazing idea that everyone can be a leader. This really does start to challenge some old thinking. Everyone can do something in their circumstances that can make something happen – to the benefit of all concerned.

Leaders encounter real challenges all the time. Especially if their leadership is founded on older principles. Just as coaching seems to have coincided with a degree of confidence among the wider population about themselves and their right to their own point of view.

The onset of education, in particular, spells a real death knell for some approaches to leadership. People have a growing ability to think for themselves. They no longer live in a small village – ignorant of the wider world. Leaders used to be able to bluff their way. Sound assertive and confident enough, and it should work – because your followers won't know anything, and will just fall in line. No longer!

Then came the internet! And social media. And even blogging.

If you can't take something from people in order to ensure compliance, then the real challenge for leadership becomes how to get people to follow you. Even if you are right, unless you can get people to follow you, leadership doesn't work. What does *a would–be* leader do then?

The real challenge for great leadership is to enable people to recognise and follow their own will. To engage them as their own person. This can require the coach to set a good example – be a role model of getting the best out of themselves – just like leadership requires setting a good example for others to follow.

This is starting to sound like what great coaching is about; getting people to fully engage with their selves, to make as much as they want, and as much as they are able to make of it, in their circumstances.

Sometimes there is just not the time for this approach of enabling people to learn for themselves about what the leader suggests. People will recognise this and realise at times they have to place their bet that the leader does know the answer.

I also believe that being directive in coaching can be appropriate in certain circumstances too; such as dealing with someone of supreme and mature confidence, who wants to know what you really think about their situation, and will make up their own mind without falling into simple adoption of it.

Increasingly, the really great leaders realise they need time and opportunity to get people to 'buy in' to ideas. They will often go so far as to make sure the 'followers' are given the opportunity to believe, and then lead, from their own understanding. Really great leadership can be completely invisible. In these cases the followers feel themselves to have the limelight; they feel themselves as the leaders. How much more non–directive can you get?

PART 1: Leading edges in practitioner learning and development

One thing is certainly increasingly true for leadership – it requires a real quality of attention to getting people to understand and see the way for themselves. Sometimes leaders themselves learn something important from this as well. They may even be great enough to accept they don't have all the answers right from the start.

So next time you set out to make something happen, what will your approach be? Ask yourself: Which sort of leader are you?

**PART 1: Leading edges in practitioner learning and development**

# How coaching is becoming an essential basis for much bigger scale interventions

## *Sue Young*

**I have just been** watching the final speeches from the Paris Climate Change Conference and was struck by the scale of the task and achievement. 195 countries and their representatives, the national interests, the translators, the negotiators all coming to an agreement. There was such a strong sense of personal and individual connection having been made.

## WHERE COACHING INVOLVES SPECIAL AND CAREFUL USE OF ESSENTIAL BEHAVIOURS

I was also struck by the different style and attention to personal relationships conventionally untypical of such large scale international conferences. For example:

- A real sense of handling and working with individual differences.

- A great deal of attention being given to ensure that the voices of the traditionally weakest were heard.

- An explicit recognition that the nature of circumstances and challenges involved are very diverse.

- That there was clear demonstrated respect, empathy and trust amongst the players at the end.

The urgent non–negotiable imperative of climate change and increasing demand from democratic nations is driving the use of behaviours (most of which are taking place in individual conversations in 'safer' space behind the scenes) that we very much associate with coaching – mutual respect, active listening, helping others articulate their perspective and rapport building between individuals with different interests and perspectives.

## SEEING THE SCOPE FOR THESE SPECIAL BEHAVIOURS

I see strong parallels between such large scale world events and in the 'coaching approach' at use in organisations. This goes way beyond the traditional coaching format of confidential one to one sessions which may be contracted for in particular contexts such as in the executive, sport and health fields.

## COACHING BEHAVIOURS CAN BE A NATURAL CHOICE

They have always been there as part of the mix of people in a society. The diplomat, the local 'wise' woman or man, who is regarded as source of wise counsel, the local priest or vicar as a source of confidential 'space'. The difference today is the explicit attention to this form of interaction as an organisational behaviour, operating not only with individuals, but teams and, increasingly, as a key part of some organisational cultures.

Getting these quality behaviours into organisations is still a challenge; coaching has been increasing hugely in popularity in recent years[1]. Coaching skills and a coaching mind set are becoming increasingly regarded as an important part of leadership and management. The awareness is there, but the readiness, by individuals and organisations to make the adjustments required is still a major issue occupying the

---

1 See blogs in the good coach

growing number of organisations seeking to integrate more of a coaching approach as part of their culture.

## Examples of how they are beginning to become a fundamental part of wider organisation interventions

So what is driving this wider attention to the subject of coaching and the use of such behaviours? Wide reference is made in writing and research to the impact of such factors as the pace of change, greater global connectivity, increased uncertainty and volatility. There is a greater requirement for managers to quickly learn, and to be able to do this collaboratively with a wider and more interdependent, complex range of stakeholders. All of this at a relentless pace. As a coaching practitioner and facilitator, I hear about and work first hand with how this plays out in organisations on the ground.

For example:

- **High potential manger development:** Coaching is increasingly part of the mix of interventions used on high potentials and middle to senior leadership development programmes.

- **Leadership development:** Coaching is often part of the core subject matter on leadership development programmes, where it is increasingly regarded as a core leadership capability.

- **Internal coaches:** The training of internal coaches has grown in organisations as more businesses see the value of having dedicated internal coaching resources. Most people in organisations take this on as a part–time role, in addition to their mainstream role. A few organisations, such as the major professional firms, have sufficient enough demand that they now seek to add value through use of a dedicated team of internal coaches.

- **Coaching skills programmes:** Increased availability of dedicated coaching skills programmes made available to people at all management levels.

- **Action learning or peer learning groups:** I see an increase in use of 'action learning' or 'peer learning' groups where the aim for that small group (typically six to eight in size) is to support each other in their learning goals and act as co–coaches. The emphasised role of the group is to help each other to think. They seek to only bring to an individual's slot what that individual wants. The facilitator/ supervisor's role is to ensure that space is held. Intervention on the process only happens when, for example, there is a rush in enthusiasm for group members to impose their solutions. Although it is not always called that, undoubtedly these kinds of learning groups use and model their own coaching approach.

- **Organisational learning interventions:** Increasingly, I am involved in work related organisational learning interventions that take a coaching approach. Team coaching would be one such, where the emphasis is on working with both the team collectively and individually on progressing organisational priorities e.g. developing strategies and key relationships and their ways of working to be more aligned whilst collectively developing their agenda as a team. These projects tend to be highly dynamic and responsive as they need to work closely with the messiness of the realities of how the individual, team and the organisation works – and particularly where it doesn't work!

- **Organisational change interventions:** I am noticing a rise in increasingly organisational change interventions where there is an emphasis on use of coaching approaches as a core part of the overall organisational direction and strategy.

*To give an example of this:*

A regional healthcare group in the National Health Services (NHS) I am working with is piloting an intervention aimed at individuals on the front line in a range of professional healthcare roles. The goal is to better equip and enable these individuals, encouraging them to experiment with ways to extend their use of coaching approaches. These includes both with fellow healthcare professionals and to increase the use of health coaching approaches with patients.

Seventy percent of national and local healthcare spending is taken up on medication and health professionals' time supporting people with long–term chronic health conditions. These are usually not immediately life threatening, but they are situations where successful outcomes, both for the individual and for the wider NHS system in terms of effectiveness, depend on the individual's capabilities and motivation to self–manage a health regime that suits the individual's life circumstances as much as possible.

This is a dramatic culture shift from the traditional 'expert' led medical model. There are an increasing number of service businesses deploying a coaching approach as part of their service delivery, where a high degree of individual attention is part of the proposition or where close interdependent relationships in the supply chain are vital to delivery.

So what are these still elusive coaching 'qualities' that all of these example interventions illustrate and represent as a direction in the future for coaching? There is a multitude of definitions of coaching[1]. All of these focus in on the nature and qualities of the coaching process.

I would see the following as underpinning wider themes that define an organisational–wide 'coaching approach' moving into the future:

- **Recognising it is a process of continuous learning, not a simple formula approach**: the recognition that there are no 'quick fix' solutions; an iterative evolving approach is required as on–going learning, both individually and collectively, is going to be crucial to organisational and business success.

- **Attention to creating a learning environment:** where the design and testing of new approaches is seen as critical and individuals are actively encouraged to experiment; there is no failure but what matters is the learning we're taking forward from this experience.

- **Actively seeking to engage individuals, in a manner appropriate to each individual's needs**: gaining the value of their knowledge and experience, as core to any change initiative or programme.

---

1 "How we can define coaching – 'Define It For Yourself'" by Jeremy Ridge

The leaders' and managers' ability to do this well is regarded and assessed as a major performance measure.

- **The ability, motivation and courage to put wider organisational priorities before a narrow more self–interested priority**: coaching capabilities and values of staying open, genuinely respecting and valuing differences, building rapport and good questioning and active listening are the skills underpinning this fundamental orientation.

- **Use of feedback:** e.g. 360, team reviews, as a way of working being widely used.

- Learning is regarded as synonymous with change.

- **Coaching support is available in a range of formats suited to the range of context requirements:** regarded as an integral part of organisational development, learning and business strategy, needing to be tailored to the circumstances, stage of development and resulting needs of the organisation.

We should recognise where and how this is happening – spontaneously.

In writing this, it's emerging in a way that could sound idealistic. I contend that all these elements are presently in place in different mixes in different places. There is currently a clear direction present for those with eyes to see it, if they raise their outlook to a larger perspective. It requires those of us involved in coaching, in all its different manifestations, to see what we are already doing as part of something bigger.

For example, I am reminded of the mind set power embedded in Steve Jobs' comment to John Sculley. At the time Jobs was trying to entice Sculley to leave his high–profile, comfortably–successful role in Pepsi to join Apple, then a small fringe player in the computing world.

*"Do you want to sell sugared water all your life, or do you want to change the world?"*

**All of us in coaching choose to have our own vision of how we see the future of coaching and take this into our practice whether we be leaders, managers, independent coaches, organisational coaches, or even just do coaching as part of what we do.**

Achieving the potential coaching has to offer happens in millions of events and interactions already. Bringing these individual voices together into professional and organisational communities in a way that raises the dialogue to this larger perspective will massively add to the speed of embracing all that a coaching approach is capable of achieving. I see 'the good coach' (mentioned above) as potentially one of these communities, representing what experienced coach practitioners can bring to the table to build these differences into a bigger whole.

# How we can define coaching – 'Do it Yourself' (DIY)

## Jeremy Ridge

**C**oaching starts with: "*What is it – exactly?*" Let's get technical straightaway. After all, being special at something means we know what we are doing. OK?

And *the* technical term for all of this is... definition!

However we still have major problems agreeing a definition. Coaching is almost in its fourth decade. What are we missing? A consensus in the field, realising that:

- Coaching is not the same for everyone.

- Definition is not a statement at such a general level; it doesn't identify clearly what is involved.

In my experience of working with other coaches I have come across a wide range of definitions. I am always eager to see how well formed their own is – a definition that works for them and their market. So let's move on from trying to find the simple, single, final solution and recognise, even celebrate, this diversity.

**PART 1: Leading edges in practitioner learning and development**

The future will have to go in this direction. Each person will find their own definition that works for them. (It's called the inexorable march of constructivism in another language!) The irony of diversity is how it keeps things simple – through focus on the single and unique entity of a person.

Actually, everyone seems to have their own, for examples, go to Karen Wise's blog[1] where she has compiled a list of the range of definitions of coaching.

Literature, whether as books or simply ideas, offer concepts that may help some of us make sense of things. It allows us an opportunity of expression for data and patterns we already have but have yet to organise.

Be wary of anyone that gives final solutions!

It is easy to write at a level of generality. It is easy to write with that hint of a crucial breakthrough that the final solution is here, which is then followed by next year's book... and solution. Why? It's not built on sound definition. Even bodies that award credentials change their requirements. This happens every year.

Then there are the times when the marketplace has its own expectations of coaching – which may override everything – resulting in different forms of practices calling themselves coaching.

The marketplace may yet drive us to better ourselves as expectations sharpen.

## WHY DOES DEFINITION MATTER?

Agreeing a definition of 'definition' may be overwhelming for some, but the marketplace/users/regulators want to know what this is that we say we do, whether this has been proven, who can evidence this – all so they can trust what we are doing.

---

[1] [website] https://karenwise.wordpress.com/2010/05/20/what-is-coaching-10-definitions/

## THEN WHY IS IT SO DIFFICULT TO DEFINE COACHING?

The multitude of events that take place in a moment or two of human interaction are still too dynamic for us to easily untangle.

For example, we accept 'contracting' as an essential feature of the coaching process. This is halfway to definition because you are making an important start to defining what is going on between the two people involved.

Of course, contracting is often more tacit than explicit; more in the way that users themselves are capable with (rather than a language everyone could make sense of). However, we know that we also have to make sense to the user. This matters! And I'm including the non–verbal factors too (see Andrews University for a simple outline definition of Non–Verbal Communication Modes[1]).

How often do you include that in the contracting? And then there is the difference at the semantic level. Tone and timing of voice expression is another major feature.

Even then there is still a real problem with the ideal of definition. Sometimes knowledge is still too complex for us to yet study with the methods we have available. This is the issue with coaching.

On the one side, there are people who think that knowledge is something that is common and only exists when anyone can reproduce it from an agreed definition. There are also those on the other side of things, who say it is all too complex and that definition hinges on learning by experience – which is impossible to reproduce because experience is unique to each person.

We need to find the middle ground. The importance of the first position is that the knowledge can be trusted. However, if this method cannot produce the knowledge, then we need to examine why and how to find alternative approaches. But alternative approaches must also provide essential rigour.

---

1 [website] http://www.andrews.edu/~tidwell/bsad560/NonVerbal.html

## HOW TO FIND THE BEST DEFINITION OF COACHING...
## 'DO IT YOURSELF' AND CONSTRUCT YOUR OWN!

The question needs to be *what is it for you*? If you already have one, start to share it with us in the comment box below.

Coaches can do a lot to solve the problem of definition by working out what it is for them, and then sharing that rather than waiting.

I often hear coaches say such things as, *"It's about making a difference"*, with such an intensity of feeling that it indicates a real cathedral of understanding inside their heads about this simple entry point. That's what needs to be shared: 'What is it that makes a difference?'

It's about getting to that level and quality of a definition because each definition is based on unique relationships – according to the unique people involved, as well as being highly dynamic because of influences on mood and concentration levels – that exist from moment to moment.

To begin, take a simple approach to definition such as the basis for contracting. Then, apply 'SMART' levels of definition for some of the patterns you see in the pattern of your practice.

The November 1981 issue of *Management Review* contained a paper by George T. Doran called "There's a SMART way to write management's goals and objectives[1]." It discussed the importance of objectives and the difficulty of setting them.

Ideally speaking, each corporate, department and section objective should be:

- *Specific* – target of a specific area for improvement.

- *Measurable* – quantify or at least suggest an indicator of progress.

- *Attainable* – assuring that an end can be achieved.

- *Realistic* – state what results can realistically be achieved, given available resources.

---

[1] George T. Doran. "There's a SMART Way to Write Management Goals and Objectives", in *Management Review* (AMA Forum, November 1981) pps. 35-36

**PART 1: Leading edges in practitioner learning and development**

- *Time–related* – specify when the result(s) can be achieved.

Work at being SMART in the way you define the patterns of how you do coaching. Are you able to talk about the patterns of how you work with people at this level?

The reality is that each coach has their own formula that is a function of themselves. It's just that we still haven't got here yet. We're still in the game that 'there must be one definition, in the traditional sense.'

## HOW TO DO IT YOURSELF

This will require a particular discipline, one which we are still learning. As with anything we need to build progressively. It goes through stages, not in a single leap (refer to last blog).

We still have a long way to go to get to ways of achieving comparability and validation but we have to make a start somewhere. Traditional forms of research are not designed for this kind of complexity.

Here are some ways to get it started:

1. Find someone to talk to about it who appreciates and can sincerely relate to the way you do things.

2. Get a coach who can engage with you, personally. That way you can really communicate with the level of insight needed as you break down the patterns of smaller events, which may have happened over a few seconds, in relation to larger ones.

3. Find help for putting into words the things that are still just too intuitive for you to explain.

What are the essential common features of your approach? For myself, I always start with how to get someone to smile. It is a universal cue, even though it happens so differently with different people, that the movements of those particular facial muscles, and it has to be done with the eyes too, prelude the breaking down of barriers.

I am still amazed by how effectively certain behaviours get across empathy and respect, sometimes far more than what the other person is used to getting, and how that leverages the process.

- So what do you do in those wonderful cases where it works?

- Do you know your own method intimately enough to explain how it works?

- And could you do so in a real live case such as in a video?

# CHAPTER 2

# PRACTITIONER'S RELATING THEIR COACHING (CODES OF) PRACTICE / APPROACH

## Adult Learning – the real leading edge of coaching

*Sue Young*

From my earliest days with a major multinational organisation, I've worked with a wide range of people. Along the way I've developed my interest in the reality of the issues and challenges others faced in their roles. As a manager I made active use of those perspectives in my business plans. In hindsight I was a good listener. I found that others readily opened up to me – perhaps the beginning of my coaching?

This experience informed my move into management consultancy, where I increasingly saw that people were the biggest potential enablers or saboteurs of business strategy. I saw a need to plan how to get them on board. I moved increasingly into the area of management development. In this I was helping to raise managers' awareness that the changing reality was that nothing in their careers was going to automatically happen. They needed to take charge of their development and careers. That was the start of my interest in self–managed learning.

After about ten years in practice, I decided to take time out to study the formal knowledge and theory of Organisation Development, by undertaking a master's in the field. It was at that time that I discovered the formal body of knowledge around adult learning – wow! It affirmed and resonated for me many of the principles that had been core to my way of working and learning throughout my career.

So why is the body of knowledge around adult learning so invisible when it comes to reading and training materials about coaching, let alone discussions and media coverage and writings in the field?

The key features of the theory of adult learning are not nearly as widely disseminated in coach education and the industry media as the different techniques that can be used in coaching. Take for example the behavioural approach of GROW, NLP, Solutions–focused coaching, TA etc. In addition there's a great deal written about the skills and competencies of coaching. The ICF, EMCC and AC have followed this through in their competencies frameworks. Poorly used, they can be prone to be input led rather than learner–needs led. This risks missing out on the whole point of coaching – enabling the client to take charge of their learning.

So, what does the field of adult learning add? The field of adult learning is an integrative one, drawn from the fields of clinical, developmental and social psychology, sociology and humanist psychology. The focus of its approach is trying to understand, from observation and research, the conditions that enable adult learning (andragogy).

The andragogic model of adult learning makes a number of assumptions:

1. **The need to know** – Adults need to know why they need to learn something before undertaking to learn it. The first task is to help learners become aware of "the need to know" (Tough 1979).

2. **The learners' self–concept** – Adults have a self–concept of being responsible for their own decisions, for their own lives. They become responsible for their learning and are naturally self–directed learners. If people do not feel safe, and are not treated with sufficient respect, they can revert to resistance or passive dependence.

3. **The role of the learners' experience** – The richest source of learning resides within the learners themselves. This experience will be unique to them. Habits of thinking accumulate, some of which may get in the way of seeing new perspectives. Deeper levels of learning involve exploring the meaning of our experience, questioning assumptions and beliefs.

4. **Readiness to learn** – The assumption is that people learn in a staged way. Until we have learned some basics we will not be ready to jump straight into the more advanced tasks. This progression can be accelerated by the right support.

5. **Clear context for learning** – Unless people can see the relevance of the learning to what they want to achieve, they will be unlikely to engage. To achieve maximum outcomes the learner needs to see that the learning they achieve will contribute to something they see as high priority.

6. **Motivation** – While people are responsive to external motivators – e.g. better jobs, more money, they naturally also want to keep growing and developing. In fact today's younger generation sees opportunities to develop as one of their top criteria when judging attractiveness of jobs. In addition, learning is frequently held back by limiting self–belief, and lack of opportunity.

You may notice that it could be referring to coaching. Probably because coaching, out all of the approaches to learning, most closely aligns with adult learning principles.

For me the theory of adult learning provides a bigger context and rationale for a coaching approach to learning. If our coaching is not having the impact we want, I suggest the answer may well lie in reviewing our practice against the underpinning principles of adult learning.

The following few questions may be useful to check out yourself against:

1. **Whose needs am I meeting here?** The coach can get so caught up in the tools and techniques, or approaches they are using, that they may get in their own way of truly seeking to understand and connect to the client's reality. Have our egos become over identified with our chosen techniques and approaches, so much so that we're not open to hearing the real information our client is giving us about their needs? Are we imposing our reality on the client, and getting in the way of their learning?

2. **Am I leaving my client more able and equipped to self–manage their continuing development after my work with them is complete?** Some coaches get so caught up in the impact they want to have on the client in the immediate, they can accidentally encourage dependence. Well in that case, it's not generating sustainable learning and change.

3. **Have I really connected to, and understood the emotions of the client in relation to their learning goals?** Learning can be a strongly emotional issue. This is the territory for the biggest potential shifts in awareness and capabilities, but it requires the right environment to be created. Have I invested sufficiently in the relationship so there is a foundation of rapport and trust we can build on? This can be easily underestimated, particularly as people are experts at masking their more difficult feelings, uncertainties and anxieties. Have I proactively created the safe space for the client to explore their feelings in relation to their objectives?

4. **Have I sufficiently helped the client tap into the depth and value their experience brings?** In our 'expert led' society it is easy for people to massively discount the expertise, knowledge and qualities they bring from their experience. Helping them raise their conscious awareness and connect to the power of their implicit knowledge and be able to articulate and express that is one of the most powerful sources of learning for experienced people. Are we helping our clients maximising learning from their experience sufficiently – both in immediate and longer term life/career contexts?

5.  **Have I got a sense of their readiness to learn and change?** This is about where they are at, where they want to get to and the nature of the gap. If people set themselves stretching goals without chunking it down into tangible sub–goals defining progress, then they may be setting themselves to fail. Or, as a coach, am I being unrealistic in my expectations of them, given where they are? (Emotional readiness can be a major factor here – see 2.)

So, that's an overview of the key features of adult learning theory and a few questions that may be a useful 'health check' on your coaching approach. Particularly for those cases where you feel slightly disappointed in the outcomes, it may help develop your thinking about your expectations and identify things you may test out doing differently.

# Critical assumptions in coaching*

## *Dr. Lucille Maddalena*

A **significant part of** our task as a coach is to enable our clients to examine the critical assumptions they make about themselves.

As an executive coach I work with senior leaders. In spite of their success, their immense experience and their talent, they are like most of us who perhaps created a self–definition as a child and somehow failed to challenge that assumption as we grew.

The learning process of pedagogy is directive: we sit in a classroom and absorb primarily through memorization, specific facts and knowledge. High levels of education provide greater opportunity for exploration, testing and pursuing independent thought, typically in pursuit of knowledge within a framework or discipline.

* [website] Dr. Lucille Maddalena. "WHAT THE !%*# IS ANDRAGOGY" Retrieved from: www.mtmcoach.com (2015)

## ANDRAGOGY

The term andragogy[1] was coined in the 1800s by Alexander Knapp, a German educator, to refer to "*methods or techniques used to teach adults*", later popularized in the 1960s by an American educator, Malcolm Knowles. With the exception of a brief period in the 1970s, the term andragogy is rarely used or instead acknowledges that educators and academicians continue to apply the term pedagogy, defined as teaching techniques for children, when referring to adult education.

With the acknowledgement that learning is a life–long process, there is renewed interest in how adults learn through the directive knowledge attainment common to traditional education, by guided experiences such as encompassed in the coaching process, or by personally assessing how the very real, experiential random exposure and challenges of living influence our actions and reactions.

To understand the future it is best to examine the roots of how we view the adult learning process. Knowles joins many in voicing the opinion that there is much we can do to improve the way information is presented to and utilized by adults: "*Indeed, in my estimation, the main reason why adult education has not achieved the impact of our civilizations of which it is capable is that most teachers of adults have only known how to teach adults as if they were children.*"

Knowles' work, when viewed as a theory or set of assumptions about learning, can be effectively applied to coaching as we guide our clients to explore innovative approaches that encourage self–development. Andragogy appears to be the only term and body of knowledge that describes the unique adult learning experience that can be captured in a coaching relationship.

---

1 The term Andragogy (or Andragogology) is a combination of the classical Green noun *agage*, which is the activity of leading, and *andr*, the word for adult. *The modern practice of adult education: From pedagogy to andragogy* 1980 by Malcolm Shepherd Knowles.

## WHO IS THE COACH?

Serving as master coach, I hire accredited coaches as leadership coach sub–contractors to work with individuals my clients identify as high potentials. In this intermediary position, it is my task to introduce the concept of coaching to those unaware or intimidated by the process with the misconception that it is a punishment or indicator of the need for remedial work.

During this early introductory meeting I seek to explain how coaching is a development process designed to prepare the individual for future success. I find Knowles' five crucial assumptions[2] describing characteristics of adult learners useful, as they are aligned with the qualifiers we apply when considering an individual to coach.

This tool was especially useful recently when a middle–level manager rejected the leadership coach I recommended to work with him. The manager, responsible for two hundred workers in a high–pressure environment, stated that if he was going to invest time in coaching he wanted to work with a former CEO. He explained that a retired corporate president was the only one who "*has been through it all and could offer some realistic guidance for me to develop my career*".

The individual was recommended for coaching because his leaders saw his potential and believed that he would be able to accept greater responsibility. However, his direct manager observed that he was repeating actions that could derail a promising career: he was not respected by some of his team as he did not effectively control his emotions and he seemed to make hasty decisions while preventing team members from questioning his orders. Of greatest concern to his direct manager was that he did not seem to accept feedback and challenged performance reviews that suggested any weaknesses.

Aware that his managers thought highly of his work, this individual proudly recognized that he was considered a high-performer. Comfortable with his success he looked to the future without defining the present: he did not take into account that the skills and talents of

---

[2] *The modern practice of adult education: From pedagogy to andragogy* (1980) by Malcolm Shepherd Knowles. Self–concept, Experience, Readiness to learn, Orientation to learning, Motivation to learn.

someone functioning as a CEO would not be the same as a manager in the field working with a team on a specific project.

## CRUCIAL ASSUMPTIONS

The first task before beginning his coaching experience was to enable the manger to discuss his work, his life goals and the choices he made that brought him to this position in his career. He clearly had a position of high–responsibility leading a significant number of trained professionals to achieve their goals. The question I sought to answer was how he described himself, his successes and his areas for growth.

**Self–concept:** As a person matures his self–concept moves from one of being a dependent personality toward one of being a self–directed human being.

*Coaching seeks self–awareness and acceptance.*

I met with the manager at his work site to discuss his coaching goals. As we talked, I proposed that we examine the competencies required to achieve his assigned goals, to develop his staff and satisfy the requirements of his leaders. Initially he was quick to respond by stating his job description. As I asked more directive questions about how he performed the assigned tasks, he became more contemplative and took longer to respond.

**Experience:** As a person matures he accumulates a growing reservoir of experience that becomes an increasing resource for learning.

*Coaching provides the opportunity to evaluate what we have learned, what we should retain or change, and what we could learn.*

By articulating his role, his daily tasks, and the experience he gained to achieve his current level of success, he was able to step back and appreciate his personal skills and talents. I then asked him to consider how the work he did now will be useful to achieve his future career goals. The discussion encouraged him to identify what new skills and competencies he would need to master, as well as what approaches he could revise to ensure his readiness to move to the next level in his career.

**PART 1: Leading edges in practitioner learning and development**

**Readiness to learn**: As a person matures his readiness to learn becomes oriented increasingly to the developmental tasks of his social roles.

*Coaching inspires the development of new skills and recognition of a full range of options.*

His passion for his work began to surface. He shared his enthusiasm to participate in a planned future training program and described how it would prepare him to accept a highly–visible voluntary post in a new company–wide program.

**Orientation to learning:** As a person matures his time perspective changes from one of postponed application of knowledge to immediacy of application, and accordingly his orientation toward learning shifts from one of subject–centeredness to one of problem centeredness.

*Coaching encourages a world–view, embracing new opportunities for continuous growth.*

We discussed his learning goals in greater detail, talking about the different types of knowledge and unique roles required to lead a global corporation, comparing the role of a company president to his task directing operational success of one specific project. He took over the conversation, identifying specific differences between the skills required to achieve his work goals, now able to view them as building blocks for his future. He was now able to compare the talent and competencies required in different job levels working toward the role of a corporate CEO.

**Motivation to learn:** As a person matures the motivation to learn is internal.

*Coaching embraces life–long learning and self–coaching.*

By the end of our discussion, the manager was able to identify his goals for a coaching event. We reviewed the leadership coaches available: he choose an experienced coach that had worked with others in similar positions.

About a year later I visited the manager in the field. At the time he was immersed in a particularly complex problem, assigning duties to his team to work through the issues that would lead to resolution. We talked about his coaching experience. He described the opportunity as *"life changing"*, explaining that he had a better understanding of his personal goals and what he needed to do to achieve his long–term goals. He explained that he was now able to see the 'big picture' more clearly.

## THE ROLE OF COACHING

Andragogy appears to have enjoyed a much more rapid acceptance and growth in Europe than in the US. In the US, the developing fields of management and organizational development, as well as psychotherapy and social psychology, have inspired new interest. Addressing interpersonal as well as intrapersonal aspects of an individual's level of understanding requires our awareness of how adults learn as individuals and as contributing members of a community or organization.

These five assumptions are successfully applied by coaching practitioners representing all of the contributing disciplines, employing an andragogic approach using new mediums as we seek to inspire leadership and self–direction. Concurrently within business and industry programs, such as LEAN promote continuous learning for quality production, academic researchers pursue studies to expand our field. Coaching technology is in a never–ending evolution of learning and exploration that provides a means to share our knowledge.

# Leading for change, with the (social) brain in mind

*Aurora Aritao*

How many change initiatives do you know of that were successfully implemented with zero conflict, with all targets achieved, within budget and on schedule?

Despite all our best intentions, studies consistently show between fifty–to–seventy percent of planned change efforts fail. It's no surprise that rapid organizational change is the *No. 2* leadership development challenge in the next two to five years[1].

Many managers get busy focusing on change management, the operational or structural side of change, but give significantly disproportionate resources and effort to the people side of change. Fundamental to this is the challenge of how to motivate people throughout the many phases of change.

In my role as people manager in various large multinationals, I saw contextually varying levels of commitment and performance from employees. I wondered for some time what truly drives motivation. The

---

[1] David Dinwoodie, William Posmore, Laura Quinn, and Ron Rabin. "Navigating Change: A Leader's Role." In: *CCL White Paper* (2015) p2

more I searched the closer I got to the brain. I looked deeper into two basic concepts that helped me understand why some people embrace change, and others don't:

- A core organizing principle of the brain, as coined by Dr Evian Gordon, CEO of Brain Resource Limited, is to maximize reward and minimize threat[2].

- Our brain is our social organ. We are wired to connect.

## THREAT VS REWARD

When we feel danger, the amygdala in the brain's limbic system, involved in the processing of intense emotions such as fear, gets activated. It puts us in a fight or flight mode (stress response). It exhibits a bias toward detecting cues signalling potential threats. Imagine our fast reflexive reaction when a snake drops from a tree in front of us. In milliseconds, our brain automatically kicks off its primary appraisal of this stimulus for its inherent threat value. We are ready for fight, flight or freeze.

On the other hand, we unconsciously move towards experiences that we perceive as helpful for our survival or that generates a feeling of reward – not just food and money but also connection, acknowledgment, getting a good reputation, love, security, freedom etc.

## BAD IS STRONGER THAN GOOD

Under threat we may experience stress. All that matters are the basics, and the most critical physiological and behavioural responses are initiated. Our body will turn off non–essential functions like reproduction, digestion or tissue repair, to focus on survival. Our lungs work overtime and our heart races to pump oxygen into the bloodstream. Our blood pressure goes up to deliver that energy to critical parts of our body so our muscles can respond instantly. Stress as a defensive response, has evolved as a means of adapting to immediate, life–threatening stressors.

---

[2] Evian Gordon. *Integrative Neuroscience: Bringing together biological, psychological and clinical models of the human brain.* (Singapore: Harwood Academic Publishers, 2000)

Trouble is, while we no longer worry about tigers eating us for lunch, we continue to have the stress response and the amygdala fire up in the same way whenever we feel threatened – whether by a domineering boss, or receiving negative feedback, or by an ill–written email message for example.

Today, we turn the stress response on for psychological reasons (worrying that someone does not like us, that something terrible might happen to us in the future) and not for real physiological reasons. We can arguably say that the stress response is more dangerous to us than the stressors.

Researchers have documented that the threat response often triggered in social situations, tends to be more intense and long lasting than the reward response. Data gathered through measures of brain activity – by using fMRI and electro–encephalo–graph (EEG) machines or by gauging hormonal secretions – suggests that the same neural responses that drive us toward food or away from predators are triggered by our perception of the way we are treated by other people[3].

## THE BRAIN, AFTER ALL, IS OUR SOCIAL ORGAN

Brain studies have shown that we instinctively make sense of our social world like a reflex. In 1997, Professor Gordon L Shulman and his colleagues at Washington University carried out a study using a PET scanner: participants were asked to perform a routine cognitive task for a minute (like motor, memory and visual tasks), then rest for a minute, before starting the cognitive task again. During rest times, they found a region to be highly active, a region known as the Default Mode Network (DMN). This area is almost identical to that which fires up when people think about themselves, other people and their relation with others. Psychologists call this social cognition[4]. It would seem that the default setting in our brain is to instinctively make sense of ourselves and others, nudging our attention toward the social world.

---

[3] David Rock. "Managing with the Brain in Mind." In: *Strategy+Business*. (2009) p3
[4] Matthew Lieberman. *Social: Why Our Brains are Wired to Connect*. US. (Oxford University Press, 2013) p9–25

## A LOW–COST REWARD SYSTEM

The best experience of organizational change I have had was back ten years ago in Australia, when a multinational telecommunications company I worked for embarked on a major rebranding, trying to differentiate itself in an industry of largely homogenous products. As a young Product Manager I remember being fully engaged because I felt that I was an integral part of the change from the start. I was consulted for my views and suggestions. Forums were organized for sharing ideas. The whole organization was regularly informed of the progress by the CEO himself. I was given a role to play in it, all the while encouraged to provide on–going feedback to the program team. I owned part of the change and I was highly motivated to make it work. I felt included and valued. I felt an inner sense of achievement in knowing that part of its success was due to my team's efforts. This supports the idea that financial rewards as the key incentive for driving performance or engagement may be overstated. What about transparency, inclusivity, autonomy, fairness and equity?

Being treated with respect and as a valued member of the organization may activate reward systems in the brain that promote stronger learning of behaviours that predict more of these social rewards in the future. And obviously, providing social rewards is an extremely cost effective measure, requiring only a bit of time and thoughtfulness[5].

## THE CONDUIT OF INFLUENCE

Understandably the role of a leader is significantly impacted by these perspectives. Even under normal circumstances employees' relationship with their leader is inherently threat–evoking. The overly vigilant and easily–triggered amygdala, which is more sensitive to threats than rewards, operates below consciousness. Speaking to one's supervisor or someone of higher status can often activate a threat response. Perhaps there is always an inherent threat on peoples' status in the way hierarchical organizations create and value job roles. Perhaps it is also threatening to our sense of control and autonomy having to answer to a boss who may eventually rate our performance against our peers.

---

[5] Matthew Lieberman and Naomi Eisenberger. "The pains and pleasures of social life: a social cognitive neuroscience approach." In: *NL Journal.* (2008) p7

One study showed that people trust a stranger in the street more than their boss[6].

Successful leaders offset this inherent threat by increasing relatedness or connectedness, which can come from identifying and focusing on shared goals, and also by being authentic and open so that people share positive human experiences[7].

An article by Harvard Social Psychologist Amy Cuddy et al, suggest that when we judge others – especially our leaders – we look first at two characteristics: how lovable they are (their warmth, communion, or trustworthiness) and how fearsome they are (their strength, agency, or competence). These two dimensions of social judgment account for more than ninety percent of the variance in the positive or negative impressions we form of people around us[8].

Most organizations are designed such that aspiring leaders strive to first prove their competence and demonstrate their excellence. When fear of the leader develops, chances are the leader (whether on purpose or not) has imposed her strength, competence and superiority before establishing trust. Yet fear can stunt creativity, openness and risk–taking. On the other hand, warmth, connectedness, empathy – these enable trust to develop, open up communication and make way for the sharing of ideas.

So which one is better: to be warm or to be strong, to be trusted or to be admired? As Cuddy asked in her HBR article: to be loved or to be feared? The best answer, the research tells us, is to be both, and in this order: connect first, then lead. When warmth is established first, you are paving the way for a deeper trusting relationship by demonstrating that you are listening, that you care.

*"Once you establish your warmth, your strength is received as a welcome reassurance. Your leadership becomes not a threat but a gift,"* Cuddy adds.

Connectedness is the conduit of influence.

---

[6] Michael Segalla. "How Europeans do layoff." In: *Harvard Business Review.* (2009)
[7] David Rock and Christine Cox. "SCARF® in 2012: updating the social neuroscience of collaborating with others." In: *NeuroLeadership Journal.* (2012) p6
[8] Amy J.C. Cuddy, Matthew Kohut and John Neffinger. "Connect, Then Lead." In: *Harvard Business Review.* (2013)

# Mindfulness is no longer a 'nice–to–have'

## Charlotte Rydlund

What is mindfulness to you? What does it mean for your everyday life? Mindfulness has become a buzz word in many professional spheres – be it in executive coaching or leadership development. Personally I've always found that the word is abstract and 'fluffy', and that when it gets overused it loses its value or meaning altogether. Perhaps it's not the meaning of the word that's important or relevant, instead maybe it's the sentiment or feeling behind the word that matters. If this is the case then mindfulness is no longer an abstraction because it is tied to a tangible feeling.

The Oxford dictionary defines mindfulness,
"*A mental state achieved by focusing one's awareness on the present moment, while calmly acknowledging and accepting one's feelings, thoughts, and bodily sensations, used as a therapeutic technique.*"

Within this definition, I see other words that I would use instead of mindfulness – like presence and self–awareness. Again, these words can have many meanings depending on your context, and some people might group them all into the 'fluffy' category.

How do these 'fluffy' terms like mindfulness, presence and self–awareness matter in a professional way? I believe that mindfulness is a key differentiator between being a good leader and being a great one. The Harvard business review recently published an article[1] on how "*Mindfulness can change your brain, literally*". It discusses new research in neuroscience that collated more than twenty studies conducted around the world in the last few years which showed a direct correlation between practicing mindfulness and changes in the brain. The research goes on to make direct links between the changes in the brain and the impacts these changes have on relating to others, reducing stress and making better decisions.

I've noticed that when I don't practice yoga for a week or two, or if I don't take time for myself regularly, I become more irritable. I communicate less clearly. I get frustrated more easily. I find it more challenging to think creatively to solve problems. I get stuck in a rut more easily. As soon as I begin practicing yoga again, almost immediately, I'm a different person; more calm, more prepared to take whatever comes my way. What differences do you notice about yourself when you are more or less mindful?

The HBR article makes the argument that, "*Mindfulness should no longer be considered a 'nice–to–have' for executives. It's a 'must–have'...*" If this is really true, how can we support each other in becoming more mindful and better leaders? Returning to the definition of mindfulness, there are two elements that we might seek out to help us: one is being present in the moment, the other is accepting what you are feeling or experiencing in the present.

Sometimes, at least for me, it might feel like being present and accepting whatever feelings or sentiments in the moment that take too much time. This is especially true with a lot of things going on. That being said, I've found that there are several things that have supported me in working on bettering my mindfulness, and they all revolve around focus and choice: focusing on one thing at a time, keeping my daily to–do list short (maximum three items), and, of course, practicing yoga regularly, which I admit has not been the case lately. Visualizing a place

---

1 [website] https://hbr.org/2015/01/mindfulness–can–literally–change–your–brain

or view that helps you focus also helps (mine is the Åhus beach in southern Sweden).

In the end, I don't believe mastering mindfulness is possible. It's not like you're done when you climb a mountain and reach the top. Improving your mindfulness is an on–going developmental process which is crucial to becoming a better manager and a better leader, and, in the end, a better person.

So I leave you with these questions:

- What does mindfulness mean to you?

- What steps could you take to improving your mindfulness?

- What benefits do you/would you expect to experience for yourself from practicing mindfulness regularly?

- What actions might you take to support others at home and at work to practice mindfulness?

# Smiling and laughter really matter in coaching

*Jeremy Ridge*

Smiling and laughing (spontaneously expressed by the other person – not because you do it, or want to) is arguably the most important evidence, or data, that we can get about the progress of a coaching dialogue. Certainly it is for me. Though, *I'm not out to be a comedian!*

It is a serious element of my practice. Though it may be mixed with more straight forward dialogue, periodically it becomes an important part of checking out, of self–supervising – that the other person is also in a good place with it all.

I may not know you well enough to get a smile or a laugh from you, but for me getting a laugh out of you means getting more personal with you. It means you're opening up to me in the sense that our dialogue might matter for you.

However, I am amazed, and this is not a laughing matter, that laughter is so absent from all the books, journals and research in the coaching field. This is true even with the positive psychology movements and appreciative enquiry. Let alone the wider related fields such as counselling and therapy etc.

Other fields always seem to prefer to get to the negatives of experience and behaviour – the emotional, the serious and invisible 'problems'. Dealing with positives (more to do with opportunities) is what coaching specialises in. So we need to create a means of appreciating these positives. Smiling and laughing are often the first, early, indicators about being on the right track.

Let's get it onto the table and realise its significance. We all use it. We all measure it – sometimes more or less knowingly! Some can articulate and differentiate the extraordinary detail involved, especially when it's the 'eyes' that smile; or it can be in the tone of voice, even!

It is such spontaneous behaviour, and therefore of good valid evidence of what is happening. It is often less controlled. It signals some important positives. It signals a trust in the dialogue, for example – when someone can release these reactions to you. It's often an early signal of pleasurable 'feelings' (smiling). Laughing allows you a whole lot more understanding of where some of the other person's boundaries may lie. (Laughter has been said to be an expression of some sort of a 'surprise'.)

Smiling and laughter are connected. One is more of a physical act of expression than the other. Both forms are driven by very human physical features.

- **Yes,** it can be acted. Yes it is complex – which is why it is below the current radar of formal study, but so are many things until we learn about them. People used to believe the earth was flat since they never saw beyond their village; the evidence wasn't yet convincing. We have to start somewhere. Hence the attempt to see if it is also something seen as important elsewhere.

- **Yes,** people do smiling and laughing differently. Yes there are massive cultural variations (even my next door neighbours have a unique profile for how they do it). And some personalities do it so internally, the trace is merely a moment's hesitation – as they process.

**PART 1: Leading edges in practitioner learning and development**

- **Yes,** it's the leading edge of how I personally practice. The first thing I do is work out how to get a real and positive smile, then a laugh reaction about something.

Coaching is about bringing such excitement, and expression about it, into life – the excitement of continuous learning and of sharing this excitement with others. It's about the positive feelings and surprise we can always find in life and in work.

I trust this day is bringing such a reaction for you, too – enjoy a smile and a laugh!

# Beyond personality assessments: What the coach can learn about patterns of behaviour and their implications

*Lynne Hindmarch*

**T**he purpose is not to defend or promote the use of assessments in coaching. Lots of coaches are very successful without using them at all. What I am interested in sharing (and debating) is:

- How they can be used.

- What they can teach the experienced practitioner about patterns of behaviour.

I will discuss what we mean by psychometric assessments, give some examples of ones that are appropriate for coaching, and show how coaches can deepen their understanding of behaviour by using assessments.

*Psychometric tests* are designed to measure differences between people. The term covers both ability tests and personality assessments. I will focus on personality assessments, as ability tests (such as verbal, numerical and abstract reasoning) are not generally used as part of a coaching programme. Examples of personality assessments that are frequently used in coaching are: the Myers Briggs Type Indicator, the 16PF, the OPQ and NEO. They are different to most of the free tests that can be accessed online in that they have to meet certain technical criteria in the way they have been developed. They must be:

1. Reliable (consistent across time with different people and different applications),

2. Valid (measure what they say they are measuring),

3. Free from bias such as gender and race, and

4. Standardised to minimise human error and bias.

This is why access to psychometric assessments is only provided to people who have been trained in their use. Training involves learning about the technical and statistical underpinning of the assessments, and how to feed back the results to the client.

Using a personality assessment allows the trained practitioner to form hypotheses about the client's behavioural style, and that is what is explored in the feedback session. Basically, the assessments form the framework for a good conversation; the focus of that conversation will be determined by the purpose of the coaching, such as personal development or career exploration.

## COACHING AS A GOAL–ORIENTED ACTIVITY

Early in a coaching programme the coach is likely to ask the client in some form: "*Where are you now? And where do you want to be?*" There are different ways to explore where a client is now, such as gathering biographical information and using a model such as the 'Wheel of Life'. Using a personality assessment (or a combination of assessments) is an additional approach to help raise the client's self–awareness and help the coach better understand the client.

However, my interest in the benefits of using personality assessments is rather more than that. Many coaches train in assessments once they have qualified with a coach training institute. Personality assessments are viewed as an additional tool in their kitbag.

## MY OWN EXPERIENCE IS SOMEWHAT DIFFERENT

I was first trained in personality assessments over twenty–five years ago. I had been using them extensively for a long time before I became involved in coaching, team building and coaching supervision. In fact my route into coaching was through the understanding of behaviour, and patterns of behaviour, that using personality assessments had provided. I started working as an associate for a major outplacement consultancy, using assessments (at that time mainly the 16PF and the MBTI) with redundant senior executives. The feedback conversation usually focused on:

- What their behavioural style meant in terms of organisational 'fit',

- How they would approach the job search (interview style, networking inclination, commitment to the process), and

- Career implications.

I found the process of giving feedback, and the interaction with the client, absolutely fascinating. The consultancy allowed a generous amount of time with clients: an initial session lasting about two hours, enabling me to obtain biographical information and administer the tests – paper and pencil in those days! This was followed a week or so later by a three hour feedback session, providing a good amount of time for me to explore the implications of the results with the client. These sessions were, in effect, mini coaching sessions. From this, I was asked to take on actual coaching programmes, particularly in the area known as emotional intelligence, still using the assessments as an initial part of the coaching relationship. As this part of my practice developed, I took further qualifications in coaching and coaching supervision.

One of the exciting things that a lengthy experience of using personality assessments can give the practitioner is a deepening understanding of behaviour and patterns of behaviour. These can provide insights that feed into the coaching goals. The opportunities for the coach to learn more about people's behaviour are presented every time he or she carries out feedback. Using assessments in a development setting, the client is more likely to be open in discussing the results than when it is used in selection. The alert practitioner can learn a lot from each feedback meeting. Each discussion can yield rich information about how the client 'lives' the profile. Over time, this depth of understanding can provide great insight into how behaviours impact on each other, and what that means in the way the individual manages themselves and their relationships.

For example, what does it mean for the coach if a person is low on self–discipline, is emotionally resilient and is also a conceptual thinker? I can tell you as I saw such a client recently. I'll call him Peter. It was the first time I'd met Peter, as I was profiling him for his coach, who isn't trained in psychometrics. I analysed his personality assessments before I met him, so I knew it was likely that he would be late for our session (he was). He was late because typically he doesn't plan ahead (so he hadn't allowed time for parking), has a positive outlook (so doesn't factor in negative possibilities such as traffic delays) and is absent–minded (likely to mislay his car keys).

This is a light–hearted example, and of course this pattern of behaviour has much wider implications. But the point is that a depth of understanding of personality assessments can provide the coach with insight into the client's behavioural style, with implications for how the client is likely to interact with the coach and the coaching programme. These understandings can clarify what their development needs may be in relation to their coaching goals. In the example I gave above, the feedback to Peter on these particular aspects of his behaviour included discussion about the positive aspects of his creativity, flexibility and generally upbeat outlook, and also how those around him might perceive these in a negative light on occasion. I suggested that it was possible he might come across as having somewhat eccentric, unrealistic ideas, that he may not follow through on commitments, and that he may overlook or ignore potential difficulties.

I had contracted with Peter to share the results with his coach. I was able to share with her that Peter was likely to be effective at coming up with imaginative options for addressing his coaching goals. One of the coaching challenges would be to help him break down his ideas into practical steps that he could work through. Planning his goals and the steps to reach them would also be helpful in encouraging him to focus and organise himself more effectively. His positive outlook is likely to help him in believing it is possible for him to achieve his goals, but may mean he underestimates the difficulties along the way.

Over time, as one's understanding of personality increases, it is fascinating to be able to observe just one aspect of a person's behaviour (without using assessments) and see how a pattern may emerge. Let me share some other examples:

- If you note that a person is idea–oriented rather than practical, they may be imaginative but also absent–minded, accident–prone and unrealistic. (They don't generally like DIY. You wouldn't trust them with a hammer.)

- Observing that a person doesn't plan very much suggests that they may be flexible and adaptable, but also disorganised, last–minute and only motivated to complete something if they really enjoy it.

- Those who have a positive outlook may be cheerful and upbeat but may not be aware of drawbacks and may take risks.

This is just to provide a taster of what I plan to cover. My purpose is to share insights I have gleaned over the years into the subtleties of behaviour, and how observing one aspect of behaviour can provide an understanding of associated characteristics. That is the really fun bit!

# Looking at Chelsea Flower Show through just one lens

*Doug Montgomery*

My wife gave me a day–long masterclass with a renowned garden photographer as a Christmas present last year. I've had my camera for about ten years and have always used it in automatic mode. The workshop taught me how to frame and make best use of the light for garden photographs. It taught me how to use more than just the two buttons I am used to using. It gave me lots of hints, tips and ideas in a very accessible way. So I learned how to use various other settings. I learned how to use the information that the camera provides to take wonderful pictures of gardens and flowers. And I came away with a renewed enthusiasm and ability to use more of my camera's potential.

Not long after the class, we visited the Chelsea Flower Show and had a wonderful time exploring the show gardens, grand marquee and stalls. To travel light (seven hours on foot!), I only took only one camera lens and left the tripod at home as the crowds are always extensive. That evening, I was really disappointed when looking through the photos on the laptop. While some were beautifully clear images of specific flowers, in crisp focus and gloriously isolated from their surroundings, other photos were nicely framed but with the majority of the picture out of focus or with no clear focal point.

Other photos were blurred. They were obviously suffering from 'camera shake' due to too long a shutter speed. What I was learning, was the limitations of the zoom lens I had taken and the impact of having compromised the depth of field in order to achieve a quick enough shutter speed to hand hold my camera. The lens was great for picking out and isolating a bloom or plant, but not so good for capturing the whole garden in all its glory. By taking one lens and leaving my tripod behind I limited myself to fast shutter speeds and a narrow depth of field. A good lesson for my photographic ambitions, and an interesting metaphor for my coaching.

It got me thinking about where else I am looking through only one lens and at a limited range of what that lens offers.

- Which lens am I using most often and what am I missing as a result?

- Am I missing the wide view by focusing on too small (and interesting) a detail?

- Is this the lens I am using when I notice that I am getting caught in my client's story?

The same zoom lens allows me to ask the client to narrow in on a word or a phrase and say more about what it means to them.

Am I seeing enough of my client's personal or organisational context – what would I see through my wide–angle lens?

I often invite my clients to fit a different lens, for example, by asking them to imagine sitting in the other person's chair, or by taking the perspective of an interested observer.

It's not just as coaches that we need to be aware of the different lenses available to us. Peter Hawkins's *Seven Eyes of Supervision Model*, first published in 1985, describes seven different lenses through which a supervisor may look within a session to explore the supervisee's work. A coaching supervisor's role is to support the coach to be the best coach they can be for their clients. One way they do this is to help the coach to reflect on all aspects of the coaching work and their relationship with their client. Hawkins uses:

- A macro lens to look close up in detail at the players; at the coachee, at the coach and at the supervisor.

- A mid–range lens is taken to picture the respective relationships between coach and client, and between coach and supervisor.

- The wide angle lens is used to look at the coachee's context.

With each of these lenses he brings different aspects into focus at different times and explores different depths of focus. His model uses the full capability of all three lenses to explore what is present, to hypothesise about alternative interventions, to explore parallel processes and transference, and develop the coach's self–awareness and capability. The supervisor is challenged to look inside themselves for what is happening that may be informative and useful for the coach (perhaps the analogy here is an endoscope!)

Similarly, as a coach, I want to use all the lenses at my disposal to see the full range from isolated detail, to the whole picture of my coachee and his story and the reaction it is creating in me.

I get great joy in taking garden photographs; of being in beautiful places, experiencing beautiful colours, textures and structures in combination, and seeing how seasons and weather change the view over time. I also find joy in getting home and looking through the photographs. It's only at home with the laptop that I clearly see the images I have captured. Then I can compare that image with the scene I was trying to capture. Once I've gone through the pictures, I analyse the settings, I check which lens I used and start to learn about what worked, what did not, and what I could do differently next time.

And so it is in my practice of reflection after coaching sessions and my learning through supervision. My personal reflection and reflective learning with my supervisor enable me to look at what lens and setting I was using and what I was seeing clearly and what is blurred. It helps me to swap lenses and to look at and challenge myself as a coach and to supportively challenge my coachee's thinking. I know I have lots more to learn about swapping lenses thoughtfully and with purpose.

Interestingly, in sitting down to write this, I found myself looking through a familiar old lens – the one that questions why anyone would be interested in what I have to say, believes that writing is erudite, academic and intellectually challenging, and fears the humiliation of rejection. Realising that this lens was not useful, I changed it for the one that says I'm interested in what I have to say, that I won't know what others think until I've posted the article. And anyway, who cares if no one finds it interesting or useful; I've enjoyed and learned for the experience and want to share it.

Not only have I a lot to learn about the lenses I have available, and when and how to use them, but my old camera has lots of useful features I was unaware of. It just goes to show that *this old dog* has been taught new tricks.

So let me leave you with these questions:

- As a coach, how is your default lens limiting your view?

- What other lenses could you look through that will give you and your clients new views, sharp focus and different depths of fields?

# Uncovering your motivators from a situation that frustrates you

*Nicholas Wai*

**I have written about** motivation – in "Our Needs and Our Behaviours[1]" I wrote about how a better understanding of our hierarchy of needs will help us create stronger motivators for behavioural change, and in "Why We Do What We Do – How To Make Use of This Knowledge To Set Our New Year Resolution?[2]" I wrote about how intrinsically motivating goals are better than extrinsically imposed goals in driving performance and behaviour change. In both cases, through reflecting on day to day personal experiences, I arrived at insights that helped uncover my motivating factors.

I hope my stories have prompted you to start thinking about the topic. However, you may also be thinking: "*It's all very well for you, but I have never found it easy to know what truly motivates me.*" I agree with you. For almost all of us, including me, it is much easier to identify what irritates us than uncovering what it is that specifically drives us forward. Nevertheless, a very experienced coach has showed me that what

---

[1] [website] http://the-goodcoach.com/tgcblog/2014/11/27/our-needs-and-our-behaviours-by-nicholas-wai.html
[2] [website] http://the-goodcoach.com/tgcblog/2014/12/31/why-we-do-what-we-do-how-to-make-use-of-this-knowledge-to-se.html

**PART 1: Leading edges in practitioner learning and development**

irritates us, or pushes us into conflict with someone, would in fact also shows us what our dearly held values and motivating factors. They are two sides of the same coin.

I have had the privilege of experiencing a taster session led by its creator Dr. Paul Jeong, from his accredited Certified Professional Coach Training Program, earlier this month. His school is currently one of the largest providers of coach training in China and he will be bringing his program to Hong Kong soon. To introduce the program to some of his prospective students, he conducted two very animated and activity–packed evenings to introduce some of his powerful coaching tools as a preview of what is to come in the full program. One of the exercises that really impressed me was how he turned someone's conflict situation into a learning opportunity of what makes that person excel. Through a simple visioning and reframing process, Dr. Paul, with his energetic yet caring line of questioning and guiding, demonstrated how coaching could help someone look at a frustrating situation from a very different perspective (reframing), thereby creating an opportunity and the motivation for the person to resolve the situation.

I applied this exercise to help me understand my working practices. I hate being forced into agreements like accepting a project or an assignment without enough time and information to understand and accept on an intuitive basis what I am getting into (one of my hot buttons). Once I am, I take the responsibility that comes with the role very seriously to ensure its success. What is this telling me? I need enough space and freedom to think things through in my own time. The underlying values driving this need is my strong preference for freedom and self–determination, which I not only expect of myself but also hold for those whom I work with. So what motivates me are autonomy and accountability.

However, what I've also learned and have come to realise is that they are my values and not those of others. They are equally relevant for me at work and in personal situations, where conflicts are even more likely, especially with close relations and loved ones. I have come to realise that it is very important for me to consider what motivates them also, and examine how we can relate to each other better so both of our values are respected and both our needs are met. For example, I may consider giving freedom and accountability to someone as a show of love. My girlfriend however is motivated by connection and intimacy, which means her way of showing love would look very different from mine. Understanding what motivates each of us allows me to read our behaviours differently and to not react in my old ways when my hot buttons are pushed. I must admit this is easier said than done but I am happy about gaining this insight. I am starting to behave differently for the better of myself and my relationship.

For you:

- Think of a conflict you recently had with a loved one. What does it reveal about the values that you and your loved one hold dear?

- With this insight, is there anything you would like to change about how you would react if a similar situation happens again?

# How a coaching approach is important to collective intelligence – and vice–versa!

## Laurent Terseur

One of my strongest beliefs is that individuals and teams can dramatically improve performance in organisations by growing more collective intelligence.

Research has documented that collective intelligence is a stronger predictor of a team's performance than its individual members' abilities (Woolley & Al, 2016). Collective intelligence is also often subliminally eluded to in commonly heard injunctions for teams to be 'smart', 'agile', 'do more with less', or to apply the principle of '1+1=3', 'outsmart competition', etc.

This, to me, would make of collective intelligence a useful guiding star for leadership and team development.

Yet there is even more good news in Tom Atlee's definition of collective intelligence: *"The intelligence of a collective, which arises from one or more sources."* Every drop counts in that ocean!

It's fascinating indeed to consider that everyone, alone or as part of a collective and regardless of their position, can at any point in time act on increasing collective intelligence levels in their sphere of influence. This will both help them progress with their goals and achieve a much more overall positive influence.

I would like to share here some things that I observed and find useful about how a coaching approach can use the dimensions of collective intelligence as a frame of reference:

- Growing systemic.

- Leveraging complementarities.

- Developing emotional awareness.

- Fostering collaboration.

- Acquiring a learning mind set.

I realise I might introduce some of my jargon here, but I want to share the meaning behind it. To me, it's about the person in the system; what people do on the Monday morning to make an impact in their organisations.

## A BRIEF TOUCH ON WHAT COLLECTIVE INTELLIGENCE IS

Intelligence can mean different things to different minds.

I will focus here on collective intelligence in relatively small groups, within organisations. A number of definitions of collective intelligence exist. However, it doesn't seem to me that any of them has reached a level of consensus at this stage.

Two of them resonate most with me:

- *"Collective intelligence is the capacity of families, groups, organizations, communities and entire societies to act intelligently as whole, living systems"* – Tom Atlee[1]

---

[1] [website] http://www.co–intelligence.org/l–fivedimensions.html

- *"Collective intelligence captures a group's capability to collaborate and coordinate effectively across a range of tasks, which is predictive of a group's future performance."* ( Wooley & Al, 2016)

Whilst the former emphasises the systemic dimension of collective intelligence and the latter its application to performance, they both highlight that collective intelligence is a potentiality.

I look at intelligence as the ability to learn and adapt, and at collective intelligence as the ability of a collective to learn and adapt. This ability may then vary in its intensity but arises at the minute two people or more start interacting.

## USEFUL DIMENSIONS FOR BOTH INDIVIDUALS AND TEAMS TO USE AS A COMPASS TOWARDS HIGHER LEVELS OF COLLECTIVE INTELLIGENCE

I will first clarify that I personally consider leadership development as an intentional attempt to increase levels of collective intelligence by helping individuals and teams to grow their cooperation, learning and adaptation skills.

This applies to individuals and teams with the ambition to form high–performing teams, as defined by Peter Hawkins: *"a high–performing team effectively meets and communicates in a way that raises morale and alignment, engages with all the teams key stakeholder groups in a way that grows performance, and provides constant learning and development for all its members and the collective team."* (Hawkins, 2011)

So, what does it take to increase levels of collective intelligence?

### 1. It's about understanding the system

Every individual or team is part of a relationship system, a system being *"a regularly interacting or interdependent group of items forming a unified whole"* (Merriam–Webster Dictionary).

As Atlee points it, collective intelligence resulting from a system's interactions can therefore become greater (or smaller!) as a whole, than the sum of the individual intelligence of its parts.

A few examples of common situations I observed, in which the way the system is (or isn't) thought through will dramatically impact levels of collective intelligence:

- Leadership teams operating in distressed environments, having long endured a high pace of change, often combined with a significant turnover amongst the team members. Such a context can easily corner these teams into a fragmented, reactive–only mode where each team member ends up in the ropes, fighting alone his vision of the adversity. Alternatively, teams managing to keep sharing a common vision of the system will increase their resilience as they will perform as a whole.

- Leaders torn between competing loyalties as they sit in multiple and sometimes overlapping or even competing governance instances, will regain perspective and sometimes relief when seeing through the whole system's dynamics.

- Individuals or teams operating transversally in matrix organisations, with often ill–defined or ill–published accountabilities, will experience and foster different levels of collective intelligence if they look at the whole system.

### So, what does that mean practically for leaders and teams?

Leaders and teams will drive up collective intelligence levels as they enhance their awareness and understanding of the structure, the context and the dynamics of their environment/system.

They can grow this awareness by regularly asking themselves the following questions:

- Who is part of the system? – Within the team as well as outside.

- Who and where are the key stakeholders?

- Who is commissioning the team?

- What is the team's purpose in the system? – What only this team can achieve in the system.

- What are the expectations? – From within the team as well as from the external stakeholders.

- Where are the disruptions or changes, what is missing or not yet addressed?

- What are the synergies, dynamics and entanglements impacting the system?

This needs to be an ongoing team discipline, as VUCA[2]–type environments and ever more interwoven networks require real–time adjustments.

## 2. It's about leveraging complementarities

Complementarity of the members is one of the keys to an effective team: "*A team is a small number of people with complimentary skills who are committed to a common purpose, set of performance goals, and approach for which they hold themselves mutually accountable.*" (Katzenbach and Smith, 1993)

These complementary skills – and strengths – will combine with each other to create a whole that is bigger than the sum of its parts, by enabling the team to share and allocate tasks in an optimal way, taking into account the nature of tasks as well as each members' skills and credibility, "*... credibility is reflected in member's reliance on one another to be responsible for specific expertise such that collectively they possess all the information needed for their tasks.*" (Williams Wooley & al, 2016)

*So, what does that mean practically for leaders and teams?*

Dedicating time and attention (or not) to the identification of these complementarities will impact levels of collective intelligence, when selecting members of a team, and also during its lifetime. I'll mention three typical applications I could observe:

- A fast–growing company in which each director has on–boarded a specific transversal accountability and leads that space on behalf of the whole team, continuously strengthening their individual credibility vis–a–vis one another.

---

[2] VUCA : Volatile, Uncertain, Complex, Ambiguous

- A program I was asked to design, to support the heads of support functions of a high–performing matrix organisation. Over the years the cost agenda had significantly streamlined their resources, yet transversal projects were booming, spreading the daunting taste of having to deliver more with less (or more shared) resources. That management team hardly had time for activities other than fire–fighting, let alone to talk to each other. But they all shared common projects and internal clients. Each of them had the knowledge of a portion of the institution, totally unknown to the others, yet which could help them.

Investing in getting to know each other, and learning to ask for and provide help to one another, was the key to unlock the synergies resulting from their complementarities in skill, knowledge and style. This turned isolated functions into one powerful and cohesive infrastructure team.

- *"It's my time management..."* or is it? I observed many leaders struggling to create more impact and trying to squeeze their time management further, hoping to create more bandwidth. But there is only so much one can do in a day. Instead, the discussion took a completely different perspective when they started thinking their team complementarities through. If making an impact is down to moving selected important rocks, whilst at the same time dealing with the 'day–to–day' rocks, quite an epiphany can happen when the team manages to find who is good at carrying which rock, or helping others by clearing the path.

### 3. It's about building emotional awareness

Research has documented the link between collective intelligence and a group's performance, evidencing in particular a correlation between the level of social sensitivity of group members and their performance (Williams–Woolley et al, 2010).

Tom Atlee also defines resonant intelligence as a form of *"intelligence that grows stronger or fuller as it resonates with other sources or forms of intelligence, or which deepens in empathic response to life"*, making the point that experiences of high collective intelligence in groups are almost always accompanied by powerful experiences of resonance and a strong sense of 'flow'.

### So what does that mean practically for leaders and teams?

If I think of the effective teams I have been given to work with, they all would have scored high on the following dimensions:

- Quality of communication, both in terms of frequency, directness and relatedness – it's ok to listen to each other in these teams!

- Sense of sharing, belonging and being one – they would easily pass the 'late lounge' test and still feel as one team even when on their own.

- Levels of empathy – sharing the joy as well as the pain – it's ok to care for one another in these teams!

Interestingly, these teams often had started with less empathy – it takes time, effort and bumps included, to build a healthy dynamic. The larger the organisation, the higher the pressure, the less clear the structure, the less supportive the context, the more volatile the environment, the more effort it will take to grow and protect that form of collective intelligence.

Useful questions to be regularly brought in to enhance emotional awareness can be:

- How do I feel in this collective?

- How are others likely to feel in this collective?

- Are we aware of our tensions, sharing our emotions and what drives them?

- What is missing, that would create a safer and more constructive dynamic ?

- What would make us grow more empathy?

- Are we feeling as one team?

- Are we still feeling as one, even when separate?

- What is needed for this collective to share and bond more?

- Is it clear what makes each member's success important to the rest of the collective?

## 4. It's about fostering collaboration

Similarly, research has evidenced that groups in which a few people dominate the conversation are likely to be less collectively intelligent than those with a more equal distribution of conversational turn–taking (Williams–Wooley et al, 2010).

At the same time, *"Politeness is the poison of collaboration"* according to Edwin Land. Collective intelligence doesn't equal avoidance of confrontation. Team members need to feel it's ok to air their opinions, in which case they will feel considered and will feel committed to the teams' decisions.

To me, fostering collaboration in a collective means creating the space for each member to fully contribute, for optimal cross–fertilisation to happen, and also for looking at the combination of individual and collective tasks that maximises the pool of strengths this specific team has for each situation.

### *So, what does that mean practically for leaders and teams?*

Collaboration transcend and make great orchestras. Each musician has an outstanding mastery of their instrument, yet the quality of the overall harmony will rely on the group to cooperate and find the right flow, pushing the right note at the right time, anticipating each other's input.

I have observed many teams struggling with the right distribution of conversational turn–takings.

Some typical examples are:

- Senior teams often welcome a collection of competing strong personalities and egos. The best solo artists in the world certainly have egos to deal with, but they preferably avoid singing over each other. They agree on the greater good (delivering outstanding performance and unforgettable emotions), accept that each voice or instrument nurtures one another, and they put time and efforts in learning the partition and rehearsing until they have achieved the perfect harmony.

- At the other end, more junior teams can easily be dominated and inhibited by one or few bullying team leaders or members, making the team's collective intelligence plummet as the conversation is taken hostage.

- Too often, team leaders and members don't pay enough attention to leaving the space open for other's contributions. Here it will be key to remember what the impact is that the team wants to create, that earns the loyalty of its members – particularly in matrix organisations. And then, back to our previous example, if the impact is about moving key rocks, some heavy rocks require two or more pair of hands to be moved, some require only one, other ones only can be moved in a second step, etc.

Teams willing to foster more collaboration, will find it useful to implement the discipline of regularly reviewing common tasks, communications and accountabilities, screening and defining:

- What is currently shared by this collective, that earns the loyalty of its members,

- Joint or separate ownerships,

- Timing, and in particular sequences of actions, by whom and in which order,

- Separate, majority or consensus decisions.

## 5.  It's about learning and maturing

Collective intelligence is also about the willingness to grow a learning mind set as a team, so as to stay fit and adapt to the ongoing change. It also involves a notion of stewardship and moral awareness and the ability to factor in the bigger picture and longer–term implications of the collective's decisions (or non–decisions).

*So, what does that mean practically for leaders and teams?*

From my observation, high–performing teams create the discipline of learning together with both a clear purpose and an acceptance that, as change happens permanently, they are on a permanent learning curve.

They also implement the discipline of regularly using noticeable events or stages of development to review:

- How the situation benchmarks against the team's purpose (if a development serves the purpose its challenges are part of the learning curve; if it doesn't it's a different conversation),

- What has been done differently by the team, or could have been done differently,

- What has been learned,

- What can be done differently.

They can also explore how the collective can get out of its comfort zone in a constructive way. This allows them creativity to bring in external stakeholders or sources of inspiration to help the collective identify their blind spots and expand their thinking.

Collective stewardship is commonly the seat of tensions between the pressure for immediate short–term performance and the need to take into account the longer term implications. Amongst the typical challenges are the disconnects between ambitious corporate values and their practical translation in day–to–day behaviours and decisions. These disconnects can generate either a lack of adoption or a genuine frustration in the absence of clear leadership expectations. Again, adopting the discipline of looking at it as a learning curve can make create a great opportunity for a team to grow its collective intelligence.

## IN CONCLUSION

As organisations evolve in more and more VUCA environments, and as the top–down, command & control type of leadership is being shelved by new information technologies and the resulting loose, lateral, networks leadership, I believe that collective intelligence is both a useful compass and a great outcome for leadership development. And I also firmly believe it is applicable to any team at any point of their life and performance.

I like the idea that it is not about offering pre–formatted tools. Instead it's about encouraging people to create their own questions, which will work in their contexts. There can be a mindfulness here of collective intelligence dimensions as rich, thought–provoking sources of inspiration.

I also am very encouraged by seeing collective intelligence as a quite universal lever, available for everyone to pull. I find it very powerful to think that everyone, individually or collectively, can act.

I will continue with this exploration, and hope the ideas discussed here will stimulate readers to exchange on the different ways to use coaching to increase levels of collective intelligence.

Interestingly, I also experience it works the other way round: focusing on these dimensions of collective intelligence is a powerful way to inform a coaching approach.

What do you think?

- Do you look at collective intelligence as an inspiration to your leadership or coaching practice?

- How practically do you use it?

- Do you see useful ways to bring it in your practice?

# Snapshots of you at your best – and the real profile of your best practice in coaching

*Jeremy Ridge*

N o–one can be all things to all people. One of the current complications is that we often have to fit to what others may be looking for. The temptation to put across the image of being all things to all people is still very high in coaching. So the next question is what exactly can each of us be, and to whom? What *can* you do at your best? Is there a pattern, or a profile, for how this works? Is this important? How should this be used/shared?

This idea ties in closely with the idea of being professional. A professional knows what they are doing. Professional standards are created for us to evidence and validate independently, and objectively, that we know what we are doing. Even the early attempts at setting professional standards can create methods what work for some and yet do not really appreciate the diversity of what can be really involved in powerful coaching.

## HOW TO FORM A PICTURE OF YOU AT YOUR BEST

Simply start an exercise of reviewing your best cases.

### Step 1:

The first stage in this exercise is to consider what your best cases are as you yourself consider them. This may not be the cases that bring you the highest reputation for your work, of course. This is about outcomes you are proud of being involved in creating – even if not easily visible to others. Even coachees cannot always understand what draws them in to value the opportunities presented to them.

Think of around a *dozen* different coaching cases where you think you were able to achieve what you believe you can achieve at your best, and where the circumstances were also supportive in enabling this to happen.

Even dare to think more about *where* you believe you were able to create the conditions, because of who you are and what you typically do, with another person that was very significant for them. This may not just be in the formally controlled conditions of many coaching sessions. It may also not be when you started referring to yourself as a coach!

It's really important to go beyond general coaching words and objectively ask what is really involved. Think of the actual events and behaviours that made the difference. Sometimes these can be complex and very subtle. There may be an example of a behaviour that was a peak moment, at a particular point in time. There are also stages. So what was important at the start? What built progress? And what about the outcomes?

You may already have done this. Otherwise, take the exercise in stages, step by step.

### Step 2:

Consider what it was you did in more detail that had such important impact. For example, to begin with, aim to list the three to five most important things you believe you did that you believe made the most important impact.

Do this for each case separately. You may do this at different times, so as to come with a fresh look. Even then go back to add more detail as you build the case description.

Consider also the circumstances – and what was important in being able to deliver what was important. Circumstances can be a major set of factors independent to what you can bring.

All this can be a real test for whether you do actually know what made an important difference to the other person. It can be like using that all important powerful lens to see through to what can be invisible to a superficial examination of the events.

It's a chance to celebrate yourself after all! This is not a simple exercise. But it should be a very enjoyable exercise.

### Step 3:

The third stage is to begin identifying the patterns of what you do that make a difference and that occur frequently across these cases.

This starts to really identify that profile of your own best practice. **Your practice profile**.

### A further step:

Share your review, and thoughts, with someone who really knows you well. Bring them into the conversation about what was really happening.

You may even have evidence from the coachee involved. Although that evidence can still be difficult to obtain, it will also become important looking ahead.

At some point, we will all have an opportunity to express this level of appreciation about how we really operate, in depth. This is where professional standards need to evolve towards.

# CHAPTER 3

# PRACTITIONERS' NEXT STEPS:
# REFINING THEIR PRACTICE / APPROACH

## Asking for feedback: My invitation to coaches wanting to be even more useful to their clients

*Doug Montgomery*

**I often meet new** coaches who are excited about getting started with clients. They wonder how they will know if they are doing a good job or not. Like me, they want to be the best coach they can be for our clients. To access such information requires asking the client for feedback, a topic not always included in coach training and one of the things that many new coaches struggle with.

It has taken me a bit of trial and error to find ways to get this vital information on how clients are progressing. The same goes for the usefulness and effectiveness of my own behaviour and coaching style. It has taken an awareness of my own responses to giving and receiving feedback.

Experienced coaches will no doubt be familiar with the value of asking for and being open to receiving feedback from their clients. While this article is mainly directed towards coaches setting out on their journey, old hands will hopefully also find these thoughts useful as they reflect on their own practices. Let's begin exploring what I have learned about asking for feedback from clients.

## My coaching journey – what has changed for me?

When I started coaching as an internal coach with a full–time day job, I had the opportunity to coach a few colleagues across the company. I used to look forward to the results of the post coaching feedback questionnaire. It took a few months to arrive as there needed to be three different coachee responses to maintain anonymity. The report would arrive and I would find out how the three clients had rated:

- The effectiveness of the coaching (1–5), and

- The quality of the coach (1–5), and

- To what extent their goals were met (1–5), and then

- Any comment they had written. E.g. *"Doug was great"*, *"The coaching helped me to be better at..."*.

After a while it dawned on me that while this was nice and gave me a warm feeling of doing a good job, it didn't really tell me anything about what I was actually doing. I also realised that I was waiting a long time after the event to get this feedback, and that some of my clients did not complete the questionnaire. In those cases, since I had no idea what they thought, I assumed the worst. I also worried a lot about what a score of less than 5 meant and assumed that I had failed in some way.

Not very satisfactory, and certainly not useful for my learning and developing as a coach. How could I fill this gap? Obviously I could ask the clients for feedback directly.

And yet, I was not!

## What was stopping me?

When I thought about it there were lots of barriers and limiting beliefs going through my head about asking for feedback:

- Do I really need it – I can tell that it is working – can't I?

- Fear of what they might say – what if I'm not very good?

- What if they are wrong? I'll need to put them right and that could result in an argument.

- They may not be honest with me – especially if it's negative feedback – we don't do negative feedback around here!

- If they do tell me it will just reinforce what I already know I'm bad at – do I really want to know that?

- It will feel a bit embarrassing hearing that I did something really well.

- They might not be good at giving feedback or used to being asked – that could be awkward.

And when I thought about how felt when I was asked for feedback I realised that:

- I was often anxious about the response I would get – would it start a fight or an argument in which I would need to defend my feedback?

- What if I've got it wrong – how embarrassing that would be!

- I felt horrible when I've been told I'm not good at something before – I don't want to impose that on others.

Then it struck me. My relationship with giving and receiving feedback was largely driven by my experiences of being judged when receiving feedback. I'm sure I am not alone here. It was around this time that I was introduced to David Kolb's experiential learning theory[1] (ELT) (1984) in a group supervision session and feedback really started to make sense.

My relationship with feedback is now very different. Feedback is critical to my learning, so I do ask for it regularly and I offer it regularly. The biggest shift for me is that feedback is just data, it may feel like a judgement of me at times, yet it is just data that feeds my learning and development.

---

[1] David Kolb. *Experiential Learning: Experience As The Source Of Learning And Development.* (Pearson Education Ltd., 1984)

**PART 1: Leading edges in practitioner learning and development**

## WHY RECEIVING FEEDBACK AS A COACH IS IMPORTANT?

As a coach, I want to learn from my clients experience of being coached by me and so I want to know when I am doing a good job for my client and when less so. One of the best ways to find out is through feedback.

- Feedback on progress towards their stated goals.

- Feedback on what I am doing that is proving useful to them.

- Feedback on what is not working so well, things that are both getting in the way of trust and in the way of creating the space for them to really think and change.

All these aspects are important for me to know how effective the coaching has been and how to make it as effective as we can from here onwards. Asking for such feedback gives me information and also raises my client's awareness of what is going on for them. Without feedback I have only my instincts and assumptions about whether the work is on track and that my client is having a useful experience.

Experience has told me that I can be wrong in my assumptions about progress! E.g. I have commented to a client that I was sorry that the progress we were making was so slow, only to be told they were feeling so much clearer and further on than they could have believed possible. I've also had that cold water feeling when a session I thought was going well, turned out to be heading in completely the wrong direction for the client. The feedback woke me up to the fact that I had got caught in an aspect of their story that was of great interest to me at the expense of where they wanted to focus!

## WHAT DOES USEFUL FEEDBACK LOOK LIKE?

Over many years as an employee and as a line manager, my observation is that the art of effective feedback is poorly understood and poorly practiced.

For feedback to be useful to me, whatever role I am in, it needs to be:

1. Timely,

2. Specific,

3. Honest, and

4. Focused on my behaviours and impact on the client.

**Timely feedback** is really important, particularly when things I am doing are not working so well for the client. It allows me to respond immediately and adjust my behaviour to something more useful. Much better than finding out at the end of a six session assignment that I was not challenging enough throughout the last six months! It's too late to change.

**Specificity** takes us to the key value of the feedback. If I ask, "*Please give me some feedback on my coaching?*" I may be told that "*it was brilliant*" or "*it really worked*" or that my client "*loved the session*". My ego can bask in such praise. However this feedback is not helping me to be a better coach. It's much more useful to know what it was I did specifically that made that session really useful for the client. By asking specific questions I can get specific feedback. So I may ask:

- "*What did I do that was most useful for you today?*" or

- "What did I do that was not so useful to you today?" or

- "*Where have you have got to so far with respect to your first goal?*"

Specificity allows me to take risks and know that I can adjust quickly. For example, if a client has asked to be very challenging in today's session, I can, ask them what that means – maybe scale it compared to my normal level of challenge (from 1–10).

As the session progresses, I will ask how challenging they are finding me so far. We can use the scale again to describe the level of challenge and I can compare what it feels like to me with what it feels like for them. I can ask what I can do to close any gap between where we are now and where they want me to be. It's all useful data that informs my style in that session.

**Honesty** needs to be encouraged for feedback to hone learning. Feedback thought by the giver to be critical or negative, may feel very awkward or hurtful to give. It may feel easier to say "*it was ok*" or "*it was good*" to save the feeling of the coach when in fact the session wasn't very productive or the coach's particular style wasn't very useful or the client felt rubbed up the wrong way.

This fear of being honest is particularly unhelpful to me and my client. This is because I will be unaware that my behaviour is not helping them and I am very likely to carry on being unhelpful. Dissatisfaction in my client may result, at best, in them making less progress than they could and, at worst, they could leave the relationship feeling deeply unhappy with me and unfulfilled in themselves.

This is why it is really important to create the conditions in which the client can share what is not working for them honestly, and know that their feedback is *welcomed* by me as valuable insight. A client who believes that they will need to justify any negative feedback is less likely to offer it. So I work hard to be remain open minded and non–judgemental of all the feedback I am offered.

I can choose how I hear it, and I choose to hear it as data to reflect on and not as a judgement of me.

By asking for specific information, I can focus the feedback on what I did or did not do. This helps the client to offer feedback on my behaviour rather than on me as a person or coach.

**By focusing my behaviour,** there is a greater chance of receiving useful data that I can do something with as part of my learning and development. Let me share another example. Feedback presented as a compliment e.g. "*You are a brilliant coach*", or an attack e.g. "*You are a useless coach*", is focused on who I am. These examples are nice and painful respectively but both are unhelpful if I want to develop as a coach. And while these statements may both be hard to hear, they hint at some potentially useful data that a follow up question may elicit.

**PART 1: Leading edges in practitioner learning and development**

For example:

- *"What is it that made my coaching brilliant for you?"*

- *"What was it about my coaching that you found useless?"*

By treating these statements as data rather than good or bad judgements of me, I can allow myself the space to ask about my behaviour and its impact that lie behind either statement.

**Knowing the impact of my behaviour in a timely fashion** is much easier to hear, learn from and to do something about. It is relatively easy for me to change my behaviour when I know what to change. So a little education of my client on how to provide me with the feedback I need may be a good investment for us both. An added bonus may be that we are creating a positive experience for my client as they enjoy a safe place to learn and practice offering effective feedback and discovering that it is welcomed.

## WHEN TO ASK FOR FEEDBACK

For sure, there are lots of opportunities to ask for feedback.

I was taught to check in on progress during each coaching session, around half way through or more frequently in longer sessions. **The check in** asks the client for feedback on progress so far towards the stated goal of the session and allows for adjustment of direction as necessary.

I often ask, *"Where are you now in relation to the goal?"* or, *"Are we still on track?"* to find out what the client is thinking. A positive response allows me to proceed in confidence, a negative response allows adjustment in direction and ask about where the client wants to focus for the remainder of the session. This is also an opportunity to ask if what I am doing is useful and what could be more useful.

**The end of the session** is an obvious time to ask about where the client has reached in the session, what has changed for them, what they are taking away, what they are learning about themselves and how that will be useful elsewhere in their lives. This is both useful feedback and leaves the accountability for determining progress and learning in the hands of the client. My focus at the end of the session tends to be on the clients progress rather than on what I did so that they leave with their attention on themselves and their action plan.

**A review of progress towards the overall goals** for the coaching assignment half way through a series of sessions (say end of third or beginning of the fourth session out of six sessions) is good practice. It's another opportunity to reflect on what you did that was useful and not so useful.

And of course **reviewing progress at the end of the assignment** gives the coach feedback on the effectiveness of the relationship. I use a short questionnaire at the end of the assignment to gather feedback on progress towards goals, changes the client has noticed, learnings and feedback on what I did that was effective and what could have been more effective for the client. This is a useful prompt for the end of session conversation and gets the client thinking about the resources they are taking into the future. I'm noticing that when I have been active in seeking feedback throughout, there are fewer surprises that thrown up.

There are opportunities to get feedback on what you are doing throughout the lifetime of the coaching relationship.

All you have to do is ask.

## Contracting for feedback

I contract with my clients at the outset of the coaching relationship about how we will work together. Part of this psychological contract is about feedback.

I usually start by asking about their own experience and relationship with feedback. I will be especially asking for feedback on how what I am doing is impacting them and their thinking.

Exploring with them how they would like me to share my observations of their behaviour, body language, stories and any apparent contradictions with them is a good segue into asking them for feedback, and explaining what makes it important to me and that I want it 'warts and all'.

Talking frankly and honestly about what could go wrong and what we will do when it does – through feedback – is part of creating an equal partnership of peers in which anything can be raised.

By setting the expectations of feedback to each other, I feel free to experiment and to seek instant feedback. This, in turn, allows me to be more risk taking, knowing that I can readjust quickly if it is not working for the client.

## THE ART OF ASKING FOR USEFUL AND EFFECTIVE FEEDBACK FEEDS MY DEVELOPMENT AS A COACH

To become the best coach I can be for each and every one of my clients, I need timely, honest, specific feedback that focuses on my behaviour and its impact.

Including feedback in the psychological contract at the outset of the relationship is one of the stepping stones towards the trusting equal partnership I want to create with my clients.

Asking for and receiving feedback as data feeds my professional learning and development. There are many opportunities for seeking feedback that enhance the quality of the coaching for me and my clients.

So let me leave you with some questions to reflect on.

- What is your relationship with feedback?

- What are you doing to get more of it?

- What are you hearing when you get it?

- How are you using it to learn and develop your coaching approach?

**PART 1: Leading edges in practitioner learning and development**

# What got you here won't get you there

## Nicholas Wai

This title is of course taken from one of Marshall Goldsmith's bestsellers. Goldsmith is one of the pioneers and most well–known executive coaches in our field. It was 2007 when I first read his book, which also happened to be part of my favourite class at London Business School – *Creativity and Personal Mastery*.

Goldsmith actually visited our class when I was a student (and some of the subsequent ones when I was the teaching assistant); he led us on several simple yet powerful exercises that invited us to examine who we were as people and leaders. To Goldsmith, what was important for a leader (and at the end of the day a person) was being self–aware, making continuous personal development and upholding his/her personal values and promises. These all seem very basic as concepts. It's easy for us talk, often harder to keep and share through our behaviours and actions, especially as we face competing demands and choices in our everyday lives. More often than not personal or leadership failures can be traced back to them.

You may think by using this title I am writing a review of some sort of his book. Well, not directly. I picked this title, "*What got you here won't get you there[1]*", because, although I intellectually understand and accept what the title was saying back in 2007, it was not until a recent encounter and realization that I fully understood and embraced the concept.

I had been leading a team of trainee coaches as their mentor coach since earlier this year. I did not feel it had been as successful as I had expected it to be. As a group, we successfully managed our objectives: skills and knowledge development, which from their demonstration and through their reflections the coaches showed progress and improvement towards a level of mastery. However, as a team, I was more concerned with the lack of involvement and proactiveness amongst individual team members. This outcome, which I considered unsatisfactory and had talked about to the team a few times, prompted me to respond the way I normally did. I pushed harder. I believed in my mind that I'd done everything required of me and hence assigned the responsibility for the outcome to others. This behaviour just made it worse and the coaches became more disengaged.

I questioned for some time why this was happening. It gradually dawned on me that I was responding to my 'problem' automatically by resorting to what worked for me before: Push harder. On reflection, I realized that this belief was formed quite some time ago, at a time when I was working in a large organization with a formal structure and corporate culture. Because it had worked before, this particular pattern of behaviour just came up automatically. Without my processing the fact that I am now in a very different profession and operating in a different environment, where the participants were actually my clients.

In this environment my clients had a much greater freedom in choosing how much they wanted to be engaged and motivated. Seen in this light by reframing the situation, the problem was actually made worse by my not understanding my team's motivation, which would have then led me to think of a different way in response to the situation.

---

1 [website] A video review of the book on YouTube can be found at:
https://www.youtube.com/watch?v=AleZ95q2QvE

**PART 1: Leading edges in practitioner learning and development**

I am not too happy that, in hindsight, my behaviour was not entirely coach–like. However, I do really appreciate the opportunity that helped me discover a blind spot and the possibility to make a more effective choice next time.

For self–reflection:

- Can you recall an experience where you did not get a different outcome even when you tried harder? What's the belief that's at work here?

- *What Got You Here Won't Get You There* – does it resonant with you? What came up for you?

- What experience of past success is stopping you from succeeding right now?

# Are structured coaching sessions reducing the potential for real coaching?

## Yvonne Thackray

Coaching should start where the client is, especially for our mature clients. Coaching shouldn't really be considered as an explicit structured process that the client needs to work through. The presumption that all clients want to work within a set number of sessions every 'x' number of weeks over a fixed period is perhaps one of the greatest fallacies in our field. I can see the benefits, right at the start, to have more structure when the coach and the client are beginning to get to know each other. It is a way to begin sampling, testing and deciding whether they, the clients, want to work with you, the coach, on a specific challenge for a short period of time or on a longer term basis across a broader range of challenges.

The onus is thus on the coach to role model and deliver a safe and confidential space that the client wants to enter and work within, in order to repeatedly come away from each session moving forward in some way. Not just the other way round! To me, this it is really the contracting period for coaching (that lasts over two or three session or the equivalent of 3-5hrs) not the contract itself.

For any sessions that follow after that initial contracting period, there is generally a shift in the coaching relationship. The client has now become more psychologically invested in their outcomes, and the coach has earned some of their client's trust and respect. The client has also indicated that he/she is coming to the sessions on his/her own terms and that they are being treated in a respectful way, and also that they are the expert of their content and most knowledgeable of their context. The coach is there to continually build the necessary trust and space for the client to be able to talk about what it is they are facing.

Simultaneously the coach assesses the readiness of the client by asking probing questions (of which there are different shades) which allow them to look at it from various points of views, angles, representatives, and impressions of what it is they are trying to answer. When the client naturally laughs and smiles following a coaching conversation, especially after a hard session, this to the coach is evidence of a good coaching relationship.

Coaching isn't a miracle drug. Like any other intervention (of which there are many, though less for healthy individuals) it takes time to work through a client's challenge. The client has to decide whether the conversation has been valuable in achieving their desired result. If, and only if, the client sees and believes that the coach is doing that has the coaching has moved beyond the generalised structure.

Clients form their own structure, meaning and ways to check their outcomes. As the clients are working their way through a specifically challenging situation, the coach needs to recognise the client's structure and behavioural patterns, and demonstrate empathy and remain objective during those conversations that will continually help the client make that initial move forward. How many steps might that include? Well, that needs to be checked.

Depending on the client's needs, the scheduled sessions fits into their diary. This means it could be within two or three days, or every six to eight weeks. Some clients have kept their scheduled coaching times in their diary for a planned reflection knowing that the focus is on them, and only them. For them, it's about what he or she needs to revitalise themselves and keep them moving forward, and it's about the quality of attention that coaching offers to the individual. It provides them with a plethora of positive behaviours and experiences (confidence, assertiveness, awareness, credibility, thoughtfulness). It becomes part of their re–energisation process to keep moving forward in their role and life. For example, one of my clients travelled at least an hour each way for an hour–and–half session every six to eight weeks for a whole year.

There are also times when coaching works just in one session. Those are serendipitous meetings. For example, a business owner had been working through a problem for a long time with his partner in the restaurant business. He was very much in the moment and desperately trying to find out what was missing. He attended a coach training taster session to see if he could find a way to answer the question. He was invited by someone he knew, and then he was referred to me during the break. One thing led to another, and we ended up having a coaching conversation. As he talked, he outlined his situation and shared all the different ways he tried to tackle this problem. I listened and simply jotted down his key points onto a piece of paper (we used the 'Wheel of Life'). After he finished speaking, he looked at what was on the paper when he suddenly realised that he hadn't put down 'communication'. He hadn't spoken to his business partner about the challenges. As soon as he realised that was his next step he thanked me and rushed off to speak to his business partner. In that moment he got what he was looking for and he knew what he needed to do next.

Some coaches might think, "*Hey, you should have coached him around how he should be communicating with his business partner*". Others might be thinking, can you call that coaching if it hasn't been properly contracted for? But for me, the client knew what it was that he was looking for and I happened to be in the right place at the right time. The right conditions were created for him to work on his pressing problem, and it was he who decided that I had provided the right behaviours for him to trust me in that moment. And this is just one example.

A key principle in coaching is to always start from where the client's readiness is. That's where contracting really needs to start too, as well as establishing a more collaborative and flexible business model that reflects more accurately the realities of coaching.

**PART 1: Leading edges in practitioner learning and development**

# Wellbeing shouldn't be a 'hidden' agenda

*Liz Pick*

There are times in my professional life when I feel like I'm operating undercover because some aspects of employee wellbeing are still taboo subjects for employers and staff. When I'm contacted by an organisation and asked to coach someone, it is almost invariably to help them perform more effectively at work. However, many of my coaching clients tell me, in confidence, about the wellbeing challenges they are living with and struggling to manage such as stress, physical or mental health problems, caring for a family member or marital breakdown.

Clients are wary of informing their employer, for fear of negative consequences, so coaches are in a unique position; they can address these issues without the need for disclosure and, most importantly, the focus is on helping the client achieve sustainable performance. So if my client discloses that they have a chronic illness, I assume it is because they feel this is impeding them rather than because they want my sympathy. It's a golden opportunity to develop their capacity to manage their health and resilience alongside their other commitments. I can then help them prioritise tasks more effectively, make better use of the available time and resources, or develop strategies to conserve their energy when the going gets tougher.

It's clear to me that my clients can only perform to the best of their ability if we actively consider and address *all* the factors affecting their work. In short, wellbeing is an important part of the equation, alongside available resources and competencies such as leadership and communication skills. In my experience, this holistic approach is more rewarding for clients but we also need to help organisations to understand the benefits of offering employees confidential development and support that will allow individuals to discretely address whatever is inhibiting their performance.

This matters because a study by health insurer, AXA PPP and reported in *The Times*[1] revealed that only one third of 1,000 employees questioned would be honest with their employer if they needed time off for depression, stress or anxiety. One in four feared they would be judged as weak, while 7 percent said they feared their manager's reaction. And I am only scratching the surface. According to UK statistics, there are millions of people who are at work and grappling with significant life challenges, often without confiding in their colleagues. Do any of us know whether we work alongside one of the seven million carers in the UK[2]; or one of the estimated one in five people who have anxiety or depression[3]?

I believe more needs to be done at organisational level so that employees can have access to confidential support if they need it, while remaining in work.

As a coach I have been working undercover too long – now it's time for the profession to speak out about the link between performance and wellbeing, and help bridge the gap between employees and employers.

---

[1] [website] The Times. "Bosses lack concern for mentally ill staff." (The Times, 31 March 2015) http://www.thetimes.co.uk/tto/health/mental-health/article4397453.ece
[2] [website] Carers Trust "Key facts about carers." (2010) http://www.carers.org/key-facts-about-carers
[3] Joanne Evans, Ian Macrory and Chris Randall. "Measuring National Well-being: Life in the UK, 2015" (Office for National Statistics, 2015) p17 http://www.ons.gov.uk/ons/dcp171766_398059.pdf

# Does your job stress or energize you?

## Nicholas Wai

*"Working hard for something we don't care about is called stress; working hard for something we love is called passion."*

**T**his quote by Simon Sinek, author of the popular business strategy book *Start with Why* and its related TED talk, showed up on my Facebook page this morning. It resonated with me so much that I felt compelled to share my thoughts and feelings. Why did I react to it so much? Looking back at my career, I can recall a long period of time when I was under constant stress that it felt normal to be working in such a condition. I even told myself that I needed the stress to perform, to play the game. Although I was doing well and getting promotions and recognitions, I was always tired and didn't sleep well.

Since switching career into coaching and training four years ago, even though I am as busy, if not more so, as before, I can feel a source of energy from deep within me that sustains and propels me forward. Compared with before, I feel more alive, more able to handle pressure and more confident in taking up challenges. Although I have also made some lifestyle changes that contributed to my better wellbeing, such as being more disciplined about my rest time, doing regular exercise and eating more healthily, I believe my willingness to change and sustain my new lifestyle has a lot to do with the fact that I want to be physically and mentally strong so I can be more ready and equipped to do the work I love.

You may ask, is doing what you love enough? And what can you do if you are not ready to jump into a completely different career? Regarding the first question, I would like to refer to a model I used in a recent talk about finding your dream job I did at a local university. So, is just doing what you love enough? Probably not, because you would also need to do it well, meaning you will need to have the knowledge, skills and experience the work requires. And on top of this, a dream job would not be a dream job if it does not at least pay you well enough to sustain you financially, let alone really well. Understanding the three components will help you find your sweet spot that is your dream job.

How do we help our clients find and work towards this sweet spot, you might ask? A suggestion, is to first, use techniques to help the clients find their important values and motivations. Then, ask the question – what problems are you good at solving for others, or what problems are you passionate in helping others solve? With these component parts brought to awareness, we can then help our clients identify any knowledge/skill/experience gaps that need to be developed, or meaningful work that the clients could change to or expand into by recrafting their jobs if they are not ready to take the jump. By this stage, the client will be able to more confidently and precisely come up with action steps that lead them towards their sweet spots.

By breaking down a question that at first seems impossible into more manageable steps, the clients will not only have the motivation but also the pathways to their ultimate dream job. So my questions to you:

- What are the problems you are good at solving at your job right now?

- What problems are you passionate in helping others solve?

- How motivated are you in finding and living your dream life?

# Reframing success

*Charlotte Rydlund*

**H**ow do you know when you've made it? Is it the new car, the promotion, the raise? Is it that one–in–a–lifetime vacation, or that dream job, house or yacht?

'Having made it' really depends on your context and even age. Think about a time in high school or university where something was very important to you; when you thought you'd made it. What was it, and what about it was so important? What about something that you're striving for now? How are these two instances similar or different?

Irrespective of life stage and context, how we define success is hugely influenced by our environment and at least to some extent our own values and morals.

So, what happens when you've reached that next level? It might be awesome for a short while, enjoying driving that convertible on a summer's day (I know I'd love that!), but what happens after the novelty wears off? In my experience, it can quickly become the new norm. It's no longer something to yearn for or achieve. It doesn't feel as special as it once did. Why is that? Is it because somebody else has a similar thing or experience or prestige? Has it become less fun?

Every time I achieve or get something I've been aiming for, I realize that while I've gotten that thing and achieved what I self–define as success, it never ends. Instead it easily becomes a competition between you and others instead of something you truly want. That's where this classic measure of success falls apart for me. I'm not at all opposed to setting and reaching goals, but my question is – what is so important about that thing of success? *What do you want to get out of it?*

So, in asking that question, *what do you want out of it?* I challenge you to reframe your concept of success. Instead of just going for that promotion, ask yourself *what do you want to get out of it? What do you want to get out of* travelling to that once–in–a–lifetime place? *What do you want to get out of* getting that car?

I certainly continue to follow my dreams and strive for success. That being said, it has helped me choose where I focus and what I consider success after asking myself *what I want to get out of it.*

It struck me recently – what would happen if we were all to replace the concept of success, with the concept of creating a legacy; something to be known for after you've bought and sold that car, after you've been promoted five times over, after you've sailed the yacht across the Atlantic? I might still get that car and travel to India, but it will be with a more defined purpose.

As a clever gentleman once said, it's not where you go, it's what you take away. "*What will your legacy be?*"

# Contracting to avoid gossiping

## *Eamon O'Brien, Doug Montgomery and Yvonne Thackray*

**H**ere is the story of how three coaches formed a small coaching discussion group which started as a couple of one–to–ones over coffee chats, and how it developed into an important part of our CPPD.

### THE 'ROBUSTA' CHALLENGE

It can be so lonely being an executive coach. Caring for people day in day out – attending to the other person's agenda every minute of every conversation. The only other person you come into contact with is the coach supervisor; one who makes you work in examining every breath you take, the questions you've asked, how the responses were given, any somatic twitches. All great stuff, but sometimes all you really want to do is to indulge in having an ordinary conversation about coaching, with a bit of care and attention sprinkled in.

Maybe like other professions it is hard to have an engagingly good chat about coaching other than with likeminded and passionate coaches. Importantly, for one of the three of us, it was about having those exchanges that move beyond the starter conversation: "*'What do you do?' 'I am an executive coach.' '... and I can see them thinking of a fifty–two–seater bus with an on board loo!'*" Hence the call for action, and what was clearly of paramount importance to us:

> *"We coaching nerds need to get a chance to talk shop with people who speak the coaching lingo."*

## The 'blend' approach

The three of us met at the APECS symposium in 2014. The set up was serendipitous rather than planned. It started with an intention. Eamon, trio numero uno, had determined that he was going to make more use of this professional body's network. So he used the period after the symposium was finished to set up coffees with others he had met. Yvonne and Doug (numero dos and tres, or trois and deux) had coffee with Eamon. We all realised that we would bore each other senseless if it were just the two of us! Just joking... In any case, the wise notion of inviting the third member to the next coffee was hit upon and so the trio was born.

As a group, we did not set out to create what we eventually named a 'peer exploration group'. As Eamon noted: "*Funny, I think an end of the pier exploration group might also be an option*" before pausing to ponder and say, "*Funny how it is necessary to dream up a label for three people having a chat in a bean brewing bar. Or indeed, how it is necessary to dream up a funny name for a trio buying beverages brewed by baristas.*"

I think you can already begin to note how our conversations were going! Humour plays a significant role in our group interactions!

## Contracting to avoid gossiping

Somehow as our conversations about weather, business, family and hobbies started to make each other's ears bleed – when Yvonne asked the question: "*If we are going to continue getting together perhaps we ought to agree why and what we might do at them?*"

"*Goodness!*" the others exclaimed – "*What a tremendous introduction to the need for us to contract.*"

As coaches we have many frameworks up our sleeves, and we quickly set about asking each other questions that helped us create the conditions we wanted to (a) belong to and (b) participate in:

- Why would it be valuable to meet?

- What am I bringing and what do I value that the others bring?

- How do we go about our discussions?

- What do I know about myself that will get in the way?

- What feedback do I want?

- What might we discuss?

- And, *very insightfully,* we also asked the question – What it is not?

It took time – approximately six months – and a level of readiness for each member of the trio to complete a written version of our respective expectations and requests. Thinking about what we wanted for ourselves and from the others was not a rushed affair; committing to something and setting it down on paper needed careful attention.

And thus we co–created our agreement – a living contract. During our conversations we have been referring back to it and it has enabled us to discuss, debate, disagree and argue, and still end with a mutually agreeable output.

Our outcomes from answering all those questions boiled down for us to:

- Thinking out loud about coaching with a couple of people who have a similar curiosity and different experience,

- A chance to stay contemporary, and

- To explore new perspectives together.

PART 1: Leading edges in practitioner learning and development

Importantly...

*"We wholeheartedly agreed that this is not a space for
supervision nor a place to comply with coaching accreditation."*

This was, and has remained, hugely valuable and significant to each of us. It enabled the space to be safe, discursive and one of exploration. If you like, it forced us to take off our coaching hats at the door, hang them up and just get on to talking about what we loved to talk about. In hindsight and with no data and a load of intuition, it allowed the three of us to relax knowing we were not been assessed, nor coached – that it was ok to have **our own agenda** for once!

Collectively, we also found several things in common that we were looking for from each other:

- How we each bring different experiences and training and style to the group,

- How we are all benefiting from our common and different strengths and perspective,

- And how to achieve all this with humour.

We also wanted to create a rewarding environment where we could celebrate success together and to reflect on disappointments. It is where we come to have a laugh, good coffee and the occasional pie.

Within our agreed boundaries this included:

- Elements of fun, excitement and supportiveness.

- A place where we can hear and listen to each other and can ask the 'daft' question.

- Where we can respectively and respectfully challenge one another, and where it is ok not to know all the answers and be able to suggest the unexpected or unusual.

This may sound to you very much like a coaching contract and you are spot on! Such qualities of contracting are serving us all well in many different settings beyond coaching and supervision.

## THE 'TAMPER' TOPICS

So what sort of subjects do we discuss in our peer exploration group or PEG – since we want to hang this blog on something!

Over the past year or so our discussions have ranged from the big picture to agendas with a particular focus, and across a breadth of coaching territory. Importantly, through each of our discussions, it became evident for one of us, Doug, to realise that what we were actually doing is CPD or CPPD (continuing personal and professional development). We are taking the time to review, reflect, relate how we are each developing in our own market, and in the challenges we face as well as celebrating our successes, as we're all too humble to share it publicly. We have selected each other as peers from our community, who work in different positions in the coaching market, and have complimentary personal strengths to each other.

## CPPD

Lifelong learning is, or should be, synonymous with coaches.

- We are each individually responsible for learning. We need to keep up–to–date with relevant market news, latest research, broadening knowledge as well as improving one's skills and competence.

- We need to be aware of what is happening in each of our respective markets and our clients' environments.

- We may recommend to each other frameworks, trainings and books to read, but we will also critically review what its strength and limitations are by sharing case studies, pilots and personal experiences to demonstrate its relevance to our respective work.

For us, this is much more than a 'tick' box exercise in CPPD[1], because this is about our professional competence as executive coaches.

We also appreciate that the coaching field is still in its embryonic stage. Research carried out on CPD/CPPD in other membership bodies for e.g. the Chartered Institute of Personnel and Development (CIPD) and other professional membership bodies, indicates that the primary motivation is *"to avoid losing one's licence to practice[2]"* by recording and logging CPD points or hours rather than demonstrating *"the value"* of the development activities themselves.

Paradoxically, CPPD should demonstrate professional competence that serves and protects society. In a twenty–year review of CPE[3] (continuing professional education, the predecessor to CPD), Young (1998) concluded, *"Governmental bodies, professional associations and employers have used mandatory continuing professional education as a method to quell public concern about professional incompetence[4]."* There is still much we coaching nerds need to do, the gap may be easier to bridge in this context.

## TIME FOR SOME MACCHIATO SHOTS – FLAVOURSOME TOPICS

The following examples we hope gives you a flavour of our discussions:

### 1. What the hell is this executive coaching thing?
One of the first topics we explored was, *"What does coaching, and in particular executive coaching mean to me?"*

We discovered that we each had a specific working definition of coaching in which there are significant overlaps as well as personal differences that come from our backgrounds, training and practice.

---

[1] Judith Underhill & Sue Young. "How CPPD can make a difference", from *2014 APECS Symposium.* (2014)
[2] Peter Scales. *Continuing Professional Development in the Lifelong learning sector.* (Open University Press, 2011)
[3] Hilary Lindsay. "Adaptability: The Secret to Lifelong Learning." (PARN, 2014)
[4] William H. Young (ed.) "Continuing Professional Education in Transition," in *Continuing Professional Education in Transition: Visions for the Professions and New Strategies for Lifelong Learning.* (1998)

Broadly we agreed that coaching is about supporting a client's thinking and exploration and enabling them to change their thinking and behaviour in positive ways that take them towards their goal. It involves having the coaching mind set of trusting the client's creativity and resourcefulness and that we are there to support not fix them.

The common ground.

However *how* we do this varied, including how we carried out diagnostics, framed measures of success from coaching, and how much we should share and offer from our experience as part of the coaching process. We have all been trained in different institutions and with similar but different underpinning foundations. For example, we explored what is non–directive coaching, and where on, the spectrum of directive – model driven – non–directive we felt most comfortable and uncomfortable coaching in:

- Is it a personal thing?

- Is it something we comply with as a result of our training?

- How has our experience informed us so far?

With no right or wrong answers, just our backgrounds, experiences and how we have been trained, the discussion was rich and brought us all new perspectives that are helping us all to define what we offer and which clients are most likely to benefit from working with each of us. Only our clients and those around them can actually tell us what our impact has been!

Adding executive to coaching created an interesting distinction – is it being used as an adjective or a proper/collective noun? How does executive coaching differ from coaching?

Some of the points we considered:

- Is it our own background – I was an executive once – therefore am I 'executive' enough to be an executive coach?

- Or is what we do different from other niche coaches because there are additional stakeholders to manage and contract with? Managers to get feedback from, HR directors to negotiate with, working with leaders to meet the strategic objectives of the organisation alongside their personal development.

- The context is specific to the organisation and the title on the door may be more senior but should executive coaching really be excluding the middle and/or junior managers, or any other professional who works in the organisation and wants to help it meet its objective? Perhaps the perceived working definition has been narrowly defined by the job the client does.

For example, the Association of Professional Executive Coaches and Supervisors[5] [APECS] defines executive as: "*A person who has a level of leadership responsibility (financial/operational/people) and/or responsibility for policy formulation and/or who makes a senior level contribution to the organisation.*" We discussed whether the APECS definition of 'executive' was broad enough or too limiting based on the following:

- Could it be that in some applications it is not inclusive enough or diverse enough to meet the needs of the market of which there are multitudes of organisations?

- Does this mean that the suited and booted image of the typical executive is appropriate or can it include professional athletes, for e.g. golfers, as suitable clients for the executive coach? They are both, after all, executing a strategy in highly competitive fields and seeking to be able to perform under intense pressure.

- What of the leaders in a small NGO or a charity?

- How far down an organisation do you go before you stop finding the executives?

- Who coaches those below that point?

- Who coaches the high–potential talent early in their career before they reach the 'executive suite'?

We then followed up by asking: "*So if that is executive coaching, then what does it mean to be a professional coach?*"

---

[5] [website] www.apecs.org

We all bring a strong need to be professional in our conduct and standards of ethics and practice, and boundary management. It is important to all three of us to know what we know and where the edges of our knowledge and learning is. Peer recognition through accreditation and our ongoing personal and professional development/supervision are important aspects of being professional. We all bring this attitude from previous education and career experiences. We also realise that we consider ourselves as professional coaches and that we are without a recognized and regulated 'profession' to belong to.

## 2. Help!

On a more practical note, we have had a very different conversation supporting one of our trio as they were struggling with the question: "*How do I ask for a referral or recommendation from a client at the end of an assignment? What makes it so difficult for me to ask?*" The three–way discussion that followed shared our respective experiences, explored assumptions and beliefs. It enabled a way forward and a small experiment or two to try out. It also enabled us all to explore our own practices and then extended the discussion into how we get feedback from clients and how we use it.

## 3. Who am I now?

We are all members of APECS and have gone through a very thorough accreditation process which invites applicants to explore who they are as an executive coach. One of the most enlightening things we have done is to share our respective APECS accreditation documents with each other. As many APECS members will verify, we found the accreditation process very valuable and insightful. These personal explorations and detailed descriptions of where we have come from and who we are as a coach, at the point in time that it was written, are unique and very personal. As we read each other's document, we each asked the same question:

- If this is you at that point in time, where are you now?

- What's new? How have you grown and developed to meet the needs of your market?

- What have you left behind (for now)?

- What has changed?

- How has your coaching philosophy developed?

## "*WHAT'S NEXT?*" ASKS THE PEG BARISTA

It's been almost a year, and we've met face to face for a couple of hours every six to eight weeks, and for the last few meetings over Zoom (similar to skype). We don't have the answers yet, and this will be constantly under review as we continue on in our PEG exploration. Importantly though we bring in topics that are important to us in that moment that helps us to individually explore our market within the broader topic of the coaching market.

This content was also presented as a paper at the 2015 APECS symposium and stimulated interest from other APECS members. It has spawned two additional PEGs and inspired a group of internal coaches to form a slightly larger group.

And whilst we're still learning, new questions have emerged for us and we've shared them as question points for you to consider – hope you have a coffee in hand ready to engage:

- What are you learning from this that may add value to your own CPPD?

- How has a lack of contracting in formal/ informal relationships/ groups led to a misunderstanding later on for you in different situations?

- If two is company and three's a crowd – what is the critical mass of a peer exploration group?

## Contracting during coaching – with its real 'beating heart'

*Jeremy Ridge*

**We know how** important our hearts are to our lives. Similarly, coaching can also be seen as having a 'heart'. It possesses a rhythmic beat just below the radar which has vital significance.

For those invisible behaviours that are so much in the moment, coaching must interpret their significance. Any behaviour has so many elements to it. Behaviour is more than simply words – it is posture tone of voice, facial expression, eye contact, timing of words spoken, etc.

Coaching needs a quality of attention given to the coachee that is moment by moment. When you measure coaching in that way the moment is filled with significance; every moment then can last for quite a long period especially when you measure it as events every second. Similar to the way our hearts beat – every second – providing what our body process needs.

An underpinning at the heart of coaching is 'contracting'. Why call it contracting? Contracting is one of those words that is very formal, of course. But it is a generally accepted idea and word. It is generally understood to involve an agreed, and required, standard of attention by one party to another. It is important as a term as it is one which is both established and accepted. It is even part of normal legal systems. For example, a more precise definition of contracting is:

*"The elements of a contract are 'offer' and 'acceptance' by 'competent persons' having appropriate capacity who exchange 'consideration' to create 'mutuality of obligation'. "*

Of course, there is a great deal of contracting that already takes place as an explicit formal part of the coaching process. This is especially true with executive coaching. Normally this is undertaken at the start of a coaching contract. 'Outcomes' is the word usually used to describe outputs from coaching, defined in terms of developments of coachee behaviour outside of the coaching session. A regular check on explicit, desired and achieved outcomes will be under continuous review as part of the evolving, and growing, contract of connectedness between coach and coachee throughout the life of the assignment.

In addition, there will be other explicit contracting conditions for the coaching sessions that are set – from frequency and duration, through to ethics and non–disclosure about the contents of the process. There may well be a condition of formal review of progress – for example, after three sessions and at the conclusion.

However, do we also include contracting during the small moments, and events, that create this connectedness? It can even seem they can be still difficult to be fully aware of.

The 'chemistry' contracting meeting is a good example of how the small events can matter, where a coachee is given a quick meeting with different coaches to see which coach they prefer. The way this contracting takes place is often quite invisible. So there must be a gap in identifying what exactly the approach needed is – as we can't specify it. And then what happens at the chemistry session is so invisible a form of contracting that we have to use a metaphor like 'chemistry', like 'alchemy', to describe it. It is often difficult to describe and track. It can be very unpredictable.

The coachee may respond, unexpectedly, to a wide range of coach behaviours. The coachee may have undisclosed expectations of the coaching process that are still difficult to predict in any contracting. A great deal depends on how the coachee may interpret the signals given out by the coach. This is where we need to contract effectively. If we are not aware of these small moments of behaviour signals, between both parties, the whole process can be undermined.

The really important part of coaching starts right from the very first 'chemistry' of meeting. Expectations can be created from even before the first 'hello'. Events can happen very fast, and every event can count significantly.

Every moment–by–moment event.

We need awareness of all such small events. Happening second by second. Checking that we are on a healthy path. This is the real heart of coaching that has to keep beating. When the heartbeat stops before time it can be dangerous!

We must become more attuned to this moment–by–moment experience in coaching. For example, there are those subtle moments when the coachee starts to give subtle signals. This could include a sudden change in eye contact, a showing of a tightness in expression, a shift in how someone is sitting. It can include a comment which is ambiguous in meaning and needs to be clarified. Are you noticing these subtleties? And how are you finding a way to engage with them?

It can be as simple as riding a bicycle, of course – when you have learned to ride. We know we are doing all of this intuitively, and may not stop to think about just how we are managing this important moment–by–moment detail. We just do it. We don't think about how to stay upright. We don't think about the instinctive adjustments we make. We don't think about all that balance requires. We don't think about how we do any of it.

As you have been reading this, I would assume all manner of reactions, and thoughts, may have come to you. Now, how do I contract to hear about them? That is the question!

# PART 2

## *Cutting edge performance in practitioner delivery*

# The Organisational Leadership Journey – into Chaos!

## Isobel Gray

*It continues to surprise me*
*How some*
*Apparently intelligent*
*and personable people*
*Can transform*
*When they become*
*appointed senior leaders.*

*Oblivious (sometimes wilfully)*
*To their impact.*
*Saying nothing speaks volumes,*
*Gives messages*
*To those watching for signals*
*Of their intentions.*
*In the vacuum*
*Worst interpretations*
*Rush in,*
*Diverting*
*attention and energy*
*From organisational needs*
*To individual narrow self interest*
*Feeding short term*
*Perceived 'Survival'*
*Tactics.*

*Senior Leader behaviours*
*That confirm fears.*
*Pronouncing without*
*Connecting to*
*Real context,*
*Or others' experience,*
*Or seeking to gain*

*True Insight*
*From others experience*
*And expertise.*
*Not checking out or testing*
*Their assumptions.*

*Seeing developing*
*organisational strategy*
*As a purely top down*
*Process rather than*
*An iterative, collegiate*
*and sometimes tough process,*
*Dependent on input from*
*All levels and areas*
*In a safe, supportive*
*Environment, where people*
*Are encouraged to share*
*Different perspectives;*
*Think differently.*
*The need for an appropriate*
*Level of structure and*
*Providing the container,*
*– all ignored.*

*They say*
*the right–sounding words,*
*But don't follow through.*
*So the behaviours*
*Do not match the words.*
*Abandoning the best*
*Of what already exists;*
*Not referring to*
*The platform already achieved*
*By others before they*
*Arrived as Leaders.*

*No sharing of the bigger picture.*
*Keeping the children*
*In the dark.*
*'We do all the strategy stuff'*
*Divide and Rule*
*Is the Name of the Game.*
*Stuck in putting out*
*Their pet opinions*
*And ways of seeing things;*
*making demands.*
*Oblivious to the greater*
*Collective need.*

*Who do they think they are?*
*Egos on the rampage...*
*and another potential*
*Organisational Mess*
*in the making.*

# CHAPTER 4

# CREATING ENGAGEMENT BETWEEN THE COACH AND THE CLIENTS

**How coaching, and the intimacy it can achieve, could add to the idea of what 'Engagement' can really achieve**

*Jeremy Ridge*

The areas I want to cover are:

- The importance of recognising how coaching can, at its best, achieve important levels of intimacy between the coach and coachee, and what this involves.

- A full understanding of how coaching works and how this could do a lot to transform appreciation of current use of terms like engagement.

- The mechanical structures of organisations that may benefit from working better in facilitating the sort of intimacy that results in real quality engagement.

The term 'engagement' has become increasingly popular – Especially as 'employee engagement'. Organisations even invest in, albeit still simple, levels of research into levels of employee engagement through undertaking 'surveys' of employee engagement.

Of course, even introducing the term 'employee' with the term engagement immediately highlights the difficulty, and the opportunity. Employee becomes a term that might limit the appreciation of people for what they could engage with.

People often join organisations for reasons of work, for the financial priority of earning a living. What really engages and motivates their interests are often pursued outside of the organisation.

Motivating people is a well–studied topic. It is tempting for people to do as little as possible at work, rather than as much as possible, when life outside the organisation is more stimulating and satisfactory than life inside the organisation.

**The famous 'Hawthorne' research**[1] started the record of reported understanding about this topic. It showed up the startling impact of the 'placebo' effect, where an experiment using varying levels of lighting available for workers showed improvements in productivity – no matter what the level of lighting was. Performance just went on improving even when the level of lighting was lowered to dark levels. It was concluded that simply *giving attention* – of any sort – was the really *motivating, engaging factor.*

Coaching is about this idea of giving people quality attention. It is also still a challenge for coaching as to whether the coach makes the difference, or whether just giving someone the time to themselves might work by itself!

**Coaching at its best** provides a quality of attention that enables a person to express and learn about themselves in a way that they don't find easy anywhere else. Coaching can also bring important fresh perspectives to this question of getting people engaged with their context, e.g. their organisation, and finding ways to improve how they engage with it.

---

[1] [website] http://www.economist.com/node/12510632

**PART 2: Cutting edge performance in practitioner delivery**

It is still very easy though to look at coaching as being about something remedial – help a person achieve minimal requirements, or else the organisation may 'let them go' elsewhere.

**Voluntary organisations are often the best example** for how an organisation can engage with people's positive energy. After all, when people are working without normal financial rewards, it must be for something else; perhaps an inner reward. Is this the idea of 'self' that is beginning to form in our understanding of coaching and what it is about?

**This attention to the 'self'** and that form of self–motivation can really impact the sort of positive energy and focus that a person wants to bring, and then how they can bring it. Ultimately this positivity allows them to start living in their various contexts much more actively.

As coaches, we also have to keep our own selves carefully managed in such dialogues! Many managers in organisations can get so self–focused, for example, about creating a (non–personal) system, that this then denies space to any other person not thinking the same way as them or their system. This then denies the attention needed for the unique features and perspectives of any self, or selves, within that system.

**Coaching attention can involve creating confidence in the way the relationship works. This then produces a form of real – confidential – intimacy about the self, the person and the coachee involved.**

- It is something to do with showing a sincere and insightful interest and understanding of another person's possibly half–formed awareness about themselves. It is a moment in which they show interest in understanding and exploring themselves further, and in their own words.

- These are not the textbook – mechanical – questions and words coaches use when talking about coaching; it is a conversation that can start to invent private meanings between the coach and coachee.

I find when these conditions are achieved, the coaching agenda can shift significantly. More of the real whole person becomes involved with the conversation. This can provide new insights into the matter that may have started the agenda.

The question, *"How can I be more effective in my role in an organisation?"* moves more towards not only what the organisation wants, but what the coachee would enjoy bringing more to the organisation in a way all would value it.

**A good example of current thinking about employee engagement** is offered in a report by one organisation – *"Becoming irresistible: A new model for employee engagement,"* by Deloitte University Press[1].

Of course, starting with the term 'employee' in talking about 'employee engagement' already invents some big traps. The word employee can carry some serious limitations of thinking in addressing the matter.

The report suggests building an irresistible organisation is the answer, rather than talking about employee engagement. The article then goes on to emphasise a need for the right organisation 'culture', and of course that other big idea – a coaching culture.

1. **Culture is still about people!** The frontline of any culture is still down to the kind of interaction that takes place between people. This is where coaching, at its best, still needs to be held in higher focus. Employee engagement will only create a genuine quality of participation when the employee is engaged as a full person for who they are, and how they want to live their own personal energy.

2. **Even Time out!** Employee engagement for some organisations has now resulted in accepting that the 'employee' can only achieve this by being given time out of the organisation; the best way of enabling them to find an outlet for their fuller self. So employees have time out of the organisation – where they may work on a voluntary basis for some other (voluntary) organisation that more closely enables them to live their passion and real interests.

---

[1] [website] http://dupress.com/articles/employee–engagement–strategies/

As coaches, we still have a great opportunity to help others close this gap and aid organisations in tapping into the real energy that engagement could bring.

We also know how much work it can take to get this level of dialogue even in our coaching sessions, still:

- How confident are you of achieving this sort of intimacy with your coaches?

- How do you achieve this?

- How well can you get this across to others about why it is important?

# Seaside coaching – After the Storm

## *Dr. Lucille Maddalena*

**H**ave you ever watched people simply stand and stare at the sea for hours? Mesmerized with the rolling waves, warmed by the sun and cooled by the soft breeze, the sounds and smells create a meditative environment.

> *"We ourselves feel that what we are doing is just a drop in the ocean. But the ocean would be less because of that missing drop."*
>
> – Mother Theresa of Calcutta

When you are at a transition point in your life, do you seek the familiarity of your current surroundings? How do you sort through the turmoil that accompanies change to discover your own revelations?

> *"Smooth seas do not skilful sailors make."*
>
> – African proverb

Recalling my first coaching session conducted at the ocean, I wasn't certain when the useful dialogue began. The one thing I insisted on was that we walk. We didn't have to walk on the sand or to the water's edge: staying on the boardwalk or heading to a seaside restaurant was fine. As we walk, we talk: our pace moves us through time as we near the ocean.

On the first block we peer down the path to glimpse where the ocean meets the sky and hear a gentle rhythm. The conversation is light as we discuss our surroundings and living situations, exchanging private revelations that strengthen and bond our association.

On the second block the waves come into view and the volume of the breakers begins to increase. There is a slight tenseness to the conversation as petty annoyances rise to the surface then dispel. Each step is deliberate, expressing our earnest intent to address issues of burden.

By the third block, the graceful boardwalk beckons while partially blocking our view of the sand and sea. Our pace quickens. Sentences are left unfinished with short, terse expressions of verbal release; speech patterns become fast and reactive.

Now we are on the boardwalk overlooking the full display of sand, sea, sky. The impact of the stunning view silences us. It is impossible to talk or even breathe for that first moment, as we step up to the majesty before us. The breeze fills our lungs: magically, all trivial complaints are gone.

> *"Wide sea that one continuous murmur*
> *breeds along the pebbled shore of memory!"*
>
> – John Keats

I feel my own stress leave as I inhale the salt air, and we comfortably assume our roles of coach and client. We continue our path allowing the first flow of stressors to emerge. Each item is presented, contemplated and marked for future action.

For my guest, it is the time to reveal the innocence, the vulnerable individual carefully preserved by layers of training, education, experience, loss and success. We talk about those vague, soft topics that are too difficult or embarrassing to grasp in public situations: values, ethics, passion, creativity, commitment and dedication. We slowly work our way to issues of seeming importance: expectations, professionalism, goals, obstacles and priorities as we seek balance.

The close to our conversation always comes down to choices. This is our conversation as we dine by the sea. The task begins with all due gravity and seriousness; soon the natural flow beams with the joy of spontaneous creativity. Decision paths, options and outcomes are laid as we resort to writing our designs and plans on napkins to preserve the treasure of unrestricted ideas.

Our environment is still in control as we select our path home. Some guests prefer to walk barefoot to the water's edge unconcerned that we will return with seawater in our clothing and windblown hair. Others choose to stand or sit on the boardwalk to look at the ocean, allowing private thoughts to pass in silence. It is with a feeling of freedom and peace that we retrace our steps.

> *"Your reason and your passion are the rudder and*
> *the sails of your seafaring soul, if either your sails*
> *or your rudder be broken, you can but toss and drift,*
> *or else be held at a standstill in mid–seas."*
>
> – Kahlil Gibran

# Beyond personality assessments: Dominance – What the coach can learn about patterns of behaviour and their implications

*Lynne Hindmarch*

Coaches use personality assessments as an additional approach to help raise the coaching client's self–awareness and provide the coach with insights into the client's behaviour. I intend to focus here on *dominance.* The value that long usage of assessments gives in providing the psychometrics practitioner with deep understanding of behaviour and the patterns of behaviour is why this article is called 'beyond personality assessments'.

I intend to explore particular characteristics that coaches may be more inclined to see in clients. I plan to present:

- A core aspect of personality (a particular trait),

- Some of the associated behaviours, and

- What that may mean in combination with other traits, to present a cluster.

This is a personal perspective, based on my experience of using assessments over many years, both as a psychometrician and as an executive coach. There may well be areas which readers disagree with – that would be great! I'd love to debate some of my experiences with other people.

## A couple of points to start with

1. My descriptions of behaviour are based on thousands of hours of giving feedback, and listening to clients' reactions and comments. But again and again I return to the data presented in the personality assessment. Although I may now associate a wider range of behaviours with particular aspects of personality than when I started, it is vital that the interpretation does not go beyond the data. I need to be able to demonstrate to the client the basis for the hypotheses I form.

2. I am focusing on *extremes* of behaviour; that is, those aspects of behaviour that, in the normal distribution curve, fall at the upper or lower limits. Why? Because these are the behaviours that are more consistent – we are less likely to flex around them. Because they are more consistent, people are more likely to notice them (and may use them to describe us to distinguish us from other people). They are often associated with strengths – but also may trip us up (because we are consistent in adopting this type of behaviour, we are less likely to adapt it in different circumstances).

The core trait I want to explore is what is commonly known as dominance. I chose this particular aspect of personality because as a coach I see a lot of it, as I suspect many coaches do who work with middle and senior managers and executives. Dominance is pretty much what it says on the tin: it is the degree to which one wants to dominate and influence people and situations.

I will be focusing on what this means at the high end – that is, when there is a strong desire for dominance, rather than at the low end (when the individual may have very little desire to dominate) simply because that is not a result I often see in my client group. You can see that I don't feel any need to be even–handed! I prefer to follow what is most likely to occur in my practice and hopefully will resonate with those of you who work with a similar client group.

**PART 2: Cutting edge performance in practitioner delivery**

## SO WHAT BEHAVIOURS MIGHT YOU SEE IN A PERSON WITH HIGH DOMINANCE?

This individual is likely to want to take the lead in most situations.

- Often this goes back to childhood – in conversation they will often talk about captaining the sports team, leading the debating society, being head girl etc.

- They are often decisive, persuasive, competitive and ambitious (which tends to help them rise through the organisational ranks).

- Their leadership style may be directive – they have a tendency to tell people what to do rather than consult.

Some of these behaviours may become problematic and be part of the coaching programme. For example, taking one aspect of dominance; directive behaviour (telling people what to do), this can be perfectly appropriate in certain situations such as a crisis, where there is no time or opportunity for consultation or debate. But if the directive style is consistent across all situations, the problems that can occur are:

- Lack of involvement from others in decision–making leading to wrong or poor decisions.

- Lack of power–sharing with team members, leading to people not taking responsibility and waiting to be told what to do.

- Poor development of leadership skills in others.

- The desire to win at all costs rather than considering compromise, which can lead to difficult relationships with peers.

This can lead to the individual's career getting stuck or derailing. The important point to consider is that other aspects of the personality will influence how the trait dominance manifests itself in behaviour.

For example, if it is accompanied by high scores on social confidence and self–confidence, this individual will feel comfortable voicing an opinion forcefully in pretty much every situation, even when he or she doesn't know very much about the subject. The person with these characteristics can be hard to coach; the high level of self–belief means that they don't readily acknowledge the need for development. In this example the feedback can provide the framework for not only discussing the implications of high dominance, but also how high levels of confidence can act as a barrier in doing anything about it. In this way the feedback conversation can assess if this individual is likely to respond positively to a coaching programme.

To provide another example, Joanna is a marketing director whose personality assessment shows she is high in dominance. In meetings she has a strong desire to influence and persuade others over to her way of thinking. But Joanna is also shy; her social confidence is low, particularly with new people. She may feel intimidated and self–conscious. This is very frustrating for her as she feels a keen desire to assert herself, but is unable to express it. Those who know Joanna may wonder why she is quiet in certain meetings, and also she may come across as more compliant than she actually feels. On occasion the frustrated desire to express an opinion can become overwhelming and, rather like a pressure cooker that finally explodes, Joanna puts forward her point of view. However, it may come out in a rather uncontrolled and unfortunate manner – perhaps in a more challenging or aggressive way than Joanna intended or would have liked. This in turn may mean she doesn't get the acceptance of her contribution she may have wanted, and also does nothing to help increase her social confidence.

**Feedback** to Joanna on these aspects of her personality included discussion on how her lack of social confidence was affecting her ability to influence as much as she would like. Joanna knew that she was uncomfortable expressing herself in certain situations; however, until it was highlighted in the assessment, she had not recognised it as shyness. The assessment provided a way of naming it, and once it was named and identified, the coach was able to incorporate it into Joanna's coaching programme.

*Joanna's high dominance, illustrated here by a strong desire to assert herself, was likely to provide a strong motivator for working on her shyness.*

Let us consider another cluster of behaviours.

Dan is general manager of a factory. Like Joanna, his high dominance means that he wants to get his own way. His personality assessment also showed that he is task–focused and sceptical. He is very effective at anticipating difficulties and hitting targets, but he shows no interest in those who work for him. In fact he has said that he believes that emotions have no place at work and should be left at the factory gate. His employees feel that they are cogs in a machine and that their individuality is not recognised or appreciated. Dan's tendency to be sceptical of others means that he always questions people's motives. His peers find him difficult and political. He has said, (on many occasions) "*I am really good at spotting people's hidden motives.*"

This may or may not be the case; the point is that Dan always expects that people will have an ulterior motive, which shapes his behaviour towards them. Dan's career has been successful so far. However, for the first time he is managing a project team where the members do not report directly to him for 'pay and rations'. He has discovered that the attributes that have helped him in his career so far are no longer working for him and he has become stuck. He has been described as intimidating and uncompromising, and people will not put themselves out to get things done for him.

**Feedback** with Dan focused on the advantages of his style in delivering results, as well as helping him recognise its limitations in working with a new team where the lines of responsibility are less clear–cut.

*His coach may need to accept that Dan is likely to be quite challenging and questioning of the coaching process. Helping Dan recognise that building relationships with people can enhance his ability to influence will be key, although he may find the process quite difficult. Once he has recognised the need, Dan will need help in applying practical steps to develop relationships; this may start in a small way, such as making time to get to know his team as individuals.*

Finally, let us consider Trish, who is also strongly dominant. She is also a very people oriented person who comes across as warm and friendly; she is always interested in others and will often ask people about their lives. She is very likeable, and has even been described as charismatic. She has made good progress in her career. She struggles at times when her desire to get her own way upsets people.

**Feedback** with Trish on these aspects of her behaviour included discussion of the positive impact on her warm, influencing manner. People are more inclined to put themselves out for her because they like her. However, Trish may want to think about the negative aspects of this; that it may be important to her to be liked, and the impact this may have on the decisions she makes, particularly if they adversely affect those working closely with her.

*This is likely to be an important aspect of any coaching she undertakes; she may be in danger of developing favourites in her team, and she may struggle if she is called upon to make tough–headed business decisions.*

What I have attempted to do here is illustrate, with a few examples, how a core aspect of personality such as dominance is influenced by other characteristics. Sometimes the only way to access the complexity of these patterns of behaviour is through a personality assessment. The insights presented by the assessment can raise the client's self–awareness, provide a forum for discussing the implications, and help the coach shape the intervention.

# Our needs and behaviours

## Nicholas Wai

**S**omething interesting happened to me in the last few weeks. It prompted me to reflect on its meaning. I am quite famous (or infamous) for going into 'hibernation' mode whenever I attend a class or workshop. Even in concerts and operas I still manage to find some time to catch a few winks no matter how loud or dramatic the music is. I always believed that it was because I was not having enough quality sleep, but I became aware that perhaps there was more to it than that.

A few weeks ago, I broke my hibernation pattern. I failed to dose off during a weekend workshop on adult development and sense–making facilitated by a hero of mine, Joey Chan. The workshop explored works by Robert Kegan and Lisa Lahey, David Rooke and William Torbert, as well as Ken Wilber, who all wrote about quite complex concepts that I found extremely fascinating and couldn't get enough of. Frankly I was quite surprised by how alert and awake I was able to remain, and wondered if it was because of the effectiveness of the particular facilitator, the attractiveness of the particular subject matters or some other factors. Then it happened again, at the following weekend workshop that focused on system thinking and adaptive leadership, which was facilitated again by Joey – I stayed awake for the whole two days!

I was still pondering about this awareness this morning at a breakfast event organised by the local French Chamber of Commerce. A fellow coach, Ikhlas Bidau, in her presentation about managing difficult conversations, explained that our behaviours were informed by our beliefs, which in turn were prompted by our various needs. This showed me that if I dig deep enough, every behaviour I chose was rational and in response to a deep–seated need and belief. When there are competing needs, the corresponding behaviour would be determined by my own hierarchy of needs.

In my case, by choosing to stay awake and alert, I must believe that the subject matters were important for my development as a human being. This belief was in turn informed by my needs to understand and find meaning of the world I live in and how everything is connected. While the first workshop talked about how human thinking complexity developed, and hence the ability to understand the world from multiple perspectives, the second workshop covered system thinking which better explained the cause and effect of a fast changing world than other models that explained events in a more linear fashion. I now not only have a better understanding of my hierarchy of needs and where my passion lies, I have also discovered a way to create better motivation if I want to make a behaviour change – by tying the new behaviour to my more important needs.

This realisation further prompted me to look into the motivational theories I came across during my coaching degree study, and in particular the perceived locus of causality (PLOC). Before then I would like to invite you to ponder the following questions:

- So what are the needs that are driving your behaviours?

- And how would you use this insight in making behaviour changes?

# Helping coachees ask (and answer) smart questions!

## Kim Stephenson

**was recently asked** on the radio, "*What's a good investment?*" I've been asked that a lot because of my background, so it doesn't faze me. But this time I'd spent the previous ten minutes explaining that it was the wrong sort of question!

This can be an issue with coaching – do you try to direct clients (or interviewers), or do you let them find out for themselves (eventually)? And does giving direction (when you're trying to be non–directive) include answering questions that you know are too general, questions that try to get you to tell the asker what to do?

It's about getting people to ask 'smart' questions!

### DIRECTION, DIRECTION, DIRECTION

It's not that being directive with a coaching client is never appropriate. It's just that immediately directing them to an answer is fraught with problems. General answers are usually wrong. Even (especially) with expert knowledge, it's easy to give a correct answer to the wrong question.

I find that it's better to do a lot of definition and only then to help them to the right questions.

It's not that the right answers are necessarily 'inside them', or that your expertise and direction aren't required.

**It's that many smart questions are about what they really want, when, what resources they have (which affect how), who they are, how they operate and, most of all, why they are asking and what they hope to achieve. When you know all that (and so do they), then giving them ideas about possible answers to key questions might be the best thing you can do.**

### EXAMPLES OF THIS QUESTION DILEMMA!

As with, *"What's a good investment?"* clients can ask for a value judgment in a vacuum such as, *"How can I be better?"* or *"What's the best way to do X?"*

That sort of question assumes that there is a single direction of 'bad, tolerable, good, better, best', a universal Likert scale.

It's tempting to answer, particularly if you are a subject expert. Everybody likes to be asked their opinion and feel respected. But it's dangerous.

Since my 'specialist subject' is finance, I'll use examples from finance, but you can substitute anything, sport, relationships, business, whatever the topic on which clients ask you to give absolute, directive answers to vague, context independent questions.

### Example 1. What's the cheapest way to borrow money?

This is a corollary to the common 'expert' statement that nobody should take out a payday loan. The cheapest way to borrow money is probably the bank of mum and dad, but that may not be an option.

Cheapest might be to extend the mortgage because secured lending is usually cheaper. But it depends.

So I could give the 'expert' answer and talk about mortgages, secured and unsecured loans, APR (and differences between APR and AER) and sound knowledgeable. However, that doesn't help the client, who doesn't realise their question is meaningless and that they won't remember any of the three–hour lecture I could give them about their options.

So I'd point them to questions such as, "*What is the money for?*" and "*Why do they want to borrow?*" Maybe they don't really need it or, if they do, don't need to borrow. They can save up or economise on something else. If they do need it, and need to borrow it, when do they need the money? Can they pay by interest free instalments, defer payment etc. The point is that the context is all, so until I've asked why, what, where, when, who (and pretty well any other question I can think of), I've not really got a good picture of the context, so any answer I give is likely to be wrong.

What I'm trying to do is generate options. I may not need to give answers at all. In those cases, the client works out what to do. For example, most people, given enough context and the right questions, can work out for themselves not to take out a payday loan – but still millions take them out each year despite admonitions not to. If I do need to give an answer, I can give one based on the precise requirements of what cheapest means in the context of the actual situation.

### Example 2. Should I save more for pension?

The answer's probably yes! Again, an 'expert' will answer with, "*80 percent of people don't have enough for pension.*" They might even quote statistics about how little the average person will have to live on in retirement. But the client isn't an average person (for a start they don't have 1.8 children, live in a 2.6 bedroomed house or earn precisely £26,679 p/a).

In order to save money, people have to avoid spending it. Sounds simple, and it is. A common saying is, "*Save first, you can spend what you've got left after you save, but you can't save what you have left after you spend, because there will be nothing left."* We all know it would be good to put away money for a rainy day, that's a no–brainer. But when we've got cash in hand (or that substitute, a credit card) the money just goes and we're surprised that it's gone.

So you follow the advice of the expert, to, *"Set up a standing order to savings for the day after your salary hits your bank account."* Which is fine, in theory. But theory doesn't give the right question. In reality, the savings money goes out, then the bill payments and then normal spending takes place. And the account goes into overdraft. The theory is that after a month or two, the spending decreases, but the fact is that the spending continues, on credit card. So we get the situation of several thousand households in the US in 2002 with average savings of $5,000 and average rolling credit card bills of $3,000. Sure, they've saved money for a rainy day. But they're getting 3 percent on the savings and paying 23 percent for the borrowing, so it's costing $600 a year to feel that they're smart for following the guru's advice!

The question isn't, *"Should I save more?"* That's a pretty easy one to answer (whether you're an expert or not). It's questions like why, how, what, and what for, about the money that's going to be saved, and why, what, when etc. about the purpose of the saving that are relevant.

## Example 3. Is property a good investment?
An 'expert' answer could be yes; it's got a potentially great return. It could be no; try selling a property over a week–end if you need the money in a hurry. So it's a meaningless question, but every presenter on the apparently endless collection of identikit property programmes is keen to give the answer.

On your specialist subject, it's easy to get sucked into giving a context independent answer. The reality is, like just about anything, property as an investment has good and bad points. The key is to ask about the specifics to find out why, how, when, what and so on.

But wait, I hear you cry. What about your own house as an investment, surely that's great, it has tax advantages as well, so much so that most of the property programmes are about making money on your home.

Imagine your client intends to follow the route of maximising their mortgage to buy a bigger house than they really want as an 'investment'. There's no downside, if they can afford the payments, is there? OK, try these.

It's more expensive, so it's bigger than you need. It has local schools you don't use as you don't have school age children. It has things that you don't really want, but other people do so the demand has pushed up the price. What has made it expensive is non–essential for you. You're paying a bigger mortgage than you need to buy a house you won't use fully, so if you are ill, lose your job etc., you're in trouble.

You figure it is making you money. By the time you sell it to realise your profit (assuming it has gone up, a potentially big and questionable assumption) you're used to having the extra space, the convenient shops and schools, the location etc. (the things that made it more expensive than you needed) and you can't bear to part with it (humans adapt quickly to change going up and slowly going down). So you're locked in. You can't sell it fast if you need to realise any profit you have made, so even if you cut the price by a huge amount, you'll still be lucky to complete within a few months – fancy waiting that long for an expensive operation? You decide, or need, to move just when the next Northern Rock happens and house prices have plummeted, oh dear, so much for property prices can only go up.

And, of course, if they have gone up, everything else has gone up too. So you can't get as much profit as you thought, unless you go and live in a tent.

- Does that suggest any potential downsides at all?

- And does it suggest any useful questions to edge towards how directive you should be?

This is where your expertise in your field (sports, management or whatever) really comes in. It's not in answering the questions the client asks and directing them to a generic answer. It's in knowing the pros and cons, and being able to direct them to the right, smart, questions to help them decide on the right question and answer for them.

**PART 2: Cutting edge performance in practitioner delivery**

Coaching, at its best, gets to the heart of this issue. As long as the coach is also committed to getting the coachee to ask the smart questions. And the coach can resist the temptation of setting the agenda!

# Helping middle managers step up into their true organisational leadership role

## Sue Young

**P**articularly in times of rapid change middle manager effectiveness is central to organisations achieving the sustainable changes they seek. Although senior managers are responsible for setting the overall direction and mood of an organisation, how successful it is depends on the direction being taken down and through the organisation.

Middle managers have come in for a great deal of criticism in research where ineffective day–to–day line management is the most frequently found reason for de–motivation, lack of engagement and poor performance.

I have seen directly the negative impact poor line management can have – for example:

- Micro–management.

- Undermining behaviour that leads to:

  - Loss of direction,

- Loss of self–belief, and

- Eventual drain of self–confidence, even in the most capable people.

I have also seen the positive power when middle managers step up and take up their leadership role. These cases result in individual and organisational performance knock–on effects that benefit the performance and motivation of the whole team.

## MIDDLE MANAGERS ARE THE REAL LEADERSHIP GLUE

Their true added value in organisations is not always appreciated and often undervalued. If this is the case then it is possible for their role to not add any value and be seen as a 'non–role' – at worst getting in the way. From my direct coaching and facilitation experience what I want to capture here is the positive contribution middle managers, at their best, bring to their organisations.

- Middle managers potentially have the strategic perspective of being able to connect the bigger organisational picture, to the realities and pressures on the ground that any strategy or plan has to address. This knowledge is potentially their source of real added value contribution – if they recognise it, of course.

- Middle managers often find themselves in a position of being expected to lead and maintain staff morale, where the direction is unclear, and their personal future is just as uncertain as the people for whom they are meant to be providing leadership.

### The early stages of their role:

In early stages of their middle management role, and possibly as a remaining style issue, middle managers can find it difficult to let go of the 'doing' operational mind–set. It is only when they have the confidence and perspective to step back and see the need, can they really let go of the day to day. It helps them make this shift when they see more clearly what they want to be doing in their bigger leadership role. Only then do they engage more meaningfully in the true leadership value they can bring.

PART 2: Cutting edge performance in practitioner delivery

For example, are they passing on their knowledge of the bigger context and translating it in terms that will carry meaning for their people? Then, to help them take that perspective into their work, making the day to day judgement calls that need to be made on the ground.

## Pressures during the on–going role:

There's the on–going particular pressures of being 'in–between' top decision makers and the operational level that delivers the service or product to the end users. More middle manager roles today do not have a team reporting to them but rather are accountable for achieving organisational objectives through others, over whom they have no direct authority. This is unless they are amongst the minority fortunate enough to have an enlightened manager who readily passes on information and their intelligence about the bigger picture and overall direction. The most effective middle managers today are proactive in building their own strategic picture, intelligence and wider network of relationships and sources of information.

## The best managers eventually lead their teams, and those they seek to influence, in a highly collaborative way:

They use times of uncertainty to encourage fresh thinking and ideas in the team, and with colleagues across the organisation, about how ways of working can be evolved and how resulting delivery can be improved. They recognise that the core fundamentals of what they are seeking to deliver to users or customers do not change, and they do not lose sight of these fundamentals and represent this reality with their people.

## Managing and holding these kinds of tensions to do with change is probably one of the middle managers most valuable contributions in times of uncertainty:

The reality is that 'them' up the chain do not have definitive answers either. They know the overall direction but do not have all the answers. Sometimes this is not conveyed in the ways some senior managers behave! Once they have a clearer sense of the overall direction, managers can best judge for themselves what is most likely to be changing and, most importantly, reminding others of the fundamental purpose and needs, the things that are unchanging and that are within their control.

They are in the powerful position of often needing to be the translators of the pronouncements put out by senior management. Pronouncements that can sound very general and lacking with regard to the big question for most people: 'What does this mean for me?'

Line managers who are honest and open and there for their people can make a massive difference. They can step in with their personal 'take' on the overall message and what it means in terms that will make sense to their people. In reality, what the clear direction is for us, even if the detail of the 'how' is at this point unclear. It is our job to develop and craft the 'how' in our area of the business.

**The personal challenges – and where coaching can add real value:**
The middle manager probably has the greatest impact with their behaviour and the tone they set.

- Are they true to themselves, open and genuine?

- Do they treat their team members and colleagues with respect?

- Do they disclose their feelings selectively and appropriately to the situation?

- Do they know and share their personal values which shape their leadership approach and are they consistent with this?

- How do they deal with failure? Do they attempt to cover up and bluff their way out or are they open – *"We did not get it right this time; what is important is the learning we take from this experience..."*

- And do they follow this up in wanting to work with the team to understand and get to the bottom of what happened and why?

- Not to play the 'blame game' but to learn for the future.

## Coaching middle managers to do more coaching:

As well as ensuring on–going 'business as usual', engaging their team in continuous development and improvement in delivery of on–going service, middle managers can lead in the tone and culture they set in their leadership approach.

Part of the main purpose of middle managers, as line managers, is to support the continuous learning and improvement of their team, both individually and collectively. At an individual level this will mean treating everyone as an individual with different strengths, working with them flexibly according to their needs. To do this well can be highly personally demanding, particularly when the individual is very different in style and strengths to them. Of course this requires a coaching approach!

At a team level it will be ensuring regular meetings don't deteriorate into low level ritual but find space for keeping review of bigger priority issues. These meetings should generate fresh thinking about longer term focus and ways of working. If managers are in a role where they have no direct authority, they have to influence decision makers. A coaching approach can be an important part of this!

## Middle managers role in 'coaching' their seniors:

Finally, middle managers are a conduit of valuable information and challenge and support upwards. It can take courage to feedback on what is not working well with policies that have been set higher up.

The best managers always look to make the best of a situation. However, they see it as part of their responsibility to feed back to the bigger organisation the real information on what is working and not working. This, together with their thinking about how to approach the issue, are how middle managers recommend to the higher ups on how best to progress.

They also need to be informing the centre of changing trends their people are picking up on. While they largely delegate to their people they are sure to want to keep in close touch with what is happening on the ground.

For example, one of my clients maintains a few selective direct customer relationships to ensure they keep their hand in, and do not lose their first–hand experience of the challenges and issues on the ground.

## COACHING CREATES VITAL SPACE FOR MIDDLE MANAGERS

Managers are busy people who can get so caught up in the 'doing' and do not take the time out to think about themselves and their approach. They may take time out to consider a particular problem they face. However, it can take some good quality coaching conversations, to help managers be more explicitly aware of what it is they do that contributes to their success and where they can best seek to 'stretch' themselves to develop their leadership effectiveness. Of course, as coaches, part of our role is to help middle manager clients broaden and deepen their self–awareness and perspectives on their own particular context, and find their own unique leadership approach and contribution. A definite life journey on which we are only companions for a brief part.

So, as a coach, how and what are you adding to middle managers' true leadership contribution and potential?

# CHAPTER 5

# CREATING AND MAINTAINING THAT QUALITY OF ATTENTION

### *"Attention!"* – What really makes coaching work, or not!

*Jeremy Ridge*

**A**ttention is what I think really makes the difference. It is the real fuel that drives life into all those engines of theories, models and skills etc. Without giving attention to the moment, and all its data, theories are powerless.

Real, healthy, normal people are their own person. If you want this coaching thing to work you must realise that healthy people are too sophisticated to reduce to a generality.

Organising my attention is the most powerful way of getting at what my practice in 'coaching' is wholly concerned with. It is also what I find most stimulating about coaching – testing my attention, exercising it and getting it right.

However, it is not easy getting attention to this theme of attention, despite it being such a key element.

For example:

- Have I got your attention, right now, for the next few mins, here!

- How long will I have?

- How did I get it?

- How do I find this out?

Every living moment is about attention. So just live it. Don't fuss. Just get on with it!

## SO HOW EXACTLY IS ATTENTION IMPORTANT?

At its best coaching provides a quality of attention that enables a person to express and learn about themselves in a way that they don't find easy to do anywhere else. This is where coaching and attention intersect.

Attention is getting people to fully engage with their own self, and to make as much as they want, and are able to make of it, in the circumstances. Coaching needs a quality of attention given to the coachee. Quite a long period if you measure attention as events every second.

- **I know the typical ways I give attention, in coaching** – for example I work hard at learning the language, and even single words, the person I am with is using – the particular meanings and experiences behind another person's expression that generate them.

- **I am constantly exploring and playing back with people their meanings** – appreciating how different their experiences and meaning making is from my own.

- **Especially as the only measure of giving attention is by the receiver's response** – not the theory and good intentions of the sender. *You can't say I am giving you attention, if it doesn't work for you!*

## WHAT IS ATTENTION ABOUT? AND WHAT ARE OTHER WAYS IT IS GIVEN?

I have long since looked around elsewhere for what attention the term gets elsewhere – but it still seems limited.

I consider that the term attention is a more valuable word than many similar concepts (see the definition, below). This is because attention carries a meaning of focus to external signals and particular events, which is not just what the coach is doing but also the reactions they are receiving and how they are making sense of them.

Starting with the dictionary (http://www.oxforddictionaries.com)

a.   notice taken of someone or something; the regarding of someone or something as interesting or important *"he drew attention to three spelling mistakes"*

synonyms: awareness, notice, observation, heed, regard

b.  the action of dealing with or taking special care of someone or something *"the business needed her attention"*

synonyms: consideration, contemplation, deliberation, thought, study, observation, scrutiny, investigation, action, care, treatment, ministration, succor, relief, aid, help, assistance

The English language is often rich with the nuances of meanings among different words, for the same sort of meaning.

These definitions don't really get my attention. They don't give that clear direction for how to do it!

The meaning of language, and words, can be very coded – people are often cautious and want to say what they think is the 'right' thing to say. It may not be what they really believe. It is often their contrasting tone, or non–verbal behaviour which indicates this. For example, when there is no tone of interest or excitement about saying what they really think.

Personal attention, and how you come across, is another vital component of marshalling how to give attention to others. After all, coaches can sometimes seems to have a form of 'authority' that the coachee has to obey. It is so important to work towards the other person and their real self.

Yet we all use attention in everyday life – even driving a car is a use of attention!

## THE FORMAL STUDY OF ATTENTION IS STILL LIMITED

The earliest research and definition of attention (attention to attention) is generally recognised as stemming from when understanding people was becoming more of a learned (research–based) work – such as the emergence of psychology.

As early as 1890, William James, in his textbook *The Principles of Psychology*[1], remarked:

> *"Everyone knows what attention is. It is the taking possession by the mind, in clear and vivid form, of one out of what seem several simultaneously possible objects or trains of thought. Focalization, concentration, of consciousness are of its essence. It implies withdrawal from some things in order to deal effectively with others, and is a condition which has a real opposite in the confused, dazed, scatterbrained state which in French is called distraction, and Zerstreutheit in German."*

James further differentiated between 'sensorial' attention and 'intellectual' attention. Sensorial attention is when attention is directed to objects of sense, stimuli that are physically present.

Intellectual attention is attention directed to ideal or represented objects which are stimuli that are not physically present.

James also distinguished between immediate or derived attention: attention to the present versus attention to something not physically present. According to James, attention has five major effects. Attention works to make us perceive, conceive, distinguish, remember and shorten reaction time.

---

[1]William James. "Chapter 11: Attention," in *The Principles of Psychology*. (Henry Holt and Company, 1890)

Even with these classic sub–categories, psychology is still a very young – even an adolescent – science. It is forced to reduce its interest to what conventional scientific methods can measure. So studies are drawn into where attention can best be measured – specifically where there are obvious patterns of behaviour. This makes some forms of behaviour more attractive, such as behaviours that are fairly stuck and often dysfunctional.

The complexity of human senses and the meaning of any expression by another person has produced limited formal research for everyday coaching use – or to guide attention for 'healthy' and normal people.

For example, attention to 'happiness' is still more in the hands of marketing surveys and government indexes, rather than formal psychology research and at the level of attention that makes those critical differences in coaching.

Positive psychology (and many other concepts at a general level) has really only just started as a venture into this difficult realm. However, one thing seems sure. Happiness can vary for different people. It can vary at different times for any one person. It is thus still difficult to measure meaningfully.

## ATTENTION TO PEOPLE IN COACHING

The detail involved still inhibits its full understanding. The data in any moment of a meeting is immense. Coaching is often research moment by moment, researching what sort of attention will work for the other person, how to relate effectively, moment by moment.

Attention, like trust, is very easy to lose. It can take a lot of effort to get right.

One of the best explanations I have found about what is involved in the various attempts to recognise the stages attention goes through is DREYFUS[2] – an engineer working for the US air force on developing important features of attention in tasks where particular performance was especially critical.

---

[2] [website] https://en.wikipedia.org/wiki/Dreyfus_model_of_skill_acquisition

A summary is presented, below:

1. **Novice:** "*Rigid adherence to taught rules or plans*" no exercise of "*discretionary judgment*".

2. **Advanced beginner:** Limited "*situational perception*" all aspects of work treated separately with equal importance.

3. **Competent:** "*Coping with crowdedness*" (multiple activities, accumulation of information) some perception of actions in relation to goals deliberate planning formulates routines.

4. **Proficient:** Holistic view of situation prioritizes importance of aspects "*perceives deviations from the normal pattern*" employs maxims for guidance, with meanings that adapt to the situation at hand.

5. **Expert:** Transcends reliance on rules, guidelines, and maxims, "*intuitive grasp of situations based on deep, tacit understanding*"has, "*vision of what is possible*" uses, "*analytical approaches*" in new situations or in case of problems.

This summary is a simplification of the reality of the stages of what Dreyfus reported is involved in building high levels of attention.

The framework was also referring to tasks generally, not necessarily coaching. But it does seem to be a useful model for what is involved in the various ways attention can be built in coaching, and another discipline from which coaching can learn from.

It shows more clearly what is involved in building quality attention to complex realities. And real people have real, complex, diversity in the worlds they carry with them.

It also indicates how attention is still often seen as an invisible process – 'tacit' and 'intuitive' are the key terms.

I still hear a lot about coaching that falls back into these sort of explanations for how things worked, among coaches talking about what exactly happened.

PART 2: Cutting edge performance in practitioner delivery

And after all that, intuition, and tacit, awareness are not always right – just because it was intuitive or tacit.

## HOW TO EXERCISE THE 'ATTENTION' REQUIRED FOR COACHING

The most informing times are often conversations with colleagues (for example in coaching teams) where the coaches/facilitators can share and clarify the detailed experiences of the ways they work differently with different people.

Similarly, seeing other coaches in action often shows the particular ways they go about their 'attention' to the task at hand. Quite often, people with real skill in giving attention can be unaware, or just lost for being able to explain what they do, still.

Foremost, I want more than just the simple advice to 'reflect'. There must be more to be given to the process than the word – reflect!

At the end of the day it's all about 'practice' – where you are, yourself, your best supervisor, mentor and/or coach in the way things work or not, for you.

We still have a long way to go to have the real insights, and conversations, about what we do in coaching!

- How do you study your ways of giving attention?

- Do you know what works best for you?

- Is it the same each time?

- How it is sometimes different and why?

## Raising the profile for how coaching can add value: Doing more with typical coaching issues: a 'difficult boss'

*Sue Young*

I **would like to** continue sharing my experience of typical coaching issues: 'Managing a difficult boss'. I have selected this particular issue because nine out of ten times this is the way the matter is initially raised.

How might this be addressed through coaching? In my approach I share how I see coaching moving towards having a wider impact than just on the immediate individual client.

- In Part 1 I start with a typical case – that also was part of a 'peer coaching' process – managing a difficult boss. This is a difficult issue to raise, let alone discuss. Yet when a peer coaching community context starts to support its importance it becomes less of a 'personal' issue and something that is possibly a wider issue for the organisation.

- In Part 2 I refer to some current research into this important, and widespread issue, and how coaching can potentially add value to this issue.

- In Part 3 I give some practical examples of how I have experienced both 1–2–1 and peer coaching groups can help people progress such a typical workplace issue of 'managing a difficult boss'.

## PART 1. A RECENT CASE

### Building confidence to raising the issue:

It was the third meeting of this particular peer coaching group that I was working with. An individual eventually felt enough confidence in the group to disclose an issue with their boss. They said they had explored and tested a number of approaches and been through some considerable personal stress as a result. They were resigned to biding their time until the end of the financial year, then seriously setting about finding themselves a new job.

As a senior manager this person protected their team as much as possible from this boss's negative impact. The boss was a dominating presence and did not pay individuals any personal attention or listen to them. Two of the team were now on long–term sick leave as a direct result of the pressures and stress caused by this boss's behaviour and constant undermining interference.

### Attempts to manage the boss:

This client was a highly experienced and capable manager, with a good track record in leading teams to achieve good results. They had particular strengths in managing a high performing team with a naturally collaborative leadership style. Their boss turned out to be highly controlling in style and treated the client like a helpless incapable child.

When the client confronted the boss about this behaviour, the boss modified their tone but nothing substantially changed. For example, there were major longer term strategic issues, some of which my client would normally have expected to be leading on. The boss just ignored all their comments and suggestions. They were left in the dark, and certainly not involved.

## The group identified with the issues:

The group began to explore with the client the possibilities around escalating the issue upwards, informally to start with. Simply discussing options it became increasingly evident that the overall culture was very negative, and more so the next level up. This was endorsed by somebody else in the group, who knew this part of the organisation very well.

## Managing the Big Issue with the Big Question:

How much effort should this client continue to invest in trying to resolve the immediate situation with their boss, having reported testing different constructive approaches without achieving sustainable shifts in their boss's attitude and behaviour? It may be time to take fundamental stock of their options:

- Do they persevere; is there something fundamental missing in what they're doing?

- Or is it better to accept that the situation is what it is and that you've reasonably done all you can to make progress? Maybe it's time to cut losses and invest attention and energy into seeking to make a move?

As the client explored and recounted their situation, I made a verbal observation of how weary, weighed down, and lacking in energy they were coming across. On receiving this feedback it was like I'd pressed a release valve. They affirmed emphatically how completely drained they were feeling by the whole situation. They are a naturally enthusiastic and positive team leader, always seeking out fresh thinking and different approaches to problem solving, always drawing attention to opportunities. The controlling climate being set by their boss was not allowing the 'space' for their preferred leadership approach.

This reminded me of other situations I had encountered in my 1–2–1 coaching practice. Individuals stuck in this kind of situation over a longer period of time feel progressively undermined and lose their self–confidence – it can be very personally eroding. This self–doubt and lack of personal motivation can perpetuate a vicious downward cycle, without external support and validation.

## PART 2. WHAT CAN CURRENT RESEARCH OFFER TO INFORM COACHING ABOUT THE IMPACT OF LINE MANAGERS?

- According to CIPD research (2014)[1] about 65 percent of employees say they are satisfied or very satisfied with their line manager. Well, what follows is that just over a third of people feel some level of dissatisfaction with their line manager.

- The CIPD research[2] report goes on to report *"employee views on line manager behaviours (percent of employees who say their line manager 'always' or 'usually' displays these behaviours)"*, from a list of fifteen behaviours. The highest rated were 'committed to organisation' at 70 percent, 'treats me fairly' at 69 percent, then 'supportive if I have a problem' at 65 percent.

  Lowest rated were 'coaches me' at 29 percent, 'discusses training and development needs' at 35 percent, then 'gives feedback on performance' at 44 percent.

- Research from Great Place to Work Institute (2014)[3] shows that 62 percent of employees do not think their line manager shows sufficient interest in them as people. Two thirds do not think they get sufficient appreciation for what they do. 70 percent do not plan to stay with their employer for a long period of time.

- According to the 2015 Towers Watson Global Workforce Study[4] a third of the UK workforce is likely to leave their current employer within the next two years due to their poor relationship with their line manager.

So what is missing? What are managers doing or not doing to build engagement, performance, job and satisfaction? And how can coaching make its contribution to this?

---

[1] "CIPD Employee Outlook survey", from *CIPD*. (Autumn 2014)
[2] "CIPD Employee Outlook survey", from *CIPD*. (Summer 2014)
[3] [website] http://www.personneltoday.com/hr/line-managers-roles-are-key-to-a-great-workplace/
[4] [website] http://www.cipd.co.uk/pm/peoplemanagement/b/weblog/archive/2015/02/20/one-in-five-line-managers-ineffective-according-to-employees.aspx

**PART 2: Cutting edge performance in practitioner delivery**

Great Place to Work's research shows that a great deal of what coaching is about is in their recommended approach. They refer to this as 'trust' – which is the outcome of the right kinds of behaviour that actively build empowerment and engagement.

They identified a number of key behaviours that actively build trust and effective working relationships[5]:

- Providing appropriate resources so that employees can do their jobs properly;

- Allowing people to get on with their jobs without constantly looking over their shoulders;

- Involving employees in decisions that involve them and so give them a voice in the business;

- Being honest and ethical in what they do;

- Treating everyone fairly with no favouritism;

- Treating people as individuals;

- Keeping promises or commitments;

- Actions matching their words;

- Recognising achievements; and

- Supporting employees, particularly at difficult times in their lives.

Additional research, both from my own experience (see 'Helping Middle Managers Step into their True Organisational Leadership Role[6]') and observation distilled from the above broader research sources, show line manager behaviours that have a particular negative impact:

- Micro–management.

- Absence of direction setting, and engagement in contributing to the longer term direction.

---

[5] "Personnel Today" article. Retrieved on May 2015. http://www.personneltoday.com/hr/line-managers-roles-are-key-to-a-great-workplace
[6] [website] http://the-goodcoach.com/tgcblog/2015/11/9/helping-middle-managers-step-up-into-their-true-organisational-leadership-role-by-sue-young

- Absence – their priorities and attention are elsewhere.

- Lack of demonstrated interest in me and what I can contribute.

- Directly undermining behaviours that lead to:

    - Loss of direction,

    - Loss of self–belief,

    - Eventual drain of self–confidence, even in the most capable people.

At extremes this can become dominating, bullying behaviour. One of my recent cases, includes elements of all of these.

What this wider research tells me is:

### "Coaching needs to be more assertive about the expertise it brings to organisations."

The stats repeatedly tell us as coaches to consider that, if one third of line managers are poorly regarded by their reports, surely the probability is that approximately one in three of our clients may hold similar 'blindspots', or have acquired some bad habits.

We need to be wary of taking things literally as presented by our clients, and open up the conversation to explore how they may be contributing to the difficult situation. Otherwise we are at risk of colluding, and not helping our clients to explore and think differently at a deeper level.

We also have to take into account that it is only comparatively recently that line managers' handling of their people has come under such detailed scrutiny. The traditional route to success has been, and is still in many organisations, simple task achievement, never mind the people.

Coaching represents a bigger organisational (and social) trend to seek to engage people more and enable them be more self–directing. Both of these are essential in an increasingly complex, competitive and inter–dependent world. Also, the skills of coaching have a great deal to bring as part of the range of leadership behaviours brought by line managers.

## PART 3.  WHAT IN PRACTICE, ARE THE KINDS OF APPROACH THAT CAN BE TAKEN TO MANAGE A DIFFICULT BOSS?

Contracting is central to all forms of coaching engagement. Whether in one to one, and/or peer coaching support, reaching connected people – such as a difficult boss may involve careful consideration. There are many ways that the principles involved in coaching can be introduced in contexts beyond a straight forward 1–2–1 contract.

In a peer coaching group, particular added value comes from sharing with and hearing different perspectives from peers. In a peer coaching group people are from different parts of the organisation, so they are sufficiently separate to feel more inclined to personally disclose as there are fewer organisational and political issues leading to potential conflict of interests.

The role of the group coach/facilitator is to hold the 'space'. This means mainly making interventions and observations in the spirit of helping the group participants recognise and work more explicitly with the process, creating the conditions to help the group maximise the individual and collective learning experience. In my experience it can extend with 1–2–1's, where individuals can more freely explore deeper personal questions and dilemmas.

In coaching conversations, both peer groups and 1–2–1's, my clients have found the following approaches to be particularly helpful in managing difficult relationships with their boss.

### 1.  As independent leaders themselves, getting themselves in a 'leadership mind set'

In relation to their boss, as opposed to a 'victim' or 'blamer' mind set. Your client can see themselves as coaching them!

### 2.  Self–affirmation work

If the relationship has been personally undermining over a longer period, help your client re–connect to their achievements, strengths, values and overall sense of direction.

### 3. Clients opening up to want to understand where their managers are really coming from

This requires your client to step back and get out of a defensive mind set. It may not be a one hit/one meeting approach but needs to be built progressively.

### 4. Understand the bigger organisational strategic picture and direction (relates closely to 3)

Initiate those inquiring conversations, with the aim of understanding more about how they see the priorities. This kind of bigger perspective may help your client better understand the true pressures their line manager is under.

### 5. Understand their line manager's personal style and motivation

What are their strengths and limitations? Building perspectives and strategies around these perspectives can often be part of coaching conversations.

### 6. How is your client's line manager seen by key others

360 instruments and the resulting data, increasingly used by organisations, can be very helpful to bring these wider perspectives, more difficult messages and greater objectivity into coaching conversations.

### 7. Acknowledge and release any negative emotional responses in a safe environment

This needs to be an explicit part of the contracting process. This release of feelings can help people move on to be in a more open and constructive problem–solving mode.

### 8. From your client's assessment of the above they can arrange a feedback session with their line manager

This conversation needs to be discussed, and prepared, by both your client and their line manager.

The following are examples of cue questions that both your client and their line manager need to consider and be prepared to share their answers as part of their conversation.

## Your client's:

- What are the top two or three things you most value about how your line manager works with you?

- What are two or three things they do you have occasional difficulty with?

- What changes would you like to see in their approach/behaviour that would help you deliver more successful outcomes in your role?

Get your client to do this on themselves first, i.e. self–evaluation.

## Your line manager's perspectives:

- What are the top two to three things you think your line manager values about you?

- What are two to three things they have occasional difficulty with you?

- What changes do you see you could make in your approach/behaviour that would help your line manager?

This approach requires both parties to put themselves in the other's shoes. Also, by giving advanced notice and transparency around the agenda, both can have time to reflect and evolve their thinking. Having to do this in the moment, when unpractised, can trigger surprise, defensiveness. The conversation can easily and quickly go off the rails.

Many of my clients have successfully moved to a more productive and functional working relationship with their line managers as a result of using one or more of the above approaches.

## Conclusion

All of this has implications for us as coaches.

- What similar experiences have you had when coaching people with a 'difficult boss' issue?

- What is our role as coaches in helping our clients on the 'difficult boss' issue?

- Is one of our roles to share 'best practice' perspectives around line management from the wider field, as part of our coaching process?

- How can we best be help our clients evaluate themselves as line mangers?

- While being compassionate to our clients, how can we avoid collusion, particularly where a bad situation has become entrenched?

# Remaining honest in organisational politics – is it naïve?

## *Yvonne Thackray*

**H**onesty requires some form of self–disclosure. There are many layers of honesty that can be shared based on the circumstances. You may choose to be honest up to a certain point, but what about the other person whom you are in a conversation with? Where are they at? What is their agenda? What is it they are looking to take away from that conversation? Are they prepared to share something of themselves to create the beginning of a mutually trusting relationship? Or are they going to simply take and manipulate to their benefit?

If we agree to take this working definition as a starting point, can we still remain as honest when engaged in organisational politics?

Everyone works in some sort of organisation. No matter how big or small, public or private, politics exists because we are working with individuals who have different needs and motivators to yourself. They will also have different interpretations and perceptions of how they need to meet and reach the goals set for the group in order to meet the purpose of their organisation. Importantly, and very crudely, knowing how to play the politics equates to building up your power base because the reality is that an organisation is not a just and fair place.

## PERCEPTION OF POWER

From David McClelland's work as a social psychologist[1], he both hypothesized and evidenced that power seeking is one of the fundamental drivers of human behaviour found in people from many cultures. The strength of that power motive will vary across individuals and their desire for high personal achievement for themselves, their team and their organisation.

If we can remain open–minded, power[2] is useful because:

- It is related to living a longer and healthier life.

- Combined with visibility and stature it can produce wealth.

- It is part of leadership and this is necessary to influence and get things done.

Acquisition of power for its own sake is widely perceived to be unhealthy and there are plenty of examples in our news cycle to choose from.

So where does honesty fit into all of this? Can you remain honest in a politically charged situation that is daily organizational life?

This is a huge topic, a thesis in its own right! So let's start with bite–size chunks that make it more relatable.

---

[1] [website] David C. McClelland and David H. Burnham."Power is the Great Motivator" (2003) https://hbr.org/2003/01/power-is-the-great-motivator
[2] Jeffrey Pfeffer. "*Power: Why Some People Have it – and others don't.*" (Harper Collins, 2010)

## EXAMPLES

Let's consider a more controlled example of a 360 feedback session. An interviewer (typically the coach/consultant) has requested a meeting to discuss the behaviours of the assessed. The assessed may be their manager, their peer or their subordinate. How honest will they be? It is presumptuous and naive of the interviewer to assume that because they

think they are acting as an independent, the interviewees are willing to present an entirely honest picture. More likely, interviewees will present what needs to be heard to be able to get on with their normal routine without consequences. Therefore, how much can the interviewer interpret as being relevant, rather than an outlier, to the person in question? An unspoken agreement has been made between the two parties in the room that this dance will be taking place.

Let's consider a more open example. What happens when you're being interviewed with an explicit agenda of gathering intelligence about one of your peers? The scenario being the interviewer wants to know how they can work well with them (your peer). Proactively asking you or someone else is a positive and efficient approach to building rapport for the purpose of the project or organisation. Being honest seems positive, particularly as the benefits is for everyone concerned. This is one end of the spectrum. The other end (not the extreme) is what happens if the conversation has an underlying agenda to confirm something that could result in a demotion or dismissal of that individual from the team or even the organisation. No matter how honest the conversation is, it has become a one–way conversation because the other party has locked into what they want to hear rather than listen to the whole story.

How can you tell when this is happening? Some clues may be they have not offered any self–disclosure, or they may not have asked any questions of how they might use that to help them working with the individual in question, or they may ask for other examples of where else they (typically negative behaviours) have occurred.

## WHAT DOES THIS MEAN?

Honesty becomes a double–edged sword; without meaning to, you have given ammunition for the opposite of the intention you went into the conversation with. This can happen if you're oblivious to all the ongoing and subtle politics happening within the organisation.

What do you do when the realisation hits you, particularly as we may not all be politically savvy to the situation!

- Are you able to disclose fully the conversation you had with the interviewer of the assessed?

  That will depend on the type of relationship you have and the capacity to deal with the consequences that ensue.

- Are you able to intervene and minimise the damage?

  Sometimes yes, sometimes no. It's sometimes completely out of your control, and there is little you can do in the form of damage limitations.

- Would you have done things differently, knowing what you know now? How much more preparation would you do? Have you considered the worst case scenario to the most positive outcome?

  Perhaps talking with the right coach would help. This is because a coach's focus is what's in the best interest for both you and the organisation simultaneously (external and internal).

Returning to the question at the start – remaining honest in organisational politics – is it naive?

Yes and no. It depends on how you want to build your power base.

*What do you think?*

## "What to choose, how to choose?" Supporting clients in 'decision limbo'

*Martina Weinberger*

At a recent book launch event, a colleague mentioned that working on personal visions in one–to–one settings is becoming ever more important in her practice. She sees a major shift in the topics her coachees bring. Previously, people came to get ready for what they wanted to achieve, build the right skills and fill potential gaps.

Today, she says, it is all about answering the following questions:

- Do I really want to be promoted?

- Do I want to stay here?

- What will happen to me if I do?

- What if I don't?

This struck a chord with me since I am experiencing very much the same in my practice.

Let me share some of my thoughts and experience on how we coaches can be helpful to people who are stuck in decision limbo, a state which I define as being stuck in an often unsatisfactory but known situation, some sort of individually deeply uncomfortable comfort zone. Those who find themselves there are unable to find a right answer to this simple, deceptively easy question: 'What next?'

What makes this such a difficult question? In my experience, it boils down to fear and uncertainty.

- **Fear:** Even outwardly very successful people are afraid that this – a job they are good at – might be the end of the line. If they stick their head above the parapet with an eye on that next promotion, they might, just might, be found lacking; despite doing everything they possibly could and should be doing. Add to this, the shame people sense to be coming their way in case they do try and then fail.

- **Fear:** It doesn't end there. If they succeed, they fear turning into a person akin to their highly driven, exhausted, personally detached leaders. The much–maligned younger generation (those primed for taking on greater responsibilities and leadership roles) often attach greater importance to and are more connected with their personal values. (Whilst this is often lamented in the corporate world, this is – in my view – actually a credit to them and their parents, but this is beside the point.) They question the legitimacy of how they are being treated by their managers and companies. My coachees frequently question whether they want to remain in environments that challenge or disregard their personal values.

- **Fear:** And then there is the ultimate fear: to rise to the top of the ladder, only to realise that the ladder is leaning against the wrong wall.

- **Uncertainty:** Beside fear, there is also uncertainty. Will there eventually be a leading position for them when the time comes?

- **Uncertainty:** About how they are actually viewed internally and if they have enough backing. Despite years of feedback training and elaborate performance review processes, conversations about performance often remain ambiguous.

**PART 2: Cutting edge performance in practitioner delivery**

- **Uncertainty:** About the loyalty of 'the system'. Companies today demand loyalty but give little loyalty in return. People are labelled and treated as workforce, as assets, head count. Yesterday's high performance and your track record are easily forgotten, only today counts whilst your ability to succeed tomorrow will be questioned – again and again. There is no certainty and there is precious little safety.

Yet we all know: Fear and uncertainty are lousy advisors when thinking about your future.

## HOW CAN WE SUPPORT OUR CLIENTS TO GET UNSTUCK?

The first step is often a closer look at what is. What keeps people where they are? Some of the most common themes I see are:

### Clients are not sure whether they would enjoy another job, or another role with greater responsibilities

- The issue here is often missing information. Can we help find suitable ways to explore their often theoretical options and assumptions?

- Herminia Ibarra's book *Act Like a Leader, Think Like a Leader* (2016), emphasises the necessity of having experience and input in order to learn and grow.

- So they might want to go on a 'learning journey', e.g. by talking with people, learning what other jobs are really like, getting involved in different kinds of projects internally, talking with clients beyond the current projects to add more data to this decision limbo.

Coachees often come back from an exploration like this much clearer about what they want and what they do not want.

**They like the job and they like the idea of rising further in their organisation, but they do not like the lifestyle that comes with it**

- Many who bring this up are using the worst work–life balance offenders in their environment as their negative example. We can help them look for different role models and saner approaches. (It has to be 'saner' *for them*: I have learned the definition of sanity varies widely and depends greatly on context.)

- We can help them look into their current reality. How much do they actually enjoy the lifestyle they have right now? More often than not I hear: *"It is pretty bad. I could not really work more as it is."* If they already work this hard, is it really about lifestyle?

- We can help them get real. Many jobs that pay well and are intellectually challenging tend to come with intense working hours. Life is often a trade–off. We can support them in finding answers to what trade–offs are acceptable for them now and in the next few years.

**They do not want to be like the bosses in their company**

There are few satisfactory role models in the corporate world, many bosses are stuck in their own fears and compensate for their 'ambiguity stress' with less–than–attractive behaviour.

- We can help define their own way. A way of leading that is in line with their personal values and still fits in their corporate context.

- We can acknowledge and share the pain that systems are indeed shaping people and be with our clients whilst they are sorting through what they absolutely want to hang on to, where they embrace being 'shaped' (learning is often highly attractive), and where they want to draw the line.

**They are too tired to look for other options**

- Depending on the environment of our coachees, this is not uncommon. If this is the reason they hang on, empathy is what is called for first and foremost. Having started working with a coach is a first step to breaking that cycle!

- Often there is shame that they cannot 'make it', that everyone else seems to like what they are doing and to thrive whilst they cannot stomach it.

- We can help clients reframe thinking of themselves as lacking, 'not good enough'. We can support them to find ways to 'forgive themselves'. It is okay not to like 'it', it is okay not to be right for certain things. Often we help by reconnecting them to their personal resources.

## A RECENT CASE

A client, who needed to make up his mind about whether or not to push for partnership in a professional service firm, came to our coaching session with two **big** questions:

1. The fear that his personal ladder was leaning against the wrong wall,

   and

2. Whether aiming specifically for this potential success was not too costly in terms of his life priorities.

He had taken some time off when his first child was born and deeply valued this experience. Yet he was also keen to fulfil his personal ambition. We went into an exploration of possible future selves: professional roles/jobs he had envisaged himself taking on since he was little, the dreams his family had, and the things he was passionate about... His possible 'walls' for 'leaning his ladder' against ranged from radio host, bar pianist, running a B&B, becoming a lecturer, a politician or a partner in his current firm. So many possible lives! So many interests, so little certainty whether any push for partnership would indeed be rewarded.

No wonder he felt stuck.

In the course of the exploration, he realised he was actually, honestly and deeply, attached to his current calling. He enjoyed it tremendously!

He also realised that it was easy to say goodbye to some possible future selves. Others were harder to let go of. In looking closer at these, he found not only what made them so dear, but also ways to integrate them into his current role. He redefined his business case, threw out his old business plan and wrote the one he actually, really wanted to see come to life. And – yes – he realised that there were a few things he wanted but could not have, and so he gave himself permission to consciously trade them off against his current needs.

**The result:** An invigorated person.

**The reality:** Did he make partner in his firm? No, he did not. The firm took a strategic decision to invest elsewhere.

Was he sad and angry?

Yes.

When he had gone through his 'mourning period' (as he called it), he realised his business plan was still solid, and still what he wanted to achieve. The last time we met, he was in the middle both of another parental leave and also of setting up his boutique consultancy with projects already being lined up.

## WHAT IS MY LEARNING FROM THESE KINDS OF CASES?

As Yvonne Thackray wisely puts it: "*In every learning and growth cycle there is a plateau where decisions need to be made. Often at times when your private life changes. The question of how motivated you are to decide whether you want to engage and progress within an organisation with increasing leadership responsibilities, or not, is a natural one.*"

I could not agree more with her:

- We can first help our clients acknowledge that this is indeed natural.

- We can then act as catalysts in going beyond decision limbo.

Finally, we can support them to stop driving themselves crazy with finding a perfect solution. Instead, we can help them find a good enough one – for now.

**Update:** I am glad to say that recent brain research[1] seems to agree with me. One of the four rituals to greater happiness is taking (good enough) decisions!

## A SUMMARY

I see my clients getting stuck in their uncomfortable comfort zones. Engaging in coaching can be the beginning of a way out from decision limbo.

- What keeps your coachees stuck?

- How do you support them to explore their current reality? And move beyond it?

---

[1] [website] http://www.businessinsider.com/a–neuroscience–researcher–reveals–4–rituals– that–will–make–you–a–happier–person–2015–9?IR=T

**PART 2: Cutting edge performance in practitioner delivery**

# Eight ways to create reflective learning space beyond coaching sessions

*Sue Young*

**J**ust this past week, I was facilitating a peer learning group of managers from across the public sector. During the group one individual proclaimed emphatically "*I'm so busy juggling all the demands and reacting, making quick decisions, I just don't have the time to stop and think about the important priorities I want to be spending time on. I've just been promoted and what I am doing was previously three people's jobs.*" This is a common theme that comes up for todays' managers in large organisations, both private and public.

I find myself saying more often to new clients, some of who don't know what to expect from coaching, it's about creating space for you to think. Most managers can relate to this in a fast–moving and highly pressurised work environment, and being surrounded on the other front by life and family demands.

I thought it worth reflecting in this blog on some of the more practical things I do with clients in sessions. Things that help them create that space for themselves, and then taking that into their day to day way of working.

## 1. Reflective thinking in advance of and following coaching sessions

Prepared minds are much better placed when coming to coaching sessions. Preparation allows coaches to take their thinking deeper and further forward in the session. It's about taking their learning into their on–going way of working. This can be done in a range of ways, for example asking the client some simple questions to reflect on and capture notes on what they've been trying out, what's worked well, what's not worked so well, what would they have done differently if they were to do it again and what they are taking forward from their experience.

## 2. More consciously observing and reviewing their experience in relation to an area of their leadership they are seeking to develop

One of my recent introverted clients was seeking to raise their contribution and profile in meetings. After talking it through he took away two areas he highlighted for development:

- Seeking to spend time with individuals he was seeking to influence as key stakeholders. This way he could understand more about their priorities and needs and connect what he wanted from them to their interests. This helped him take others' needs into account in his plans and take more from others' knowledge and experience into the business case he was putting together. Just as importantly, these conversations would help build broader consensus and working relationships.

- Plan beforehand for the two to three points he wanted to communicate in the meeting. This may be as part of a formal slot, or a more opportunistic moment in the conversation where he could get the point he wanted to get across by linking it to what somebody else was putting forward.

This approach also played to his strengths and style. Being an introvert he was more comfortable with individuals and small groups. An integral part of the task he set himself was that he was to consciously observe what he and others did more, and consider the impact of those behaviours.

### 3. Some selective reading or watching on–line videos (Ted Talks is a good source)

Between sessions, and in areas of direct relevance to areas of greatest interest to them, I always encourage clients to critique from a reflective perspective how the key points and features resonate with their experience. What are the main points of value they take. How do those points link back to their context and identified development priorities? What are they drawing out in terms of how it connects to their preferred leadership approach? This can be as much what they do not like as well as their aspirations. It helps managers choose and build more explicitly their leadership approach.

### 4. Recommend they set aside times on a regular basis to have 'meetings' with themselves

Most managers are so occupied with their ever growing and demanding 'to do' list they feel it's almost indulgent to take time for themselves. This may require some reframing conversations to help them see it as an essential part of their leadership role to find quality thinking time. Once they have gained some first–hand experience of finding and taking this time, they become more committed to achieving the felt benefits.

### 5. Keep a journal/log

Capturing personal notes after key events and thoughts on priority issues can be a useful personal review and unearthing process. This is a valuable self–expression that can clarify thinking. The key thing here is to fully express without vetting. It's only for their eyes! This increases self–awareness and ability to get to the bottom of what's really going on for us.

I find it's important to find ways of keeping a journal that works for them. For some of my clients who do a lot of travelling, airport lounges can be a good space to capture some reflective notes. Mobile devices and the world of 'apps' can greatly assist with this! Others prefer to set aside time at the start or the close of the week to make their notes.

## 6. Extension of process frameworks used in coaching sessions into working practice

Many of the frameworks and tools we use in our coaching sessions can be readily used by the client in their on–going work. This includes sharing with colleagues and their team.

In working with managers on their development goals, I will often use five cue questions against each goal they set:

- Where have I been?

- Where am I now?

- Where do I want to go? (How will I know I've arrived?)

- How am I going to get there?

- Next steps.

As well as talking through that in the session, it may be helpful for the client to do some personal reflection on the questions outside of sessions, as well as to use that structure to help them plan generally and think about important issues.

## 7. Plan to have a conversation with a person inside or outside the organisation they wouldn't normally talk to

This can be to find out more about an area with they don't have much day to day dealing but which impacts on the whole business. This can help stretch into bigger organisational, or external relationships, provide fresh perspectives and opportunities from increased exposure, as well as create an exchange and transfer of experience and knowledge. It can also lead to innovation from increasing cross–silo exchange and thinking.

## 8. Identify a mentor inside or outside the organisation

Someone with additional or different experience the individual wants to add to their experience. This needn't be formal but does need to be contracted for. I was working recently with a regional financial director who wanted to build his knowledge and experience of the central head office. He saw his development edge as being able to learn more about the central decision making process around finance, particularly around mergers and acquisitions. Whatever he went on to do he had identified that understanding more of the bigger corporate perspective would be of benefit to his career development. He selected a colleague he trusted in the central corporate finance function who was only too happy to pass on his knowledge. It turned into a peer to peer mentoring relationship as the central corporate finance manager wanted to understand more about financial operational issues at a local business unit level.

## To summarise

Maintaining a learning mind set that observes the reality closely, is a way to keep open to new ways of seeing things, of exploring assumptions and actively seeking additional input and perspectives from others. It is a highly important leadership capability in today's organisations. This doesn't just happen by itself. It's something that we need proactively to find time for.

As coaches, we can greatly add to the sustainability of our work if we help our clients extend the more reflective learning approaches they gain from coaching sessions and find practical ways to apply these in their day to day ways of working.

- What do you do in your coaching to help clients take more reflective learning space into their normal ways of working?

# CHAPTER 6

# PERSPECTIVES ON MEASURING COACHING IMPACT

## The practicalities of measuring the ROI of coaching: A reflection

*Doug Montgomery*

**W**hat is the Return on Investment (ROI) of coaching? How do you measure the ROI of coaching? I have come across these questions a great deal over the last few years. Who wants this information and why? Is ROI the right or most useful thing to measure?

### Who's asking?

In executive coaching, there are multiple parties involved and interested in how to evaluate coaching. There is the coach, the coachee, the coachee's manager, the sponsor (who may or may not be the payee), the client – who is the payee, potential new clients, the board the client is on or reports to, or other stakeholders in the client organisation etc.

- Who is it that wants to know the answer?

- And are they all asking the same question?

## Break down of ROI

ROI, Return On Investment, is the straightforward ratio of money made (or saved) divided by the cost of the activity. The cost of the coaching is the cost of the coach in terms of fees, any additional expenses (travel, room, psychometric test fees etc.) plus the cost of the time taken out of the office by the coachee. For an internal coach, the cost of their time out of their day job may be included. All relatively easily quantified: the time components though are not always included in the calculation.

The value of the coaching outcome is much more difficult to calculate. What was the bottom line impact for the organisation in terms of savings or revenue? Assuming that this can be calculated, what proportion of this was due to the coaching intervention? What proportion was due to all the other factors at play? (e.g. simultaneous leadership training or other courses, change to line management attitude or personnel, actions of others, market changes, sales peaks or troughs, other campaigns, projects or strategies etc.) Hopefully you are starting to see the challenge here.

What do you use when direct savings or revenues are not visible? How do you calculate, for example, the value of increase in motivation, the value of better relationships for a manager with her colleagues or customers, the value of a key talent finding the right career path, or the value of a new leader letting go of old activities and spending more time on what the new role needs? What is the value of coaching that results in the exit of an employee or the retention of an employee? ROI can be difficult to calculate with any certainty, so how else can we evaluate the benefit of coaching?

## Evaluating the outcomes/impacts of coaching

We can come at evaluation from lots of different angles.

- Does it work for the individual coachee?

- Does it work for the organisation?

- Will it work for me?

- What impact am I having as a coach and could I be even more effective?

To systematise this there is a hierarchy of enquiries we can make to co–design the framework for evaluating coaching with the coachee and client. (This is adapted from DL Kirkpatrick's work *Evaluating Training Programs*[1] 1994, published by Berett–Koehler).

1.  To what extent did the coachee feel the time was well spent?

2.  To what extent did the coachee learn something useful about themselves?

3.  To what extent did the coachee's behaviour change?

4.  To what extent did the behaviour affect some positive change in their local system or organisation?

5.  To what extent did the change result in some financial benefit to the organisation? (ROI can be calculated from here)

Different measures are needed as we move through questions 1 to 5, and the coach and the client gradually need more input from others as they progress towards question 5.

Questions 1 and 2 seek subjective feedback from the coachee. They can be answered during each session to check that the conversation is on track, at the end of each session and at the end of the coaching assignment.

The behavioural change asked about in Q3 and the impact on the organisation in Q4 require additional feedback from peers, reports and managers and can be elicited using specific non–leading questions. For example:

- Scaling of the desired behaviours at or before the start of coaching and close to the end are useful ways of measuring change.

- Comparing the change perceived by the coachee with that of their peers may provide additional useful information for the coachee, the coach and the organisation.

- The peer feedback gathered at the end of the assignment may show positive change; how sustainable is that change over time?

---

1 [website] http://www.businessballs.com/kirkpatricklearningevaluationmodel.htm

Inviting others to look out for changes often has a positive effect by provoking useful feedback during the process as well as it incentivising the coachee.

One aim of coaching is to resource the coachee for the future. Recently, I've been experimenting with some recent coachees by getting their permission to follow up with them six months after the coaching was completed. I am interested to find out what changes they are aware of sustaining, what resources they are accessing in themselves and where their behaviour and thinking have moved to now.

As for putting some estimation of value on the desired and actual changes in behaviour of the coachee, I am firmly of the opinion that only the coachee and their organisation (e.g. their manager or HR sponsor) can give any useful answer to this question as personal and organisational context are key factors.

None of the five questions ask about the quality of the coaching technique or the quality of the relationship.

A coach who asks for feedback focusing on levels 1 and 2 will not learn much about their coaching technique or skills and competencies (I'm thinking about the ICF core competencies). A coach who wants to know how good their technique is compared to some standard criteria or their previous level of competence, is also looking at their input. I am focussing here on the coaching output – the impact as a result of coaching. Interestingly, as far as I can tell, the majority of the professional coaching bodies (ICF, AC, EMCC) focus their accreditation on inputs. The Association for Professional Executive Coaches and Supervisors (APECS) takes a more output focussed approach to its accreditation.

## APPLYING MODES OF EVALUATION FOR COACHING IN ORGANISATIONS AND PRIVATE PRACTICE

There is no single answer on how to evaluate coaching. To a large extent it is in the eye of the beholder. If you want to bring coaching into your organisation you will probably need to sell the idea to a board or executive team to gain support and resources. What evidence do they want to see or hear? Introduction, development, growth and sustainability of a coaching program, both internal and purchased from external providers, needs a strategy that aligns coaching to the desired organisational culture and direction. Matching your lead and lag metrics to the strategy and its milestones provides useful data on progress and gaps. In addition to the five evaluation questions, measuring the geographical and organisational distribution of demand for coaching, supply of coaches, and analysis of the gaps between supply and demand all support the delivery of a coaching into the organisation.

Simple data of this nature can generate lots of useful enquiries:

- What is the demand?

- Where is demand highest and lowest?

- Where might it be needed most?

- What are the barriers to coaching being asked for?

- What is creating the demand where it is high?

## PERSUADING STAKEHOLDER ENGAGEMENT AND RESOURCING

High level sponsorship is critical for creating a sustainable coaching program. So what will be persuasive to your stakeholders? Maybe success stories from other companies? Are the competition using coaching as a competitive advantage? What example are the blue chip companies setting with coaching? Maybe having a successful personal experience of coaching themselves? Maybe they want an estimate of cost and benefit? Maybe something else?

It is easy to make assumptions about what your stakeholders want to know and will be persuaded by. Instead, ask them!

Once your program is in place and you have some assignments under your belt, convincing the stakeholders of the ongoing value of coaching can take various forms. Testimonials on the impact from the coachee, their manager, their team members and their colleagues. Summaries of satisfaction scores in post coaching surveys (Q1 and Q2), post coaching 360 surveys (Q3). Careful attention needs to be taken with such data so as to respect confidentiality and permission to share. Changes in staff attitude surveys that can be related back to coaching interventions can be powerful – GlaxoSmithKline (GSK) has generated convincing positive evidence of coaching impact through their global staff survey by comparing leadership impacts in the teams of those coached with those not coached.

In an ideal world there would be research evidence from controlled, suitably powered experiments that would provide statistical evidence about whether and to what extent coaching works. These seem to be rare. Such experiments are complicated by there being a potentially large placebo effect. In such a relational intervention simply taking someone out of their busy day job for an hour and sitting with them can have a profound effect on their thinking and reflecting. It is a very challenging experiment to design, made even more challenging by the multiple and contradictory definitions of what coaching is.

As usual, starting with the end in mind serves us well when seeking to evaluate executive coaching. *"What was the coaching setting out to change and what is the value of that change to the coachee and the organisation?"* is a good starting point for evaluating its success. Establishing at the outset how to measure that change enables the baseline and success criteria to be agreed.

When taking on a new corporate and private clients, I now ask, *"What is the value to you of achieving this goal to you (and your organisation)?"* And, *"How will you know you have succeeded?"*

When I'm asked, *"What is the ROI of coaching?"* I will continue to answer, *"What is the value of the change you wish to make?"* Because I can certainly tell you what my fee will be!

# Evaluating coaching

*Kim Stephenson*

In training about coaching, or even in discussing it, I frequently emphasise that how, what and when are useful questions. They're non–threatening and can encourage examination of methods, models and ideas.

But why is a lot more powerful – hence it's often a threat to people.

Asking why can sound like a challenge. *"Why (on earth) did you do that?"*, *"why would you believe something (stupid) like that?"* See what I mean?

But it's often a good way to get at the motivation, the rationale behind something and therefore it's a very powerful tool. As it is with the evaluation of coaching. Asking how to do it, or what to do are good. But asking 'why' can open a whole different conversation (or can of worms!) Whether you swear by Covey[1] and *"begin with the end in mind"*, copy Oprah[2] and ask *"what do you want?"* or agree with me that *"why are you*

---

[1] [website] http://www.amazon.co.uk/Habits-Highly-Effective-People/dp/0684858398
[2] [website] https://www.linkedin.com/pulse/simple-life-changing-question-hardly-anyone-can-answer-oprah-winfrey

**PART 2: Cutting edge performance in practitioner delivery**

*going to college?"* is a good way to start a book on handling college finance[3], you end up with asking *"Why are you doing it?"*

So why evaluate coaching, what is your end in mind in doing it, what do you want in evaluating it?

There are two dominant reasons for evaluation.

1. Understand the impact your coaching has, to maintain and improve quality.

2. Justify the coaching to a client, internal or external.

## QUALITY

If you've done a degree (or other research) you'll know your research *should* be a double blind, placebo–controlled study, with large, stratified samples.

If you've studied human sciences, you know that is a lovely idea but impractical.

You can't do placebo studies or deceive people about the purpose of the study (the 'blind' won't pass ethics boards), not know who is in which group (the 'double'), and you don't know whether what you did affected them in the way you expected, because you can't lock them in a lab for several months as if they were lab rats to control all the external factors (ethics again!). You also can't usually afford a big enough sample or get it adequately representative; you have to have an 'opportunity sample'.

One method is to have a 'wait group' as a control. You measure the performance of both groups initially, have your coaching intervention with one, measure both again, coach the other, measure performance again. Finding changes if, and only if, the group has had coaching suggests it has worked, because it removes noise that comes in from other performance improvement initiatives, calculated by reference to your control.

But you still can't say it has worked, even with a big sample. Only that it suggests it may have done.

---

[3] [website] http://www.amazon.com/Finance-Persona-Making-College-Beyond/dp/1440834369

Before you start, you also have to find measure of target behaviours. A common model (derived from training) is Kirkpatrick's four level model. The trouble is, while you can coach people to pass tests of knowledge (Kirkpatrick level 2) the higher levels (like Kirkpatrick level 3; behaviour, and 4; bottom–line impact), are hard to measure anyway.

How do you know behaviour has changed as a consequence of coaching? You could use a wait group and you still wouldn't know for sure. You'll get different degrees of change (even if you can identify *behaviour change*) from separate individuals in the same situation (function, company), let alone widely different individuals in different functions, in separate industries and companies, and being coached for different purposes (why again!).

So you can forget doing a meta–analysis (grouping together studies to give you big numbers, hence greater statistical power), unless you think that quality is enhanced by thinking of some numbers and doubling them (in which case your maths skills are not really adequate anyway).

Of course, you can, with sufficient funds, create a 'file–drawer' study. That way you repeat the study over and over until you get the result you want, publish that one and file the 10,000 studies that showed the opposite. Ever seen the size of the "old research" files in a large pharmaceutical company?

Generally, coaching budgets don't run to that, but it's a measure of quantity (of money), not quality (of coaching) anyway!

But then behaviour (level 3) is easy, compared to the bottom line (level 4).

Like double–blind placebo studies, Return on Investment (ROI) is a gold standard for measuring stuff like this. ROI is great (I've designed and taught it on a finance for non–financial mangers MSc). What fun we can have with hurdle rates, internal rates of return, present and future value calculations and so on.

Trouble is, it's intended for capital projects.

Accounts have conventions that are accepted, but nonsense. Assets don't depreciate in straight lines, for example. Everybody knows and accepts that these are approximations, that some figures are guesswork. Though most of the time it works well (given Enron, Northern Rock etc.).

So capital projects, like building a widget factory, with known costs, price for widgets, time to build (and penalty clauses for cost and time over runs etc.) have an element of guesswork and approximation, but everybody knows it and you can useably approximate your ROI.

Look at an example of coaching managers. You coach them to use a more coaching style.

So previously the manager yelled at staff, gave the answer to queries and in 20 seconds everybody was back at work. Now they say, *"interesting, what do you think you should do?"* and discuss it for 20 minutes. Eventually the staff become less reliant on the boss. But in the short run, both are tied up for longer doing less. So productivity goes down. So at what point is the crossover and how do you know?

If what you're doing is coaching purely mechanical skills, it's still tricky to work out what comes from what you've done. If it's something abstract and complex such as managerial skills and not purely declarative knowledge, it is impossible to be really accurate.

And you can't work out a Present Value (PV) for future improvements in performance so that you can correctly work out your ROI in terms of today's coaching spend, because you don't know when the benefits will start showing through; you can't say exactly what the behavioural changes are and don't know which bits (and how much of them) come from coaching or what they'll contribute to the bottom line.

ROI isn't designed to do that sort of thing, it includes too many guesses.

So if you genuinely want to perform a *quality* evaluation of your coaching:

- Learn (or buy in some help) to control the variables as far as possible, use a good research design and understand the statistics.

- Use a good framework for evaluation.

**PART 2: Cutting edge performance in practitioner delivery**

- Understand what it is that you're trying to do, what, exactly, is the coaching supposed to achieve?

## JUSTIFY

Over the last few hundred years (since Descartes), there's been a growing belief that logic and reason dictate human thought and action. The assumption is that intuition, 'gut instinct' etc. are inferior to logic.

To evaluate the *quality* of your coaching, for continuous improvement etc. that assumption is useful. Feeling you're a good coach, people saying you are or paying you are valueless for quality evaluation. You need scientific, rational studies, as mentioned earlier.

But if you're trying to justify it to other people, ignore that. People don't make decisions with evidence objectively and logically, with evidence. They make gut instinct decisions, then look for facts to justify them.

Produce all the data you want, if they don't want to believe it, they won't. If information convinced people to behave differently nobody would smoke, overeat, drive when drunk etc. People believe what they have decided to believe (creationist presidential candidates being an example).

I'd suggest reading Influence[4] and Risk Savvy[5] if you want to understand why.

If you go to your company CFO or the operations director of a client with data, e.g. ROI, they will make their decision and use the data to justify their decision to:

a) buy coaching,

or

b) not buy the coaching.

---

[4] [website] http://www.amazon.co.uk/gp/product/006124189X
[5] [website] http://www.amazon.co.uk/Risk-Savvy-Make-Good-Decisions/dp/0241954614

We all think we're logical and that we decide on the data. We don't. We make the decision, unconsciously and rapidly, then go back and produce a post hoc reason if needed.

It's been known in sales for millennia – that's why sales people sell the sizzle not the sausage (effective adverts have no meaningful content)!

When you try to justify coaching with logic, ROI, wait group studies etc., your audience will have made up their mind and use the study to support their decision. So if they've decided that coaching isn't the answer, they will use your figures to *prove* it.

The best way to justify to people that coaching is worthwhile is to get them to see the problems of failing to act and the benefits from coaching. Allow them to 'own' the problem and decide that they want a solution.

In that case, assuming that you do have a reasonable coaching solution, they will make the decision that they want it and will make up or manipulate the figures to 'prove' the rightness of their decision.

## IN CONCLUSION

You can suggest different purposes for evaluation other than assessing quality and justifying use. If you do, you're getting back to 'why'.

I certainly wouldn't ignore articles or discussion on 'how to' and 'what are the techniques for'. But, as with questions in coaching itself, I'd still suggest that 'why' is the most powerful question. And since it's a question to yourself, and consequently carries no risk of somebody being offended by implied slurs on their reasoning, I'd seriously consider asking "*Why am I even thinking about evaluating my coaching?*" before you start looking at how, what or when to evaluate.

## "Wellbeing, why not?"

### Yvonne Thackray (YT) and Liz Pick (LP)

"**W**ellbeing, why not?" is a phrase coined by Liz Pick in her practice as a performance and well-being executive coach. It's not a simple to unpack either because it is both an important question and a serious challenge for the coaching profession. What follows is a transcript of our conversation that took place initially as an interview and evolved into a peer-conversation. It shows the richness of our conversation and the learnings and insights that we were each developing as we talked about wellbeing and the different influences, contexts, and impacts it has on demonstrating the true impacts received from coaching.

YT: Let's start with a simple question - how do you define well-being?

LP: There are many definitions for well-being, and as an executive coach I find it helps to look at it in the context of health. The World Health Organisation definition describes health as a "*state of complete physical, mental and social well-being and not merely the absence of disease or infirmity*" (2014, pg 1). Of course that is an absolute, the ideal state, and so it's not easy to work with.

Instead, I see health as an objective assessment of someone's physical and mental state and I see well-being as a subjective sense of a person's physical and mental state. Health can be evaluated, diagnosed and treated, whereas well-being is subjective. It's the difference between "*How are you?*" and "*How do you feel?*"

YT: That's a very useful definition. It makes me think of a statement repeated by many coaches and printed in many coaching literatures: a coach works only with a mentally healthy person. How does it fit in with what you've described and how you practice as an executive coach?

LP: I find it very concerning that coaches would decide not to work with someone purely because they had a mental health condition. I would suggest that those coaches are already working with clients with some form of mental illness, they just don't know about it. If they actually stopped working with those clients, they'd end up with very few clients. People with a mental health condition can often continue to work effectively, so my starting point is to assume that if someone is well enough to work, I'll work with them. The alternative is surely a form of exclusion.

YT: Wow! I agree! Reflecting on what you've said it seems that this statement is too narrow in its definition especially when we validate it against our experiences and those of our clients. Could you share what challenges you've faced when dealing with well-being in coaching?

LP: One challenge has been working in a way that feels like being 'under the radar'. In order to deliver the agenda set by the organisation, I've often worked with clients on managing the impact of their wellbeing on their performance. But because of confidentiality, I haven't been able to report back on the relative importance of well-being in the overall mix. It's rarely the prime issue but it is important, and they (the sponsors) don't know about it.

YT: Is there no convincing evidence out there?

LP: The link between performance and wellbeing is known in academic research as the holy grail, because the challenge is how to show cause and effect: "*Did you feel a greater sense of well-being because you performed better or did you perform better because your well-being improved?"* Currently the real exciting development is the launch of the 'Health at Work' policy unit[1] led by Professor Steven Bevan from the Work Foundation and Dame Carol Black. They have done so much to transform the perception of well-being at work over the last ten years. The challenge for organisations has been that whilst the evidence was growing, organisations seemed slow to act. The beauty of what they are now doing is they're focusing on measuring the effectiveness of interventions.

And there's some interesting research out there like *Secrets and Big news* by Kate Nash[2] - and *Doing Seniority Differently* by Disability Rights UK[3] , that highlights when employees are given a choice, 75 percent of people with a non-visible condition such as backache, depression, dyslexia, will choose not to inform their manager because of the fear of negative consequences.

Executive coaches can offer those clients confidentiality which makes them uniquely placed to address the impact of these wellbeing issues on performance. But if coaches decide not to work with people who are not 'mentally healthy', then their exclusion is very concerning. And of course if employers don't know about the potential for integrated performance and well-being coaching to deliver greater benefits, they won't ask for it, coaches won't be trained in it, clients will be deprived of the support their peers get and everyone loses out!

YT: Reflecting on what we've spoken about so far, executive coaching is still 'learning' and 'understanding' how to relate and work with our clients. More likely it's something we can intuitively grasp, and haven't articulated in the succinct way you have here. This is what makes this very exciting times in our field!

I've also noticed something else, I'm sensing that statistics is quite an important indicator in our field. Let me share an example. One of the positive ROI's that demonstrates the impact of coaching is maternity coaching (lesser paternity) i.e. those who are transitioning back from motherhood coaching has a great success. What's being disclosed to

---

[1] [website] http://www.theworkfoundation.com/Research/Workforce-Effectiveness/Health-Wellbeing/Health-at-work-policy-unit
[2] [website] http://www.katenashassociates.com/book
[3] [website] http://www.disabilityrightsuk.org/doing-seniority-differently-summary

the public, the sponsors, our clients have an impact on how coaching's perceived?

LP: And isn't that a fascinating example because if you think you about it, one of the reasons why maternity return-to-work coaching is so readily available is because the statistic are easy to collect and reliable - you can't hide pregnancy from your employer. The question I would ask employers is: "*If you're providing return to work coaching for people after they've become a parent, why wouldn't you offer the same to someone coming back after absence due to stress or illness?*" The rationale would be exactly the same, it's just that the statistics aren't there. Uptake of some support services may be low because access is only provided to employees who tell their manager aspects of their wellbeing that they would prefer to keep private. And yet the coaching industry is potentially differentiating between people because of their mental health. I find this surprising, and concerning.

YT: I agree! Summing up what we've discussed so far, a hypothesis could be asserted that coaching practices are being driven by statistics?

LP: I certainly think most of us are unaware of the prevalence of high stress, physical and mental illness, disability and challenging personal circumstances. Any substantial gap between internal employee surveys and independent statistics is where I would focus next. If there was a way of collecting data to show the prevalence of single and multiple health and well-being challenges in the working population, that would be wonderful. Then to show the relative impact of various interventions that do or don't address well-being, including coaching, would move the whole agenda forward massively. It would probably change the rationales on which coaches make their decisions, in a good way.

# Collecting stories from our experience

## Dr. Lilian Abrams

L ately I have been exploring practical ways to collect evidence of our impact as executive coaches. In my paper[1], I advanced the basic idea that, in order for coaches and others to collect actual, true and valid evidence of coaching impact, it is helpful and likely necessary at this point to focus on gathering qualitative data.

## "THE NEED FOR STORIES FROM COACHES AS INDICATORS OF ROI!"

Spontaneous recollections, or stories, often and unpredictably occur during coaching sessions with a client. These stories usually reveal how that client has implemented what we had covered during prior coaching conversations in their subsequent daily life. They tend to describe the impact of those actions for the client and others in their organization. However, they don't necessarily include a description of the impact on the organization, of their changed behavior.

---

[1]Lilian Abrams "ROI: Collecting Evidence of Our Success", from APECS Symposium 2015 Papers. (2015)

For the purposes of assessing the impact of coaching, I suggest we divorce our expectations of validity (what really happens) from reliability (that it happens every time, allowing *a priori* prediction), two of the classic hallmarks of solid, well–done research. Why? Because at this point in time, isolating and identifying true behavior change in practice requires a more exploratory, qualitative approach. This should help research in the field of coaching better access the core variables and dynamics, to the point where hypothesis–testing is more realistic.

Qualitative investigation, which would include capturing actual client stories, would thus seem to be appropriate and pragmatic at this time, for both researchers and practitioners. An example of this kind of qualitative data is what I'm calling in this post, 'collecting stories from our experience'.

## WHY COACHES NEED TO BE ALERT FOR STORIES

Coaches are among the best–situated stakeholders to realize that a valuable story is being told and capture it, because:

- These stories are your client descriptions of their own thought processes and consequent behavior changes. They are examples of how the client has put into practice what they have learned, and impact from that new behavior can occur at any time.

- It is most impactful for all concerned if the coach remembers to ask questions of their client that attempt to specify the tangible impact of their new behavior in terms of meaningful business results, where it is possible to ascertain such. This can extend to dollars earned or saved, as appropriate.

## WHAT TO CAPTURE: CHARACTERISTICS OF YOUR CLIENTS' STORIES, & HOW TO TELL THEM

What I'm suggesting and sharing with you is what I am experimenting with at the moment, and what I've learned from that to date. Based on that, I thought I would put forward a few ideas on what one might want to do, to collect one's own stories of impact:

- **Be an applied anthropologist/qualitative researcher**. Among the key points that apply from my prior qualitative research courses and work is that it is always necessary to be honest about your biases. What you notice and don't notice; what you ask others and what you don't ask; what you record and don't record. All of this and more are part of your subjective, inherently biased point of view. This is okay, and inevitable. But to the degree that you can be as honest about your own biases as possible, and do your best to restrain them and make every effort to be as objective as possible, it will help your data gain validity, credibility, and durability.

- **Be a storyteller**. While you are reporting a real, true sequence of events, it is a story nonetheless. Provide the details that make it real, for yourself as well as for any reader, even while protecting confidentiality. Give the person a name (though I always freely admit to using fake names, for the sake of confidentiality.) Provide the approximate size of organization, and the type of industry (i.e., "*global pharmaceutical*") though I usually avoid giving the organization's name. Alternatively, you can name the client's function. Just ensure there is not enough information to describe exactly who they are, when there is only one of them. (i.e., "*IBM's North American head of supply chain.*")

After describing the client's basic demographics, specifically and vividly describe their behaviors and thought–processes, prior to coaching, which had been problematic, as per their stakeholder feedback and/or self–report. Describe the (presumably negative) impact of those prior behaviors as much as possible as well. Then, describe the insight or transformative experience your client had during coaching that lead to a new way of thinking and acting. Describe a situation where there was a temptation for the old behavior, but where they instead displayed new behavior in line with the transformative coaching experience they have described. Include a description of their new thought–process and/or the actual behaviors of your client. Then, include the results for the client as well as others in the organization, and/or the organization itself, from the new behaviors.

- **Ask the question:** In terms of results, this is the most important thing to do: Ask the question. You may well not hear the impact of the story on the organization, or others, if you don't ask for it. And your client is among the best placed to describe the impact and outcomes of your coaching work, and certainly the best one to describe the before–and–after thought–processes and effects. Only that person knows all the details of what they used to say and do, and what the change in their thinking and actions via coaching were. They are centrally–placed to observe the results of their own changes, for themselves and for their organization, from their application of their learning from your coaching work together.

  Their success is your success. But you may never learn what that is, unless you remember to consciously ask them the specific questions that elicit it. For example, when they tell you a story about what they have thought about and/or applied since your last conversation, remember to ask them the follow–up question about impact: So what happened, as a result of that new behavior?

  And don't forget to...

- **Quantify the impact:** In addition to asking about the impact on others, look for the impact on the organization, which includes ways to quantify their impact. For example, *"What was the amount saved/earned that was new?"*

  I have noticed that this last point is not typically an organic part of a coaching conversation – either for them to volunteer the concrete impact, or to specify a financial amount relevant to that impact. You will likely have to ask, specifically, for the indexing number. You may not get one, but you can try!

- **Be an excellent librarian.** The rest is housekeeping. Record the story immediately. Store it in a (virtual) place where you will be sure to find it again. Soon you will have a collection! So consider giving each incident keywords.

Now, I'd like to share an example of how I use storytelling (what is in bold and italics is an item that illustrates the suggestions above).

**Tony*** is **head of Supply–Chain for a global pharmaceutical company**. Over the course of our coaching conversations, he has realized that the team he inherited is comprised of nice, complacent individuals, who overall are performing their work to outdated standards. Tony and the organization both need them to step up their performance, to ensure his function's effectiveness and longer–term success.

**Tony himself is strategic, action–oriented, organized, and driven**. However, one of his personal **challenges is conflict avoidance**. In other settings, he had **allowed mediocre performers to continue long term** in his group, which, as one of his stakeholders told me, left both him and the organization **vulnerable when crises arose**. Early on in his leadership tenure, he single–handedly initiated a new vision and set of initiatives for his team, to raise their level of client service and upfront relevance to the business. Since then, however, over the course of our coaching work together, Tony has realized how far of his ideal infrastructure his team is falling short, in both mindset and behavior.

To do this, Tony needs to effect change in some of the core beliefs and behaviors in his team. Here's an example: Tony's long–tenured predecessor rewarded this team's loyalty and tenure over performance. They therefore learned to do this as leaders themselves. One manager, Gloria, needed an open position filled. At first, she wanted to promote Marcy, an existing direct report, into that spot. Tony sees Marcy as competent but not excellent in her current job, and certainly not ready for promotion. Gloria was initially taken aback by his dissent, but once she accepted it, she had to break the news to Marcy and her team that none of them would be accepted for the promotion. Gloria emailed Tony immediately after that group meeting, describing it as personally quite "*tough*" for her, since her team was very upset by the news and tearful. She then asked Tony to come himself to talk to them, presumably to explain the decision and somehow assuage their upset.

Tony saw from this request that he needed to confront and coach Gloria clearly on her assumptions and behavior as a leader. He needed to ensure she understood his new expected levels of performance for her, and therefore her team, including both making and owning leadership decisions. She also needed to clarify the new higher performance standards required of her own team, and coach, develop and/or manage them appropriately depending on their success in attaining these.

By discussing this incident and others preceding it during coaching, Tony developed a list of competencies he now wants to implement when hiring, coaching, and evaluating staff, to create a team that is better suited to the organization's current and future needs.

**I asked Tony** if there is **any way to concretize the benefit of implementing these higher performance standards**, for the organization. He pondered that, and we agreed that the benefits were likely more in the realm of long–term efficiency and effectiveness, since his goal is strengthening the team's effectiveness and capabilities into the future. We will return to the topic of quantification of these standards before the end of the coaching engagement, and see whether anything appropriate emerges.

*All names changed for confidentiality purposes.

## MOVING FORWARD:

As you read the above, what thoughts did you have regarding:

- What you might do, to start collecting your own stories of coaching impact?

- What use(s) you might put these to?

- What else you might suggest or do differently?

- What benefits do you see in sharing such stories amongst like–minded professionals?

- What difficulties, and any solutions to those, might you suggest, to explore our impact using our stories?

- Anything else?

# What's the number, today!

*Yvonne Thackray*

Elevating numbers as a target in their own right, as part of a separate strategy without questioning or critiquing how or what is possible, has shifted us, albeit unconsciously, to behave in a way that seems normal. Like any language, talking through numbers is yet another example of communication.

Numbers, then and now, have been a way to keep account of and inform one to make better decisions. Current scientific management is being taken to a partial conclusion that has metamorphosed the intention of a number. It has been elevated to the stratosphere of how we should be leading our lives and livelihood, though not fully connected to reality because number is merely an objective.

Simply linking it to the Enlightenment period has created a level of connection that has been taken out of context of that time period. It was a time where social–cultural needs were different, although it's questionable whether as humans we have really advanced any further. It has became evident that the benefits that can be derived from executive coaching (in all its different guises or approaches – limited or sophisticated) are shown to 'add value' when the changes can be measured relative to something specific. This could be something like an organisational and/or government target in which results can be both tangible such as an increase in sales, weight loss, or even intangibles such as happiness, trust, quality of relationship. Usually these are concerned with observing via objective measurements as in scaling, ROI or subjective and intuitive observations.

Allow me to demonstrate the value of executive coaching in the marketplace. There has been an explosion in the field of coaching particularly with the government's new indices around wellbeing and the science of happiness. Happiness has, for some, turned from a virtue that is experienced (a typical philosophical debate) to something that can be objectified (a scientific debate) via numbers. Advances in science are an important part of progress. However, elevating them before any certainty can be validated is the 'bust and boom' of latent potential.

Coupled with this is the rise of experts in the field that have moved from informing and serving society by protecting "*the less knowledgeable members of society*[1]" to that of a dominant profession who now tells society what must be considered as having value versus what is considered of having little or no value. Scales et al[2] (2011) describes it as "*the ideas of 'entry' to the professions being dependent on specialist knowledge and skills, professional autonomy, authority and altruism. Professionalism also implied virtuous behaviour; the much lampooned phrase, 'Trust me, I'm a professional', was probably once said without irony.*"

For example, in Britain the overall costs of mental health disorders to the economy (i.e. workplace absence, reduced productivity, medical costs) is estimated at £110 billion per year[3]. Economist Richard Layard in 2007 presented a business case for cognitive behavioural therapy (CBT) whereby it would save the UK government money by its demonstrations that its 'express' treatment and apparent success rate

[1] Ivan Illich, John McKnight and Irving Kenneth Zola. *Disabling Professions*. (Marion Boyars Publishers Ltd., 2011)
[2] Pete Scales. *Continuing Professional Development in the Lifelong Learning Sector*. (Open University Press, 2011)
[3] Royal College of Psychiatrists. "Mental health and the economic downturn: National priorities and NHS solutions." (London School of Economics, 2009)

**PART 2: Cutting edge performance in practitioner delivery**

helped keep people in work[4]. This resulted in the creation of the Increasing Access to Psychological Therapies, and escalated the rise in the number of therapists trained in only one approach and employed by the National Health Services. In 2014, the government announced that disability benefit claimants could have their payment stopped if they refused to attend sessions of CBT. Underpinning this type of government intervention is the belief that regardless of the individual's need (employed/unemployed) the *"aim is to restore their self–belief and optimism with ruthless efficiency*[5]*"*. As Davies (2015) points out, the solution is also being reached through a 'range of coaching programmes', though he doesn't expand further on what he means here.

Numbers and experts are dominating society. It is unclear whether this is for better or worse – at the end of the day it's all relative in our democratic society. Without a doubt there is value in demonstrating the benefits from coaching on principle, though we should question how, why and for whom. Understanding how coaching as a tool can provide support towards the achievement of something, rather than as a monist solution with self–certified competencies, will help with moving executive coaching towards a credible profession. How we go about implementing it as we contract with our clients will depend on how we choose to intervene in the market against the backdrop of government regulation.

---

[4] Richard Layland, David Clark, Martin Knapp and Guy Mayraz. "Cost-Benefit Analysis of Psychological Therapy." In: *CEP Discussion PAPER No 829*. (London School of Economics, 2007)
[5] William Davies. *The Happiness Industry: How the Government and Big Business Sold Us Well-Being*. (Verso Books, 2015)

**PART 2: Cutting edge performance in practitioner delivery**

# Mastering six areas for bringing in the bigger picture in leadership thinking: Helping clients take a wider, deeper and longer term view

## *Sue Young*

**I**n **my work** with senior and middle managers, I find that today's pressures in the workplace revolve around workload, complexity and forever pressing deadlines. The majority of my clients are struggling in some ways with their leadership role. Unless my clients hold their own clear picture of their bigger priorities, they can stay in a purely reactive mode and end up stressed from pressure and feelings of underachievement.

My focus is to share the areas and lines of questioning I find valuable to help my clients to get to a bigger perspective about their leadership priorities, and themselves. One of the outcomes I seek is the client's realisation that they already know a great deal. Apart from this being a truth, this awareness and affirmation is a boost to their confidence and accelerates their learning and growth as leaders.

I find this is particularly relevant for managers transitioning into more senior roles, where there can be a confidence crisis as they move into unknown territory – definite feelings of 'conscious incompetence'.

At this stage, managers have to learn to let go of some of the 'doing' capabilities that have got them to where they are today. This can be a scary step into the unknown.

The following key focus areas in coaching and lines of questioning can help clients step up in their leadership thinking and contribution:

1. **Organisational context – building a bigger picture of their role**
   - **What's the overall purpose of my role?** How does that contribute to the overall unit/department/organisational goals?

   - **Do I have an understanding of the priority goals for the levels above me** e.g. the senior management team?

   - If not, **what sources of information can I tap into** that are easily/publicly available? Who else could I speak to as a source of valuable perspectives?

   - **What are the wider market and environmental influences?**

   - **Do I know how the organisation is perceived externally?**

   - **How do these additional perspectives inform my thinking** about my priorities?

   - **What others do I now want to have conversations with** to add to my perspectives?

2. **Setting direction**
   - **What is my assessment of where my department or my unit or my organisation is right now?** A classic but nonetheless very effective framework to use for this is SWOT (Strengths, Weaknesses, Opportunities, Threats) – assessing both internal and external factors.

- **What do I see as the priority objectives in my role in**:

  - 2 years,

  - 1 year,

  - The next 6 months?

- **What will success look like?** What will be happening? What will people be saying?

The client's thinking on this will evolve as they progressively build their picture. The coach's role is to help stretch the clients thinking and imagination – what would be a bigger goal?

### 3. Key relationships – mapping the territory and influencing priorities

In organisational cultures that are overtly 'task' focussed, it is easy to lose sight of the reality that relationships are core to achieving any meaningful leadership objectives. Leadership is about getting things done through others. Key issues that the client can be encouraged to explore:

- **Identifying important stakeholders**.

- **Prioritising relationships for attention**.

- **Exploring the priorities and agendas of key others** – do I understand the agendas and priorities of our most important relationships identified for achieving our objectives? Do I understand what others need from us? What are the skills, knowledge, expertise we have that others could benefit from? Are others fully aware of the strengths we have to bring? How can we help them help us?

Coaching with exploratory questioning can help extend the client's thinking and help them become more aware of the assumptions they are making, and then question those assumptions. The resulting increased knowledge and awareness can prompt wider and deeper thinking. The right open relational approach leads to more productive and open conversations. This models the leadership behaviours that are needed in today's organisations. For example, exploring differences in assumptions, opening up knowledge, and identifying opportunities for collaboration and mutual benefits.

## 4. Self – the leader as an instrument of change

- **What are my personal longer term career objectives?** How can my current role contribute to this? What experience/skills will this role help me develop?

- **What difference do I want to make?**

- **What do I stand for?** What is my personal leadership approach, and my core values? By making this more explicit to myself will this bring greater confidence in how I communicate and add to my personal presence?

- **What are my strengths?**

## 5. Leveraging impact – involving others in building the bigger picture

- **How am I passing on my awareness and knowledge** of the wider context for our work to the team?

- **Do I set a clear direction for my people?** How do I help them connect this direction to how they set their priorities? Do I help them think about how they best share the bigger picture they're building with their people?

- **How am I encouraging my people to take a bigger perspective on their work**? Am I encouraging them to make their own judgement calls, supporting them toward stepping into their own leadership and authority?

- **Am I giving the right level of individual attention to my people?** Is there anyone on the team I'm neglecting?

- **How do I treat mistakes?** Do I treat them as opportunities for learning – what are the points we're taking forward from this, rather than get drawn into the defensive 'blame game'?

- **Am I creating the space for us as a team to have the bigger conversations** about our overall strategies, and exchange the real learning, information and experience, relevant to our collective purpose? Do we have a shared team agenda, rather than simply operating in our individual silos?

- **How can we ensure our team meetings are focused** on the bigger issues rather than the day–to–day minutiae that can be better handled elsewhere?

- **Am I supporting my team, or getting in their way?** Do I need to trust my team's capability and decision making processes more?

6. **The strategies to accomplish bigger objectives**
- **What would it take to accomplish our goals?**

- **How are we going to work in our team and with key stakeholders?** (see 3 above)

This is really the point at which the team should do most of the work in the context of a framework of agreed goals. The focus has shifted from the manager to the manager and their team. At this stage the focus of coaching is often around helping the manager enable and help individuals in the team on their priorities and issues. In addition there may be particular issues involved in managing upwards and outward facing key relationships. Throughout all of this, managers are managing themselves of course, which they bring into coaching as, if done well, it can be very personally demanding.

Many of the above lines of thinking can readily be incorporated by an enlightened manager into collective thinking and ways of working with their team. Thinking deeply and widely is not just the domain of the senior management team. It is increasingly required at all levels of the organisation.

## A SUMMARY

Coaching, as an approach, both with the individual and the team, can be a key enabler. It provides the right stimulus and 'space' for thinking and working more strategically. It's a place where managers can evolve, test out and refine their thinking and approach in a safe space. The coach models the kinds of behaviours required from managers to create the environment that will enable their people to think widely, deeply and in the long term.

- What are your favourite approaches to help their clients bring a 'bigger picture' perspective to their leadership approach?

- How do you as the coach role-model the kinds of behaviours required?

# CHAPTER 7

# PRACTITIONER'S SELF–REPORTING COACHING IMPACT FROM THEIR FRONT LINE

## 'Luck needs organising' – sharing insights from coaching in professional services

*Martina Weinberger*

**do a lot** of coaching in professional service firms. One of the big questions these clients often struggle with is how to make partner.

I had lunch with one of my coachees shortly after he had heard back from his firm, confirming him as a new partner. Over a glass of wine, and amidst humungous smiles, I asked him playfully what advice he would now give to younger professionals: "*What does it take to make partner?*"

His response was, "*Luck, and being in the right place at the right time.*"

This is coming from a hard–working and brilliant young man. I had the pleasure of working closely with him, so you can take my word for it. Why would he attribute his success to luck? Part of it is certainly because he is a naturally humble person and he would not want other people to feel bad. He knows very well that not everyone can and will get promoted.

But whilst there is an element of luck involved, this is far from the whole truth. As my favourite grandaunt used to say: "*Luck needs organising!*"

Let me share what I have learned over fifteen years of coaching in PSFs. What does it take? What are the key things that help people get lucky? And where might they need support in their journey?

## INSIGHTS FOR COACHES AND COACHEES ABOUT HOW TO 'ORGANISE YOUR LUCK'

### 1. Start early

In a way, you start organising your luck the day you start in a professional service firm. Three years ahead of the point when partnership is a realistic option, it is high time to become strategic.

### 2. Learn about the 'rules of the game'

You can only be strategic if you know the game you are playing. In my experience, many extremely hard–working professionals do not take the time to raise their heads sufficiently from the daily grind, to find out what it really takes to be promoted in their firm.

- They often loathe the politics,

- The official process (if it exists) is often not transparent, and

- There tends to be a Pandora's Box full of hidden rules.

We can help our clients develop their strategy of finding out by:

- Looking for promotion criteria,

- Finding the right people to speak with,

- Having the courage to start having different kinds of conversations, and

- Helping them be well prepared for these conversations.

### 3. Be known and connected – internally

"*All things being equal, people do business with, and refer business to, people they know, like and trust,*" says networking guru Bob Burg. In my experience, this is just as true for partner promotion processes.
A strong internal network is perhaps even more important than a strong external one.

We can help our coachees develop and implement their *internal reputation building* plan. This involves answering the question of how best to find and build a strong sponsorship network, to help them win the political game.

### 4. Don't make enemies

This tends to be difficult, especially for some of my most ambitious and able clients. They can be experienced as too pushy, even threatening. Most partnerships like success, but not if it comes dressed up aggressively.

As coaches, we can help raise awareness of this potential trap and support clients to find their personal strategies to address it, to tread the fine line between assertion and aggression.

I find this of particular importance for my female coachees. For those who are courageous and ambitious enough to get even close to partnership, 'pushiness' is a real issue. It is often an even greater career derailer than for my male clients. It is known as the double–bind effect: if a woman behaves in a 'feminine' way she won't be seen as partner material, but if she's seen as 'masculine' she's often disliked and passed over. This is certainly in play at this stage.

### 5. Gremlin management

Most of my clients go through ups and downs and periods of doubt in the process of pushing for partnership. They ask themselves, is this really what I want? Such 'gremlins' are normal and helpful, they can even be useful by creating energy to explore what it is one really wants.

However, in my experience gremlins are best managed outside the firm. Why? Pushing candidates at any professional service firm is hard work.

It takes considerable commitment of more than one partner to truly back someone. So unless sponsors are sure you want it, they will not extend the effort necessary.

This is definitely a field where we, the coaches, can be of tremendous help, allowing our coachees to explore their gremlins in a judgement–free and safe environment.

### 6. Have a 'story' and learn to tell it, aka your personal business plan

There are many people 'doing the work' but not many *entrepreneurs* in professional services. Most clients need and appreciate support in building their entrepreneurial 'muscle'.

Writing a personal business plan tends to be highly useful. Not necessarily easy, mind you, but useful. We can help our clients sort through their thinking of what kind of business they want to have in x years from now, what they want to be known for.

One of the biggest pains at this stage is that writing the plan means getting clear about what to say yes and no to. After all: "*Strategy is sacrifice,*" as my esteemed colleague and business strategy expert Charles Kingsmill always says.

As coaches we can help with exploring:

- Why some things are harder to let go of than others. What they lose by saying no to certain opportunities. This is often an emotional process, "*image of self*" can be at stake here. (e.g. "*I am a generalist*" is an often dearly held self–belief, to give but one example.)

- How to make it a plan they **want** to see implemented both with their heads and their hearts.

- The fear of 'the empty desk'. What if I say no to certain things and I find myself without work? (We coaches tend to know this fear as well.)

Once a coachee has defined their personal business plan, we can support them to best 'tell the story'. Many professionals are naturally humble. They do not give themselves credit for the great work they are doing.

There might be self-limiting assumptions that need exploring and addressing.

Informal conversations have shown me that quite a few coaches are reluctant to go in the direction of supporting business planning. (You can, of course, send them all to me or Charles, since this is very much what we do and enjoy.) Coming to coaching from a pure business background I get the fear that can be behind this reflex. In my early days as a coach, by contrast, I felt relieved when it came to business planning. It was a safer, more familiar place than the messy personal side. If you don't have a business background you might well feel out of your depth in supporting clients to write their business plan. But as always: we do not need to be the expert of their business. It is not our role to actually write their plan. We need to remember coaching is about:

- Challenging assumptions,

- Challenging focus,

- Asking good (enough) questions,

- Questioning stretch (too much, too little for what they want to achieve),

- Exploring whether the plan a coachee is developing actually resonates with their whole self or simply their head, and whether it will resonate with other relevant stakeholders.

I would encourage you to give it a go. Stay in the space where you work best, but give your coachee the support, attention and space to do their best thinking.

Remember, it is never about perfection. They cannot have a perfect plan or eliminate risk entirely. Rather it is about developing your client's thinking towards entrepreneurship, about getting ready to have different kinds of conversations with the partners of their firm, their clients and colleagues, conversations beyond imminent projects. We are catalysers for the journey, never more nor less.

## 7. Getting out of the 'safe pair of hands' trap

Some of my clients are highly frustrated when they come to me. They are putting in long hours, they catch anything their partners drop, yet nobody seems to notice and appreciate their quality work.

They might be stuck in what I call the 'safe pair of hands' trap. Their partners have much to lose but little to gain if they promote them.

In cases like these, our role is to help the client 'get real'. Accept that in their partners' shoes, they would probably do the same. It is up to them to make a significant change to get out of this trap since they are the only ones losing out.

- Some of my clients realise after some exploration, that they are indeed ok with their lot, that it is *exactly* the space in which they function best. That the need is not necessarily for promotion, but for recognition – in this case, we can support them in finding ways to be recognised, or ways to self–recognise, or get recognition elsewhere, or even start giving recognition to others.

- For clients who do want to change the current dynamics, I find writing a personal business plan is again a good place to start. The question they need to answer is: *What needs to shift so that promoting me becomes a win–win?*

## 8. Lightening up

And of course, my very wise coachee is right! It is also about luck, about being at the right place at the right time. So whilst luck needs organising, and we can do a lot to support our clients in their 'luck organisation'. Clients will never have 100 percent control over their circumstances. This might be frustrating, but it might also allow for a little reframing.

I love the idea of permission slips that Brené Brown uses in the framing of her COURAGE works Living Brave semester. We can encourage our clients to give themselves permission to think differently about 'success' and 'failure'. (Many high–achieving people have a tendency to blame themselves for failure and attribute success to good luck, which is the best way to make yourself miserable in the long run.)

**PART 2: Cutting edge performance in practitioner delivery**

A permission slip allowing them to be gentler and kinder to themselves might be useful in our ambiguous world. This might be another area that we explore with our clients in coaching.

Ideally, they give themselves a real chance at being lucky. When they succeed, they can award themselves honestly and without reservation the 'luck–needs–organising–order–of–excellence'.

If when the time comes, despite their best efforts, there is no partnership slot for them, then they have learned many useful skills, way beyond being a good or excellent professional. Moving on, they know it was a case of being unlucky. They were right, but the time and place were not. And this is, of course, easier written then absorbed!

## A RECENT CASE THAT BROADLY OUTLINES SOME OF THESE ISSUES

A highly ambitious and commercially successful professional came to me for coaching. When I first met him, it was instantly clear he had formidable presence, even from the way he entered the room.

Despite being highly successful, his promotion had just been deferred again, for another year. It rankled. He wanted coaching and yet he didn't. He wanted to get rid of the anger and try again. At the same time he had offers from other firms and was debating whether he shouldn't simply leave.

We started defining possible coaching goals. I asked him to self–score against the partner promotion criteria in his firm. He did and there was a clear pattern emerging – he was not listening enough to others and kept people too much at arm's length. In short he was simply not enough of a team player. Instead he was seen as a (successful) lone wolf.

He defined his goal as wanting to become more 'partner–like', in the sense of cooperating with others.

He said he wanted to address this. However, when we explored a little more, looking into his stories on what made him such a stellar performer, it became clear that he did not want to share his ideas, his successes. He attributed his current success to not co–operating much with others. Above all, his current approach meant if he wanted to switch to another firm he would have something to offer. If he became more 'partnering' in his current firm he might give away valuable client relationships and thus decrease his market value.

Did he want to gamble and give it a go, sharing and 'partnering'? Or didn't he? Did his current success depended on his current behaviour? Or was there another way of being successful?

We decided he would take time to think whether he wanted to push for partnership (in the firm that was providing the coaching) or whether he simply did not. I challenged him that unless he really wanted to 'become more partner–like', coaching would go nowhere. He smiled and said he would get back to me.

Three months later he called me and simply said: "*I am all in.*" He explained that being the lone wolf might eventually hurt him elsewhere and he might as well give it a go where he was. He was still worried that any change might make him less successful, but he said he wouldn't find out unless he tried.

He was painfully honest in his three–way conversation, even going so far as to get 360 feedback by interviewing people himself (we worked at length to make this an unthreatening experience for those he asked for feedback). He started digging through his past appraisals, looking for clues on when and where and how to change.

One of the lovely results that emerged from his 360 was that he was highly appreciated in many ways. It also unearthed that he had indeed neglected to connect internally. He had made some influential enemies who resented his gutsy (albeit successful) pushiness. Some people outside his direct team found him scary and all found him too hard working to be a role model or inspirational.

What were the solutions he developed for himself?

He found ways to give more space to his team members, to let them speak directly with clients. To his relief he found that this did not make him obsolete. On the contrary, it elevated his standing towards the more strategic advisory role. He also openly addressed wanting to become less 'scary' towards his wider team. This landed really well.

**PART 2: Cutting edge performance in practitioner delivery**

I should perhaps mention that, despite his driving style, he does have a lovely sense of humour.

Once he realised that this was actually appreciated by those who had never seen this side of him, he allowed himself to let more of his playfulness shine through. He also involved partners more in his decisions. Even though it grated with him in the beginning as 'time wasting', he eventually found a way to make it useful for him, his partners and their clients.

Slowing down to speed up became his mantra. He successfully cross-sold a prestigious project to one of the international offices and realised he needed to make a conscious effort to work less, both for his own well-being and as a role model for others.

At the end of the coaching process at the final three-way, his lead partner just said: "*'Peter 2.0', this is how the team talks about him now*", big smiles all round. He also claimed that the changes he and others have noticed will help in promoting him this year.

We will see.

## WHAT'S NEXT?

I have shared with you some of the learnings and experience from my practice on how we can support people in professional services firms on track for a partnership or who want to get onto partnership track.

- How do these ideas 'land' with you?

- What works for you in supporting clients on a similar path?

- Where do you/your clients struggle?

- What else do you think does it take to organise luck?

# Reviewing resilience as an outcome: the real experience is a positive outcome from deeper levels of learning

*Sue Young*

A fresh look at 'resilience'. After some recent coaching assignments, I have been left wondering about the idea of resilience – something is still missing from these definitions. Resilience is usually positioned as a necessary response to a difficult situation that involves pain and is seen in a negative light – the situation is something to be got through. However, in my view there is not enough attention given to the *growth* and *satisfaction* derived from coping with, and even coming to thrive in, conditions that we need to be resilient toward. Perhaps these conditions can rather be seen as a source of stimulating accelerated learning and even enjoyable challenge.

## A PEER COACHING STUDY

I have recently been working with a peer coaching group of managers in an organisation that is in a phase of major change and transition.

The report offered here, by the people involved, in the language of the actual people in the situation, somehow carries more immediate meaning than most of the 'professional' language about resilience (a comparison I'll expand on later). Their language speaks to what I consider I am doing when I contribute to peer coaching as well.

## The importance of a practical view

This perspective, as I've described here, has raised questions for me about the real nature of resilience. Such a reflection has made me take a more practical and positive view of resilience, especially when it is something that is part of a normal healthy approach to continuous learning, rather than something that is taken up as a vague theoretical label for the solution.

## MY CASE STUDY

### The people involved:

In one organisation, I have been working with a group of managers on their development as leaders – some for nearly three years. These managers have been going through a lot of pressure, working in a highly politicised international environment, close to government and political interests, and going through a great deal of restructuring change.

Those I am working with are highly capable people fully stretched by the scale and complexity of the task they face. There is not a clear direction and focus from the top. There is a great deal of uncertainty and insecurity, as the organisation goes through major shifts and re–aligning in the ways it operates. The perception by some that they need to come up with simple direct answers is still an illusion that holds, despite all the evidence showing that it is simply not a feasible, realistic, or even desirable way forward.

Not everyone has adapted well. In some areas, and with some people, the uncertainty has caused some individuals, and sometimes whole areas of the organisation, to be frozen in a highly defensive mind set and set of behaviours. This feeds a negative, highly politicised culture where fear causes people to be reluctant to stick their head above the parapet. Avoidance and blame behaviours dominate the culture.

This can result in the best people looking to leave, and low levels of motivation and initiative in everyone who stays.

## The report coming out from this group:

Let me share what resilience really looks like on an everyday basis for people coping with the ambitions and hopes they have for themselves and their organisation, as managers and leaders. Following a number of peer coaching sessions they shared what they had experienced and learned that helped them bounce back and retain their sense of motivation.

- The support of a trusted group and 'safe space' where I can feel free to express my feelings, doubts and thoughts in relation to the realities of what I see going on.

- Retaining my personal independent values and standards of professionalism.

- Supporting my people and being there for them.

- Seeing and connecting to the bigger picture and taking a longer term perspective.

- See the organisational politics and political manoeuvrings for what they are. Recognise and take account of them but don't be driven thoughtlessly by them.

- Maintain a positive sense of the opportunities in times of change – think out of the box.

- Connect to and be able to articulate the skills, capabilities, breadth and depth of experience I bring. If I don't do that for myself I won't be able to convey it to others.

- Maintain balance. Work is part of life, not the other way around. Retain a sense of the important things in life.

- Extract the learning from setbacks. There would be no deeper learning and true progress in life without setbacks.

- Ensure you can always step back and see things objectively, review your options and retain that sense of independence.

- You may not have the power to change the situation you're faced with but you do have the power to choose how you think and feel about it.

- Retain a sense of humour!

**PART 2: Cutting edge performance in practitioner delivery**

As capable people, none of them were helpless in the face of challenging circumstances. Including peer coaching as part of their leadership development helped them to significantly strengthen their insights, confidence and ability in regards to dealing with these challenges.

It has to be said that the challenges were partly due to the ambitions they had each formed. Without such aspirations, they may not have been so challenged.

Another thing that has stood out for me is how some people do not recognise or appreciate the strength they have shown. It is only when it is affirmed or pointed out by others that they feel it for real. This is where coaching skills that help individuals focus on their strengths and opportunities can best contribute to the way forward.

I have been so impressed and humbled by peoples' abilities to hang on and continue to deliver and grow in today's organisations.

### WHAT DOES THE BEST CURRENT THEORY ON RESILIENCE HAVE TO SAY?

I include a reference to a reasonable professional authority on the matter of resilience – the American Psychological Association (APA). Interestingly, the British Psychological Society's description of resilience was more general and 'academic'.

The American Psychological Association (APA) looks at the psychology of resilience from the perspective of extremes of personal stress but also emphasises how it can be approached very constructively as a process that helps another person re–engage with their abilities to learn. This way everyone can find resilience.

The APA also provides useful information that "describes resilience and some factors that affect how people deal with hardship." They list ten ways to build resilience as a result of the research made into people who have dealt with difficult events and had their lives changed.

A summary of their key points the "10 ways to build resilience[1]":

1. **Make connections.** Accepting help and support from those who care about you.

2. **Avoid seeing crises as insurmountable problems.** Try looking beyond the present to how future circumstances may be a little better.

3. **Accept that change is a part of living**. Accepting circumstances that cannot be changed can help you focus on circumstances that you can alter.

4. **Move toward your goals**. Develop some realistic goals.

5. **Take decisive actions**. Take decisive actions, rather than detaching completely from problems and stresses.

6. **Look for opportunities for self–discovery.** People often learn something about themselves.

7. **Nurture a positive view of yourself.** Developing confidence in your ability to solve problems.

8. **Keep things in perspective.** Try to consider the stressful situation in a broader context and keep a long–term perspective.

9. **Maintain a hopeful outlook**. Expect that good things will happen in your life rather than worrying about what you fear.

10. **Take care of yourself**. Pay attention to your own needs and feelings.

## COMPARING THE CASE REPORT WITH THE FORMAL THEORY

The APA starts from a particular position. It focuses on something that needs to be got through as a matter of survival or coping, let alone natural adjustment, or learning. It then moves to ways to enhance resilience. Comparing the summary shown with my clients report, there are some similarities with comments made, which may need to be just

---

[1] [website] http://www.apa.org/helpcenter/road–resilience.aspx

accepted as they are being very general. So where do we then get the real practical understanding from?

It is so much more meaningful when this is in the words of the people actually involved – because they relate it to their experience and the specific conditions in which they operate.

## The gap

Resilience is still too often described as only a response to high levels of stress, i.e. a crisis where a certain level of stress is about to cause some significant breakdown; when people are at some apparent stage of helplessness. The demand for resilience is put to test!

Conventional commentaries also describe resilience as what makes the difference – a special quality, by itself, of some sort. "*Resilience allows a person to rebound from adversity as a strengthened and more resourceful person.*" It's described innately as a characteristic or a particular and special human trait, some sort out input rather than output.

I still find the research and writings in the field on resilience limited compared to the reality I see in organisations and the experience of my coaching clients.

## The reality

Resilience is more an outcome, and certainly not the best way to create the learning needed. It is a sign of positive success in what has been needed. It is also something that is a normal sign of healthy functioning. People are all well capable of it. Of course there are times when circumstances produce surprises that can leave people very stressed. But then coping is more a matter of effective personal learning process than it is found through anything I have read about resilience.

In times of rapid far fetching organisational change, the ability of people to reflect on and learn from their experience is paramount – often while under time pressures. It is a long–term game, with a particular set of capabilities required.

## IN CONCLUSION

Writing this has been a chance to express the reality in everyday terms of what coaching can be – from people doing it, rather than attempting to sum it all up in a few short models. Translating the coaching theory into something more realistic:

- How have you observed how managers learn to adapt under pressure?

- What would you want to add to my group's list?

- What is your experience of the kind of characteristics, behaviours, ways of thinking and support that help people develop their ability to bounce back from setbacks, go beyond and further?

# The solitary jeweller – leading and working in a contemporary team

## Laura Bradshaw–Heap

**work within the** contemporary craft discipline. My main focus being that of contemporary jewellery. When people ask what I do for a living I usually pause for a moment. Sometimes I say I am an artist or a researcher, or a curator – in reality I am a combination of all three. Contemporary jewellery can be a research led or a practice based genre, depending on the individual's focuses and interests. It usually revolves around project work – short term, often publicly funded – cumulating in exhibitions, new bodies of jewellery or artist publications.

Jewellery is traditionally a solitary profession. Contemporary jewellery – a sub–discipline – is even more so. Spread sparsely across the globe, we practitioners are usually found working from home or in small communal studio spaces interacting with other colleagues only during conferences or events, such as Munich Jewellery Week, SIERAAD or JOYA[1], or if we work within a university.

---

[1] These are different types of jewellery selling venues that have a particular focus on promoting contemporary jewellery. For e.g. Munich Jewellery Week is an unofficial jewellery festival in Germany in which thousands come from all over the world to set up ad–hoc exhibitions and to see what is on offer. Both JOYA and SIERAAD are more formal events for the public, run by contemporary jewellery enthusiasts acting as selling fairs to expand the reach of contemporary jewellery and its customer base.

In past years, as an attempt to counter the isolating experience of solitary work, I have actively sought out ways to work with others in my field, be it through developing research projects, organizing symposiums or curating group exhibitions of work. I would like to talk a little bit about my recent experiences of working as part of a team.

I will share some of my experiences of how a small group of independent professionals, each used to solitary work, came together as collaborators and co–creators of a project. I hope to demonstrate how rewarding this experience can be – both in terms of project development and in terms of personal insight into others and one's own working practices.

## My approach and role

As an independent, opinionated practitioner, the idea of sharing the control and direction of a project was one that I certainly, at the beginning, approached with some trepidation. What if my opinions were overruled or discounted by the other team members? Would we retain equal authorship over the idea? Could I trust them to maintain interest throughout and would they care as much as I did about the final results? And, most importantly, could we work together? These are questions that no doubt trouble many who find themselves in similar positions. Despite these trepidations working in a team gave me the ability to bounce ideas off others, to test working hypotheses and to develop my skills in a safe environment.

When forming a team, it was important to understand that the aims and objectives of each team member will have similarities but also slightly different focuses. Each person will have specific ideas of the direction the work should take. For these different perspectives to combine in a way to make a project stronger – rather than clashing against each other – it was important to spend a significant amount of time listening to each other; to understand each person's perspective and each person's aims. From a personal perspective, within my most recent project, I found this sharing of ideals very rewarding. Seeing how others interpreted the project we worked on together enabled me to expand on my ideas of what it was and what it could be, encouraging me to be bolder in my own ideas of what we could achieve. Here are some examples of how.

PART 2: Cutting edge performance in practitioner delivery

One of the most tangible ways we found for doing this was through the writing of our project aims, objectives and methodology. By putting our various ideas and conceptions of the project in writing, we gave ourselves the space to then debate, develop and expand on the direction we wanted to follow during our regular meetings. This continued as we wrote funding applications and abstracts.

It was my job to do the majority of this writing, which in turn gave me a key role in shaping the foundation of the project by acting as its 'voice'. But it also placed me in a particular position within the team as it was my responsibility to allocate space for the other team member's voices by integrating their feedback and alternative viewpoints back into the writing.

This was a challenge at the beginning. Each of us has our own specific voices and as the writer I automatically wanted to iron out these differences to produce something that was more fitting with my own style. Yet finding techniques which would enable every voice to be heard became a key part of the project. It became the key for each of us to maintain co–ownership. This process evolved throughout the project and became more effective as we as team members grew to know each other better. To begin with we followed a process that anyone who has co–authored a paper will be familiar with, but for jewellery practitioners is exceedingly rare.

We first discussed our ideas face–to–face. I then mapped out these ideas into a text which would be forwarded to one colleague, who would edit and add content, and then share with the next who would also comment and edit as needed. This new draft would bounce back and forth until we were all satisfied. Inevitably we would meet and talk about the progress, flag up any content that worried us or to make alternative suggestions. We made a point of listening and considering all opinions throughout, though this did not mean that all could be integrated. Indeed there were times where ideas I had were overruled by the other team members, and this could have had the potential of causing resentment. However, as we had provided the space and time for all the alternative views to be voiced and heard, this possibility was negated. Interestingly, because all team members sought to actively listen and consider each other's opinions, there were none of the typical heated debates that can occur in such situations where 'he–who–shouts–loudest–wins'.

This was a lesson in letting go of control for me. Throughout the project I had to drop some of my own ideas and accept others. It was the same for both of my colleagues. A large level of trust had to be built between us, to have faith in each other's viewpoints and to accept majority decisions. Through this continuous iterations of learning to collaborate and work together, we developed an effective method of co–authorship which resulted in a strong methodology for the project. Subsequently we were asked to talk at a major conference and won three significant funding bids.

## WORKING TOGETHER AS A TEAM

Successful teamwork sees the integration of each person's individual abilities within a project. By working with others who had different skill sets to mine I found that I gained a renewed confidence in the things that I was specifically very good at. When working alone we become a sort of 'jack–of–all–trades', often unconsciously neglecting the jobs we are less confident in. Within a team the dynamics change as roles are designated to different team members based on individual strengths and competences.

Although basic roles were designated at the very beginning, we discovered that by maintaining a high level of communication we were able to develop an approach that adapted to each of our own strengths.

We began with monthly meetings, increasing to bi–monthly, and finally two or three a week during the most intense periods of the project. These varied between face–to–face and via Skype. In addition, when I worked with a colleague on particular aspects of the project we insured that we coordinated our time so we could work together. We often had daily Skype meetings combined with sending ridiculous amounts of emails to each other as we worked, sprinkled with the odd telephone call. How and how much we communicated was left very fluid according to particular needs at any given time. By maintaining this constant communication it became possible to then develop a flexibility within the team that enabled the shifting about of jobs as particular strengths or reluctances emerged.

While our approach required a significant amount of sensitivity so not to bruise egos or leave any team member feeling less than adequate in their skills, working this way proved invaluable. An example of this was how my colleague and I divided particular tasks when seeking sponsorship. I focused on making initial contact via letter and email, and she followed these up with a phone call – thereby negating my reluctance to use a telephone and her reluctance to write. Together we made a formable team and successfully managed to draw in a significant amount of sponsorship to the project.

Of course, this approach was not without its challenges. For one, we are not always aware of our own or others shortcomings. Shortcomings are only revealed upon reflection and after the fact. However, by maintaining an open and frank dialogue throughout and through observing each other's insecurities, a structure was put in place that gave each member the chance to play on their strengths during the project. We also provided a support structure so no team member felt in a position to take on a task they felt was outside their competences.

## WHAT I LEARNED WORKING IN A TEAM

One of the most surprising parts of working as a team was how it enabled me to observe myself and the work that I do through other people's eyes. Self—reflectivity is well understood to being key in professional development, but in reality how we observe and analyse our own actions are greatly affected by our personal biases. It can be incredibly difficult to see what we did as opposed to what we think we did and it is easy to focus on some certain aspects of what we have done more than others.

The support structure that was put in place within our team, based on constant communication and a sensitivity to each other's reluctances and strengths, not only enabled us to complete roles and tasks most suited to our abilities and strengths, it also provided a system of feedback between the team members. This feedback gave insight to what each team member accomplished during the project.

By receiving feedback on my team's perception of how I worked, I was able to develop an increased understanding of my own strengths and weaknesses. It gave me a new perspective on what I personally achieved during the project.

It is very easy to take for granted the things that come easily to us – a love of list making, a familiarity of social media, a love of writing – yet it was many of these traits that proved to be what made my contribution to the project so successful; as they complimented the skills brought by my team members.

Through honest feedback from my team members, throughout and at the end of the project, I was able to develop a much more complete picture of my role within the team. Subsequently I could take a more holistic approach to my own self–analysis and self–reflection.

So what did I learn about my own working practices? An awful lot – too much to write down here. But in the main:

- That I enjoy pushing and developing ideas and require others to bounce these ideas off for them to grow.

- That I am naturally inclined towards research and will spend hours insuring all avenues are investigated (be it for funding opportunities, sponsorship partners or research methodologies).

- That I was not always as direct as I thought I was in expressing my opinion. Which was surprising as I had always thought I was very blunt. This discrepancy in understanding between what was blunt and what was not became clear when we talked through our various cultural understandings of what 'direct' actually meant.

- That I sought to reconcile differences of opinions. Sometimes I took on the role of translator within the team when miscommunication arose.

- And most importantly, just how much I enjoyed working with others. It's now a key part of how I would like to develop my own professional practice in the future.

PART 2: Cutting edge performance in practitioner delivery

Teamwork is a complex beast. It requires equal measures of self–motivation to push a project forward during moments of disagreement or fatigue, sensitivity, the ability to listen to others and the ability to give all members the space to develop their own voice and ownership of a project – what some would call a coaching approach. While I approached this project with some trepidation as an independent practitioner, for fear of losing control, working in a team actually became an empowering experience as we achieved things I don't think any of us would have been confident enough to do on our own as a result. All the while we gained valuable insight into how we each individually work.

## The courage to challenge – how choosing to challenge a client can change the nature of your relationship – for the better

*Morton Patterson*

The reality of working as an independent or small business practitioner can bring to the fore issues of self-worth and value when it comes to pricing for and contracting work.

For many, the default position is to undervalue and offer a discounted price in the hope for future work rather than focusing on the value of the difference you will make. This is unfortunately a common behaviour amongst small business owners, and I'm not immune to it either. At times it is invaluable to have that external voice to challenge the limiting beliefs that can keep you stuck, playing small and prevent you from asserting your value when you're working with a client.

What I'd like to share in this article is a coaching conversation I had with a peer, who's based in the States whilst I am in UK, and whom I've known for many years. What I share below are those '20-30 minutes' in our Skype conversation of how the conversation came about, and how I in that moment found the courage to challenge.

## THE SITUATION

Joycelin (not her real name) is a successful coach who was asked to facilitate a strategy review for a potential client. The purpose of the review was to create a purpose and mission statement. This group, a small business consulting organisation, having existed for many years felt that they needed to improve and attract a different type of clientele. They believed that creating a 'revised' purpose statement would do the trick.

The retreat would take about five hours to facilitate. At the end they would have a clear statement to represent their vision for the future and motivate the team. What follows is the discussion we had and raises the issue of how and when do you challenge a client and is it safe to do so?

The first thing Joycelin said after mentioning the opportunity was "*I am going to discount this, as it will be huge opportunity for me and will open the door for others to get an insight into my background and skills.*"

I must admit that to hear her first instinct was to offer a discount without any consideration made me feel really uncomfortable. As I listened to her adamance that it was necessary to go in cheap to 'get her foot in the door,' and for them to get a chance to recognize her expertise, I was convinced of two things: that despite her years of expertise she did not know her own value; and most of all that I had to say something and question this belief – but how?

This was scary and increasingly uncomfortable – which I could feel throughout my entire body – that the cost of asking one more question could spiral quickly into a fully blown argument. This scenario is not uncommon in personal and business relationships, where you may innocently ask a question or challenge a client, superior, colleague or friend. The result of which is that the next time, for the sake of your relationship, continued harmony, business or friendship you keep quiet. This was the dilemma I faced. Should I or shouldn't I? Deep down I knew I had to. And the more I listened to her limiting beliefs (in effect stories) to protect herself and to play safe, the more I was convinced that Joycelin did not fully appreciate what she brought to the table. That not only was she doing herself a huge disservice, but that she was also doing her client a disservice.

Joycelin has over 25+ years experience. She worked initially as a financial planner and later as a coach with hundreds of business owners, professionals, and executives, helping them to connect with their value. She is very good.

So, with some trepidation I pushed the boat out and gently asked why are you going to offer a discount at such a low fee? Every step of the way, her response was defensive, passionate and determined and her responses were not uncommon:

> *"This will be a good opportunity for me."*
> *"I am happy charging that very low fee."*
> *"I have seen their books, it does not feel right charging*
> *them a lot of money, as I am fully abreast of their situation."*

Why do we do this? These limiting beliefs keep us rooted in the 'undercharger' box. It challenges our sense of self-worth. Depending on how we view our value these limiting beliefs can be destructive and put our focus in the wrong place – that of being beholden to the opportunity, the tasks we are going to do, and not how the client would benefit at the end.

## THE CONVERSATION

This was my personal challenge (and a common professional dilemma I'm sure we've all faced with our clients): should I or shouldn't I challenge her. Her resistance and tone in response to my gentle questioning put me in a place where I feared for the relationship. If I pushed any harder, I didn't know where we would end up but something in me snapped. I thought and felt that I had to be honest, because if I chose to say nothing, I knew that deep down I would later regret it.

And so I mustered all of my courage and decided that I had to say something resolving in my mind that as a minimum I was honest, but at the end of the day it was her decision. Mind you, this isn't something that's taught in any coach training sessions either as this would be seen as being directive.

So I said to her, "*Joycelin, because of our relationship, I am going to be really candid and say that I really disagree with this approach of offering a discount. Every time I ask you about why you are taking this approach you get very defensive and as far as I can see you are blatantly underselling yourself. It seems as though no matter what I say you only want to ask for the fee you are comfortable asking for, but your fees are too low, you are not doing yourself any favours, and ultimately the client will see you differently.*"

To her credit, she listened and said, "*Mort, you have a point. I know I was being defensive because as you challenged me all of my fears just rose to the front. I am afraid that I could lose this opportunity and I really want it.*"

Does this sound familiar?

I continued, "*Joycelin, you don't need to prove yourself anymore; they have already made a decision that they want you. You were recommended by a very credible source. The issue here is not your fee, but how much you can engage and excite them about their future. If you go in really cheap, you will not be creating the platform for them to see you as the expert.*"

She listened.

She quietly added that as well as offering a discount she wanted to do some additional background work that would be outside the project objectives to ensure that the session was perceived to be valuable. What I had said was slowly sinking in and so I gently reminded her.

"*If you want to go in at this low fee, be really clear what it entails, what you are going to do and what you are expecting them to do, but don't give away the store.*"

## ALIGNING AND ASSERTING VALUE –
## PERSONALLY, PROFESSIONALLY AND FINANCIALLY

The conversation started to lighten up. I had now created a space for us to begin talking openly about the value and the opportunity of this project. And so, she began to share how she was planning to handle their first meeting and that at the meeting she would ask how they would like the day to go. I knew instinctively, and from experience, that you must appear to have some semblance of clarity and confidence about how the facilitation needed to go. You are the expert and must at least appear to be so.

In order to offer her another perspective, I began outlying what I thought the clients would be expecting to receive from the meeting. From there we began exploring what her purpose is as the professional consultant and how they were expecting her to manage the meeting. My experience from having these initial meetings is that it is important to take charge and be the professional they are expecting even if you don't believe or feel it yet. And so, the last thing her clients would expect to do, particularly in that engagement meeting, is to advise her about the process for that day before they even know what they're going to get.

I felt safe to share an approach (three questions) I had been considering. I was confident it would be suitable for her. These questions from the outset establishes value that helps them to focus on the outcome, not the process; it gets them excited and helps to deepen the relationship. And so we worked through them:

## 1.  What's the objective for the day?

Thinking out aloud, I said to her, during the meeting, I would like to suggest that you say to them: imagine it's the end of the day, what would you like to have achieved? Try to get as concrete an answer as possible. Joycelin said that for her it was that they (her clients) came away with a clear purpose statement.

## 2.  How will the objectives be measured?

I would asked questions like: What would they like to see happen on the day? How will they measure that the retreat has been a great use of their time?

We covered some of things that might be said. For example: "We will measure it by how everyone is engaged and excited during and after the session." "Everyone who has attended the session is feeling that we have finally cracked this thing." "This has been a bug bear for so long but we just did not know how to deal with this." As I gently guided her through the process, she realised that through how they measured the objectives on the day a process would emerge. *"This is what you are bringing to the table Joycelin, the chance for them to get clear and think these thoughts through. Create the space for them to answer these questions themselves, ask the question and listen to how they would measure a successful day."*

### 3. How will this be of value?

Again we explored what we thought this might be worth to her client's organization to have this done. What difference will having this statement make, whilst bearing in mind, this is not about a statement, as the strategic retreat is much more than that. For example, some of their responses might be, *"My god, finally we are on track; we have a statement that we have been putting together for the past year, and now it is finally done." "The value is in the feeling of a renewed sense of hope."*

How did she feel after going through this? She listened intently and said, *"I get it. I was nervous and felt that if I went in and asked them to guide me, that would have been a better way to get my client's buy-in, but I can see the **value** in this approach."*

I continued – do not feel pressured to quote a fee until you are clear about these things. Taking the time to ask these three questions will add value and make you stand out.

## What happened next

How did this all end? Was it happily ever after or was she forever disappointed at my guidance? Joycelin doubled her fee and charged them substantially more than her discounted fee. She asked for 50 percent upfront and the balance before the session was started. There was no resistance. In my view, even that was a safe figure because when she quoted it they asked her, *"Are you sure?"* It sounded as if she had left a considerable sum on the table. But she said do you know what, I am happy with this. As I listened to her, I realised that at the end of the day that is all that matters that you are happy with the fee you are charging.

Sometime after, we reflected on our conversation and I expressed that I was really uncomfortable about challenging her and she said,

"*I am so thankful that you did. I am rarely challenged in this way.  Please call me out as I do not have an opportunity to have these conversations, where I have to look at my thinking. I really needed that. There is nowhere else for me to go to have these conversations.*"

Imagine that. Despite my fears, that was how she was feeling.

## What I've learnt

There can be times when a problem is presented and you have a solution in mind. You know that your clients' approach does not make sense but the travesty is that you choose not to say anything. For a myriad of reasons, we acquiesce and do not say anything primarily because of fear. Instead we nod in agreement or stay silent. In any event, we are not taking a position which represent why we are there in the first place. Which is that they need the objective view that does not pander to their ego. If it does, what value am I really providing?

We have a duty to challenge – professionally and firmly – and contrary to some of the perceived rules from the coaching market to see if what they are thinking and doing stacks up. That is why they have engaged us in the first place. Clients invest in their future now, not the present, by how much better off they will be by having engaged you. Have the courage to ask the difficult questions and see where it goes.

# Co—creating strong team foundations through peer coaching and a thinking style assessment

*Charlotte Rydlund*

S ince starting my company 'Pacta.io', I've been discovering ways to apply coaching skills in a technology start—up environment. This can range from sales to team building and more. Over the last few months we have grown the team to five full—time employees, which is sometimes hard to fathom considering we were just two people the same time last year. Since every person who joins a team will change the team dynamics, it was key for us to create a strong foundation from the very start.

When our Chief Technical Officer (CTO) came on board six months ago, he was joining two co—founders who had known each other and worked together (and have been married) for many years. Being aware of this dynamic drove me to look for a way to set a neutral foundation and balance in our new executive team of three. This had to be done before getting into the specifics of the company, our strategy or even the product. To help me build this foundation, I chose the Neethling Brain Instrument (NBI) thinking style assessment.

The NBI uses research in neuroscience to map out thinking styles in a simple graphical format. What is so compelling about this assessment is that every profile is as unique as a fingerprint. The resulting image you receive after the assessment depicts a circle in four quadrants to signify the right and left brain as well the cognitive and emotive parts (top and bottom of the brain).

What I like about this assessment is that it is quick to administer and easy to explain, which means someone who has not been trained in the assessment can quickly benefit and learn from it. There are also communication, leadership and even career implications with this assessment, which can provide further potential explanations of why we might prefer data or creative activities, strategic or process driven work.

When we began reviewing our own styles we used a peer coaching approach to help each other see each other's potential. Combining our approach with the assessment supported us to be aware of, and understand where, our own strengths and potential blind spots may lay at this stage of our business. This took us at least an hour, just reviewing our own profiles and discussing how our preferences might show up at work. By creating that neutral and safe space, it allowed us to begin openly talking about our preferences we were able to get to some of those nitty gritty questions that would impact our creativity and productivity, for example: What time of day do we like working? Do we need space to focus and therefore get annoyed with interruptions? Or conversely, do we need to discuss something immediately to progress? How do we prefer to communicate – email, messaging, face–to–face interactions? And so on.

As our own understanding of our preferences became clearer through this process, it also helped us to openly uncover as a team where we might have synergies and where we might anticipate points of friction. What was great about this part of the conversation was that it was completely without making it personal or judgemental. It was a way to appropriately address the dynamics that were driving me to find that strong foundation for our growing team.

As our session progressed, we began incorporating the elements of what had come to light about ourselves through the NBI into how that would shape and influence us as a team. Where are we strong as a team? Where might we have a blind spot? Because the NBI not only offers a detailed description, first and foremost it lays out your profile graphically, which easily allowed us to overlay each of our profiles as a collective.

It was encouraging to see that we all shared a preference for one area, while we balanced each other for the remaining quadrants. We have areas of common ground and areas that complement each other. And it shows in how we work together, even now, five months later.

As the team dynamic keeps changing we take on more people in the team and meander and adapt our product roadmap based on continuous customer feedback, using an assessment for team building that can be hugely helpful in creating a strong foundation that enables and drives that agility. It helps foster, and act as a reminder of, a learning mind set in ourselves and each other.

Questions for our readers:

- How have you used assessments in team building?

- What has worked or not worked for you?

- Which assessment is your go–to for team building?

# Coaching culture: Tangible coaching ingredients as success enhancers for leaders

## Laurent Terseur

As more and more organisations express their interest in growing a 'coaching culture' amongst their ranks, I am passionate about exploring what a coaching culture can mean practically for leaders in their own words:

- Can leaders tangibly increase their teams' effectiveness? Can they deliver higher performance by adapting their style and tapping into the benefits of a coaching approach?

- What specific coaching ingredients can they bring into their leadership approach?

- What resources are required?

- And where do these leaders start this journey?

I'd like to share some of my personal insights from having worked over the years with senior leadership teams on organisational and cultural change projects. Whilst a broader number of dimensions were key to the execution of these projects, I would like to focus here on those coaching inspirations which proved decisive in creating success.

## THE CONTEXT

Typically it can involve a new management initiative. For example, take a large division of an organisation that receives a strong mandate to move away from serving one type of customer with non—complex needs. This division might be stepping up to efficiently cover larger and more international clients, and deliver them a much fuller range of products, services and geographies.

## THE PEOPLE'S CHALLENGE

As well as recognising the need for a new model in the organisation, the challenge is also about recognising the complexity of implementing such a change on the people's side. Making the most of this change typically involves three major pieces:

### 1. 'Breaking the silos' (a frequent explicit leadership challenge in large organisations)

The model needed is more one of a global team with fluid cooperation and coordination across geographies and divisions.

The starting point is an existing staff and a leadership long being used to work as local teams with a domestic focus often limited to a narrow range of products, and no communications with the group's other divisions.

### 2. Building a competitive advantage through increased collective intelligence (a frequently implicit challenge)

Beyond the implementation of a new model and the related organisational changes, the intent needs to be to raise the teams' profile and behavioural standards, to maximise the opportunity through high degrees of cooperation, creativity and cohesion.

Typically there is a significant entrenchment, over a long time in an established culture of silos, which limits the teams' vision of how to leverage the many diverse resources across the organisation in a coordinated and proactive fashion... let alone with the confidence that they have the requisite skills to perform it.

### 3. Maximising everyone's contribution (a very frequent execution challenge)

To succeed, the implementation of the new model has to be owned by the teams, who would make it happen on the ground.

This very articulated vision can be compelling but has to translate to what it means in day–to–day business terms for the staff and existing leadership: what exactly needs to be done differently?

### HOW PEOPLE WERE ENGAGED

The key actions to engage people that I aim to bring are:

- **Sharing vision:** The new strategy and vision need to be quickly and consistently shared across the leadership by a series of face–to–face workshops and phone/video based follow–ups.

- **Involving the wider leadership:** During those first months, all the senior leadership and a large portion of the management need to be invited to contribute to establishing the medium–term strategic plan that would support the strategy. This approach enables both quality input and a high degree of buy–in, creating a solid bedrock for the change.

- **Energising and sustaining the effort:** A strong emphasis also needs to be placed on energising and creating engagement and complementarities across the teams, between those who know the organisation from the inside and the key external hires helping to bridge the gaps in terms of knowledge and experience of the desired model. This will help creating a robust foundation and securing quick wins needed to buy the necessary time with the involved stakeholders.

This sort of initiative typically indeed takes place over a substantial time period – generally a few years of sustained efforts and consistency to deliver the bulk of the value.

For example, during the first stages of the plan, the leadership must remain committed to:

- Keep sharing motivating vision and purpose.

- Maintain energy and engagement levels.

- Set clear expectations and boundaries, and enforce them when needed.

- Encourage empowerment across the whole command chain.

- Dramatically increase the pace of exchanges.

- Create forums for teams to communicate, exchange, voice concerns and help each other.

- Adapt compensation to reward higher engagement and performance.

- **Developing individuals and teams:**

  A number of key individuals in the senior leadership team need to set the example of deliberately encouraging a genuine team coaching approach. This involves considering also a number of individual coaching relationships and the design of bespoke development efforts to address specific gaps as they are surfacing.

  For example, following various feedback sessions and a purposeful use of talent reviews, specific coaching/training series are designed to:

  - Foster more cooperation.

  - Create empowerment and leadership across the client service teams.

  - Overcome cultural differences and work efficiently as a global team.

## WHAT SUCCESS LOOKS LIKE FOR THIS TYPE OF PROJECT:

- Within the time needed – which may be over several years, the P&L impact will prevail as a key measure of success (I have seen examples in which the income in scope increased multiple–fold and made qualitative leaps, shifting from mostly an addition of uncorrelated domestic revenues to the desired internationally balanced and cross–fertilised set of revenues).

- To use a sport metaphor, the teams' credibility swiftly changes leagues, with a significantly increased recognition externally as well as internally across cousin divisions.

- Many individual profiles in the staff switch from individual domestic performers to internationally mobile team leaders, or from experts/producers to respected leaders, setting many attractive examples of internal promotion success and boosting employee morale and engagement levels.

- As a result, talent retention dramatically increases – I have seen cases with no single talent loss over long periods – achieving a quite unusual retention success in the particular industry.

## SO, WHAT SORT OF RESOURCES NEED TO BE TAPPED INTO IN THIS SORT OF PROJECT?

From my experience and observations,

- **The senior leadership team** need to maintain their confidence, their usual great competitive spirit and an unalterable faith in the success all the way through the project. Combining this with an overall unassuming leadership style and a real care for their teams and their success is a winning game.

- **Staff and managers** need to tap into their courage and openness to change to take the leap of faith. Some, by leaving good positions in other organisations to join the project; others, already present in the organisation, by accepting to challenge the status quo and reinvent themselves, doing many things differently.

- **Everyone, regardless of roles and seniorities,** has to keep working hard but differently. The most decisive change agents are the individuals and the teams who manage to make the time to reflect and be creative, observe, be agile and learn all the way through.

- **Many, in particular those leading virtual and transversal teams,** need to learn to take more of a coaching approach with their colleagues and pass on the empowerment they are personally receiving. In doing so these leaders have to shift their mind set and become confident that by giving they won't be losing anything; they are investing to reap the benefits of more collective intelligence in return.

## WHAT SPECIFIC COACHING INGREDIENTS HELP TO MAKE THE DIFFERENCE?

In this sort of change project, I identify at least seven decisive coaching ingredients that work each time they are used, in different combinations and approaches:

1. **Consciously creating space to dedicate quality time and attention to the different teams and individuals.**

2. **Providing clarity and certainty by "contracting":**

   a. Setting clear expectations and targets, involving the teams inputs.

   b. Sharing clear progress markers and measures of success across the timeline.

3. **Showing appreciation, attention and consideration:**

   a. Dedicate quality management time to individuals and teams

   b. Making every virtual leader understand what their role is about, and realise how much more senior and motivating it is than what they initially thought.

   c. Giving them wider public recognition within the organisation.

   d. Deliberately celebrating all progress as it is being made, regardless of the size of it.

4. **Accentuating the positive, encouraging and stretching:**

   a. Deliberately giving encouragements, acknowledgements, accentuating the positive as often as possible.

   b. Stretching individuals and teams to grow and go bold, demonstrate responsible but ambitious leadership.

5. **Giving autonomy:**

   a. Empowering teams and individuals, so as to ensure there is leadership across the whole organisation.

   b. Giving space to express themselves within clear boundaries and clarified roles and rules of engagements.

6. **Fostering cooperation:**

   a. Making sure everyone involved would be recognised.

   b. Communicating about the differences and making them all understand.

7. **Encouraging learning:**

   a. Last but not least, accepting the principle that there will be a learning curve, and spending dedicated, personalised leadership air time whenever and wherever a gap needs to be bridged.

   b. The latter makes great impact whenever the leadership identifies that individuals and teams are presenting different strengths, challenges and needs in the change process, and manage to adapt the support given accordingly.

## WHAT I TAKE AWAY

A considerable amount of intuitive learning exists and is waiting to be extracted from live, practical experiences of change. This particular summary supports in my view the evidence that leaders can successfully draw on a more coaching orientated approach to contribute to change.

As I am reflecting on it, two key learning points stand out for me:

## 1. Leadership presence:

The coaching ingredient that I see as the most important for leaders to reflect on is the notion of leadership presence. Great leaders set a clear vision and share it widely. When it comes to execution, I believe sustainable success requires leaders too avoid the pitfall of arriving with a fixed agenda for everyone. Instead, Leaders who are eager to seek inspiration from coaching can reflect on:

- What conditions they need to create, so they can trust their teams for having the capability to become change agents in their own style and at their own pace.

   and

- How they can give them the quality space to unpack this capability.

That quality of leadership presence, consciously ensuring that as much space as possible will be created to dedicate quality time and attention to the different teams and individuals is, I believe, the first enabler to a coaching culture.

## 2. Collective intelligence:

Great leaders seek to make a positive difference by winning both hearts and minds. I believe leaders will increase their chances to achieve this if they consciously invest in fostering more collective intelligence by:

- Growing the teams' systemic awareness of their internal and external interactions.

- Leveraging the different forms of intelligence and skills in pursuit of opportunities for cross–fertilisation.

- Fostering fluid collaboration and synchronicity.

- Calling out teams' wisdom and showing trust on their ability to self–organise within the agreed boundaries.

- Encouraging the emotional connection to the vision as a means to sustainable performance.

**PART 2: Cutting edge performance in practitioner delivery**

## Other things to consider that are beyond the scope of this paper

Whilst this paper aims at sharing insights and observations from practical experience, and to help to make the concept of growing a coaching culture more palatable to leaders, it is important to point out that differences obviously exist between the respective roles and positions of leaders and coaches and their ethical implications.

Let me leave you with some questions to reflect on. If you read this as a practitioner, a leader or an executive using coaching to accompany change:

- What are those practical situations you have experienced?

- What helped implement successful and sustainable change, and was it inspired from coaching approaches?

- What did you observe, that ensured the exact level of attention needed would be dedicated to everyone whilst coping with the overall volume of the projects, size of staff, etc?

- How do you think leaders can increase their awareness of existing coaching strength and seek to grow these strengths even more?

- Given they are in a different role than the one of an external coach, what ethical safeguards should leaders have in mind when they apply coaching–inspired approaches?

# The Organisational Leadership Journey
# – into Enlightenment!

## *Isobel Gray*

*Now we are free*
*From the shackles*
*Others would impose on us.*
*But even more so*
*We have thrown off*
*The shackles*
*Of self–imposed constraints*
*We have built*
*Around ourselves in the past.*

*We now recognise the*
*Power we hold*
*If we choose*
*To see and step into the*
*Opportunities surrounding us*
*with our full Self,*
*and the strengths we bring*
*As leaders*
*In the context of*
*the relentless pace and turmoil*
*Of daily organisational life.*

*We can hold our presence*
*While those around us*
*Hold questions and doubts*
*About the future*
*Providing a positive path*
*and way forward;*
*Even though we are uncertain*
*About what will happen,*
*As events beyond our control*
*cascade and evolve.*

*Keeping our nerve,*
*Trusting our judgement*
*About the fundamentals.*

*We hold to our purpose*
*And keep that anchored*
*To the ground*
*for our people*
*And others*
*we seek to influence;*
*shielding and diverting*
*the variable winds of political*
*Manoeuvrings and positioning*
*That would otherwise*
*Batter us, leaving us*
*Flattened, disempowered*
*and knocked off course.*

*Rather we can make*
*Positive, creative use*
*of the uncertain vacuum,*
*and the opportunity*
*it provides for fresh thinking*
*That questions and challenges*
*The underlying assumptive*
*'We have always done it this way';*
*Flat earth thinking.*

*Our leadership journey*
*Has grown us.*
*More at ease with uncertainty;*
*At ease with ourselves.*
*True leadership is personal.*
*The challenge we face*
*Is how we can bring that*
*Opening up of possibilities*
*And continuous learning*

*To others as a core part*
*Of our leadership Task;*
*To bring about Change*
*As only when we better*
*enable others*
*to step up in*
*their leadership contribution*
*and be enablers*
*of sustainable*
*Organisational change.*
*Can we truly call ourselves*
*'Transformational' Leaders*

# PART 3

## *Identifying the competitive edges in the market*

# CHAPTER 8

# IDENTIFYING THE COMPETITIVE EDGES
# – MARKET REALITY

## Passionate professionals DO NOT NEED coaching

*Yvonne Thackray*

et me share a conversation I recently had with a leading expert in cybersecurity, together with their thoughts on coaching or, as they refer to it, mentoring. The definition used here to describe mentoring is key – as they're also describing their coaching approach:

- Enabling the recipient to grow and develop their potential,

- Aligning their strengths as a leader, and

- Being aware of where their weakness lies and finding those peers whose complementary strengths positively negates those deficits (a form of delegation, even).

This results in building a team that supports each other as they rely on each other delivering their responsibilities and collaboratively working together to deliver complex solutions to typically high–profile cyberattacks. This in turn meets the organisation's objectives. They also shared their observations of the cultural differences on the professional services industry in the UK and USA. The one that strikes them most is the lip service paid to 'human capital'.

Typically, company objectives are placed front and centre. Everyone who works at a company needs to align their professional objectives with that company. When a person is moving up the career ladder success is typically defined by the establishment rather than as a part of personal agency.

What they see in their field of cybersecurity, which is apparently something that is increasingly common rather than the exception, is a move away from traditional highly organised structures to a more radical and fluid organisational structure that meets the needs of their division. Yes, there are organisation objectives to be met and there is an individual who needs to be accountable to it all – however, how they achieve the objective should be left to each director overseeing the operation.

In this particular case:

- The director took a rigorous approach to selecting the right candidates for the role that started from how passionate they are about the field. Mistakes (many) are taken to be a given and expected to have occurred throughout their career. What the director is interested in is what the candidate learnt from their mistakes, how they've been able to apply those lessons in developing their role, and, through their experiences, how they've become better at managing them, which in turn reduces risk.

- They took a radical approach to developing a half billion dollar service in two years. It involved creating a culture that focussed on the team members supporting each other where there wasn't a separation into regional operations.

- They found a way to externalise the internal politicking – that typically takes between 20–30 percent of their time – in finding new clients to work with that benefited everyone, rather than a sub-group within the group.

The rigorous selection process – where passion is one of the key criteria – suggests recruiting an individual who is fairly confident and independent in their actions. They are more likely to find role models within the organisation who can mentor them into greater leadership roles rather than simply navigate promotion within the organisation's politics. In this way, they imply that leadership requires skills from coaching and/or mentoring. Context is key. Hence, those who do not seek mentoring and acquire external coaching are struggling within the organisation. It is possible to sign them up to attend a training course (provided internally/externally) to address what they're struggling with. This is also an opportunity for networking, however it will not result in any long–term sustainable behavioural changes that will help them in their organisational role.

It's encouraging listening to them share their experiences, passion and hard work in a field that wasn't even a field a decade ago. Hearing what they've been able to achieve and continue to achieve makes their organisation an absolutely amazing place for the right individuals with the right attitude to work. That they are rewarded accordingly is amazing too. If I wasn't doing what I'm currently doing and had the right skills, I think I would be working there too.

After what they've passionately shared, and their approach to adding value, let us ask the question of how or where coaching can really add value?

## UNLOCKING PASSION – WHAT I'VE LEARNT SO FAR

Passion seems to be the key word, and this is where I'd start in suggesting why coaching is valuable:

- A 2014 report from Deloitte's Center for the Edge "*Passion at work: Cultivating worker passion as a cornerstone of talent development,*" up to 88 percent of America's workforce is unable to contribute to their full potential, which means only 12 percent really possess the attributes of worker passion. Furthermore, companies do not recognise this value and rather viewed it with suspicion[1].

- The 2016 Gallup Daily: US Employee Engagement poll stated that 34.3 percent of employees are enthusiastic about and committed to their work and workplace. According to their worldwide survey carried out in 2013 only 13 percent of employees are engaged at work[2].

---

[1] [website] http://www.prnewswire.com/news-releases/new-research-from-deloitte-suggests-that-organizations-need-to-tap-into-existing-passionate-workers-for-sustained-performance-improvement-278499361.html

- 2016 Steelcase Global Report "*Engagement and the Global Workplace*" that explores the relationship between employee engagement and the work environment, found that only 13 percent of workers are highly engaged[3].

If coaching becomes defunct because individuals are passionate about their industry and have found an organisation that works with them to continually develop their potential through mentoring, as described (not the industry definition), then please fire me!

## WHY WOULD YOU NEED A COACH?

- If you are passionate and know what you want and have a strategy in place.

- If you are confident of how to get what you want from your work and you are proactively making those connections.

- If you're committed to trying – always willing to learn and grow from failures (which becomes fewer and infrequent over time) and continually delivering better success with each project/objective – within the organisational–market parameters.

- If you have a sponsor/mentor who's willing to personally support you to achieve your professional aspirations and continually become a better leader.

However, what the statistics show us, for better or worse, is that only 12–13 percent of the global workforce are passionate about what they do. This small percentage is the exception rather than the norm – although I wish that was the norm rather than the exception!

Everyone works for their own reason.

---

[2] [website] http://www.gallup.com/poll/165269/worldwide-employees-engaged-work.aspx
[3] [website] http://info.steelcase.com/global-employee-engagement-workplace-report?utm_campaign=2016-WPR-Campaign-En&utm_medium=HomeHeaderImage&utm_source=Steelcase.com#about-the-report

## To summarise:

- Coaching helps those who sit on the side lines uncertain and unsure of what it is they *really* want to do. Working through those key questions in a safe space allows the recipient to retain and regain a sense of control over their situation. They can have a coaching conversation with another who can emphasise with the context and provide that confidentiality and independent space needed for reflection, accountability, strategy and potential action.

- Coaching and mentoring complement each other; choosing one or the other seems to be based more on the degrees of passion/engagement that the individual has for their work. Importantly, both apply in a coaching approach. You need both!

- Coaching and Leadership are closely related. Building a strengths–based team that complements someone else's weakness leverages, even multiplies, the expected results: 1+1=5!

Investing in a quality of attention that can personally and professionally support people to have an edge (whether it might be potential, happiness, satisfaction or competitive) should not be uncommon. Many parents provide that for their children to get ahead within the established educational system.

I think the idea that the individual has a modicum of control in their professional life is perhaps the most frightening idea for most. It is the hardest to challenge in a stable society with established rules, expectations and norms.

What do you think?

- What was your instigator/motivator to get yourself a coach (externally/internally)?

- What was the process like for you?

- What was most challenging for you in picking a good coach for yourself?

- Do you share with others that you work with a coach, or not?

**PART 3: Identifying the competitive edges in the market**

# Using coaching skills beyond coaching

*Charlotte Rydlund*

**W**hen I began focusing on building my tech business, I thought it meant leaving coaching to the side. I recently realized that I haven't left coaching aside at all. Instead, I'm still using my coaching skills, just in a different way. Realizing there are new applications for my coaching skills has changed my perspective. It has reframed how I think about coaching; when, where and how I put my skills into practice.

When we think about the coaching space in general, and executive coaching in particular, we might forget that what we are trained to do in coaching has a plethora of applications outside each session and each coaching interaction.

## COACHING PROCESS <> SALES PROCESS

I was trained at Columbia University where a specific coaching framework[1] is applied. I also draw a lot on the GROW model[2]. So, when

---

[1] [website] http://www.tc.columbia.edu/coachingcertification/index.asp
[2] [website] https://en.wikipedia.org/wiki/GROW_model

**PART 3: Identifying the competitive edges in the market**

I was first introduced to SPIN selling I got excited because the process very much mirrors what the coaching process does.

GROW stands for Goal, Reality, Options and Will. These are the four stages of questions to proceed through to work with someone in a coaching session or to set goals.

SPIN selling is based on the influential book by Neil Rackham, using four steps of questioning to move towards a sale: Situation, Problem, Implications and Need–payoff. This kind of selling isn't what you might think sales to be in the traditional sense, like the approach of a used car salesman. Instead, this is about building trust and developing a relationship with a potential customer, taking them through a series of questions (like in coaching) to help discover and articulate what gaps or issues there might be, what the severity of the gaps is, and, together, identify whether there is a fit where the cost of these issues are significant enough that they justify a solution – one that you might be able to help with.

To illustrate the similarities between GROW coaching and SPIN selling:

| GROW Coaching | | SPIN Selling | |
|---|---|---|---|
| Goal | What do you want to achieve? Why is this important for you? | Situation | What's your current situation? How long has this been going on? |
| Reality | What's the current situation? | Problem | What are the challenges with the current approach? |
| Options | What options can you think of that might help you/ that you can try? | Implications | How do these issues impact your business? What implications are there of continuing this way? |
| Will | What will you do? How committed are you to taking these steps? | Need–payoff | How do the implications outweigh the cost of finding a solution? How much do you need this to change? |

## COACHING SKILLS <> BUILDING BUSINESS RELATIONSHIPS

Columbia University outlines nine coaching competencies, four of these are considered the core competencies: Relating, (Coaching) Presence, Questioning and Listening. Imagine if we were cognisant about practicing these four skills with our business counterparts, our colleagues, our customers.

- **Relating** is about finding common ground with your counterpart and then tailoring your message and positioning of your product/service to make it relevant for them.

- **Presence** is about being present. Being completely focused on the person you're speaking with; no distractions or multi–tasking, irrespective if this is a skype call or face–to–face.

- **Questioning** is about asking open–ended questions that display genuine interest and curiosity. It's also about choosing the questions that are appropriate for the SPIN or GROW step you're in.

- **Listening** is checking for understanding and summarizing what they are telling you.

How do you use your coaching skills outside of coaching?

## Freeing up our use of coaching! Contrasting the simple model of coaching with a more 'open' model for coaching

*Jeremy Ridge*

et's start our discussion about the opportunities and benefits of a more 'open' approach to coaching, rather than just the simple 'set piece' model for coaching. Much of the thinking about coaching still expects it to be behind closed doors – literally. Is that really necessary?

Can we not just do it in the moment, whenever and wherever the opportunity arises?

My coaching career began when someone said to me, *"Did you know that what you do is now called coaching?"*

I had three responses to this.

**My first response** was, *"No problem. I have been calling it whatever my client wants to call it."*

But whether I call it one thing or another, the choice of name doesn't change what it is I do. This is especially important to speak the language the other person uses for the sake of receptivity and understanding. I have always been using all sorts of terms to describe what I do.

Now, this was in the early days of emerging 'professional bodies' – all setting out to lay claim to the territory when it was all new. During those days, most of these bodies just had to say, 'Send us a small sum of money and you are suddenly a member of a new – self-appointed – professional body'.

**My second response,** unsurprisingly, was then to ask, 'What did *they* mean by coaching?'

The answer left me quite surprised!

I was told, "*Coaching is where you take a person into a private and carefully controlled space where, over a number of sessions, over a number of weeks or months, you have time with them that enables you to do coaching.*"

This left me slightly nonplussed. It appeared that coaching was more about the careful management of the physical and time conditions for the process than what you did in the space.

**My third response** was to understand why this 'simple' set piece model was so central to the definition.

The response I received was, "*We have to make what is done seem special by going through this formal separation, through this special fuss about it, in order to make what we do seem more specialized.*"

And so coaching has been all about this sort of private and controlled space; and often still continues to be separated this way.

## SOMETIMES A CONTROLLED SPACE IS IMPORTANT

I might accept the use of a controlled space when the person may be in some state of fragility. However, I also thought coaching was meant for people who were in a positive and robust state already, not just fragile states.

It just does not appear real, to me anyway, that the only way you can give quality attention to someone is in such restricted space.

**PART 3: Identifying the competitive edges in the market**

One of my definitions of coaching is to give a quality of attention to another person, sometimes more than what they are ever used to getting in their normal lives, so that it creates an experience for them that they really value. Sometimes this is a space in which they have the opportunity to just 'catch up with themselves'.

## SO HOW MIGHT THIS MORE OPEN APPROACH WORK IN EXECUTIVE COACHING?

### Proper concerns for essential privacy matter

The first thoughts that come to mind when it comes to executive coaching are concerns for creating the right conditions for that essential privacy – lest something is overheard and restricts freedom of expression. We may think this is especially so in the confined space of an office – especially open plan or working with a team of people who work together.

### Getting out and about in the organization

I have been invited by a lot of clients to get what I do out into the wider organisation, rather than hide it behind closed doors. Now how I do this has to be done carefully! However it then means I am often invited to roam, and meet a wide range of people, across all levels, in formal (e.g. meetings) as well as informally, just passing in the corridor, or the coffee point even. Sometimes it's even in a crowded bar after the work.

### Team Coaching

One of my jobs typically involves what is more often referred to as team coaching. Teams can vary widely in the ways they work and connect. Sometimes they are working in different continents and never even meet in the same room.

This involves a much more challenging approach to the contracting and ethics involved. But it is all there to be done. It can also involve private conversations among those involved, as well as then being with them when they are together.

## Let's recognise when the real coaching contract starts!

The real contract is created in that moment where someone begins to respond to the quality of attention you are offering – not just when the organisation, and or the coachee sets out the formal agenda.

## Multiple relationships, and the complexities involved, happen even with a single coachee:

Even when there is just a focus on coaching with the one person, I still cannot see how the simple model should be so limited.

## Engaging with the immediate client representatives:

As soon as you engage with a single person, you are likely to have engaged already with the client/organisation through either the HR system or through their hierarchy – their manager. Even at this stage the dialogue involves them as well – even though they are often not formally up for the coaching, you are still given the opportunity to engage with them as much as anyone.

## Engaging with the wider stakeholders in a person's role in the organization:

This would be people coachees have contact with as part of their everyday job. Similarly, in any coaching agenda, it involves other stakeholders directly in the conversation, or indirectly – as the coaches strive to make personal sense of themselves in the wider world they are in.

Sometimes this engagement with the wider stakeholders is very formally organised. For example, use of 360 feedback processes (i.e. a structured approach to gaining feedback for the coachee from people they work with) is one important route to stimulating coaching dialogues; which is increasingly popular these days. This process can also immediately connect you directly with often a dozen or more of their colleagues; where you talk to them about their feedback to help make sense of it and consider how best to present it.

## IN CONCLUSION

I am suggesting that we may have more opportunities to use our coaching than we might realise. It can be at any time, with any person. This doesn't mean any moment whatsoever with every person that you can get your hands on – because there is still something about having the right conditions in place that are important to build up trust. That's another topic.

However, I believe this sort of wider view already makes sense to a lot of people I meet and work with in the field. Does it make sense to you?

This could be important as it really opens up much wider scope for the way we can use opportunities for coaching than in just that restricted space. We can accept there will always be a place for the simple model of coaching. But can we also begin to appreciate the need to think more widely – the more 'open' model for how coaching can contribute to the lives and networks of the coachee.

# How do you coach happiness with money?

*Kim Stephenson*

**f you use** strengths, values and positive psychology in your coaching, you're already in a good position. Money might be a useful tool for the client – then again, it might be irrelevant.

For example, what would you do if you won several million? Decide that you'd *"do a Viv"* and *"spend, spend, spend."* Remind me, how did that end up – bankruptcy, divorce, depression wasn't it? Or would you work out what you wanted, and if you actually wanted nothing, give the money to those who did? Would you be happier with that – well, these people did[1], and they were really happy.

It only takes the realisation that money is just a tool, not a god, to get people thinking about life rather than money – just the sort of re–focus that good coaches help with.

---

[1] [website] http://www.cbsnews.com/news/couple-wins-11m-gives-almost-all-of-it-away

**PART 3: Identifying the competitive edges in the market**

## A CONCRETE EXAMPLE OF WHAT I MEAN – PENSIONS.

Imagine you're coaching somebody about pensions. Maybe you think,

*"What about all the rules, funds, tax laws, options? Should they have a policy? Take the proceeds straight away, invest more? How do you advise them on a pension?"*

Clients ask because they have heard from gurus (self–appointed experts who can't spell charlatan) that *"everybody should have a pension"*. They're bewildered and bored by details of tax, carry forward, investment options, and policies. I used to do all that professionally but I don't know the rules now (they change with every election, budget, financial statement or scandal) and I don't care, because people don't actually want a *pension*.

They want security, or freedom, or a lifestyle when they have time to do the things they don't have time for when they're at work.

Some people want to retire from the job they hate, a job they went into because it paid well – and so ignored the life they did want. Maybe they want something to keep them until they are earning enough in something they like. Some want an income that's secure and will top up with part–time work; they love what they do and spent years learning to excel, why would they ever retire completely?

They each have a vision of what their future could be like. For some, a conventional pension product might be useful. For many, tying the money up would be daft. A pension plan is just a way to put money aside. It's got tax advantages, but it has downsides too, like less flexibility.

So all the questions about *"what fund"* and *"how do you maximise tax relief"* and so on are the wrong questions. Here are some more useful questions, many of which you may use in your coaching already:

- What does a pension mean to you? Income, savings vehicle, security blanket, lifestyle choice, aspect of your compensation? Depending on what you see it as being, you may want different things from it and ask different subsidiary questions, which have different answers.

- What do you actually want from life? If you're 30 now and plan to set up your own business in a year or two, does it make sense to tie up money in a scheme where you can't get at it for twenty years? If you plan to travel round the world when you retire and do the stuff you didn't have time for when you worked full time, do you think it's a good plan to leave that to chance? Might it be better to see if you can live now on say, 70 percent of the money you have (that you don't have time to spend) so that you can put 30 percent away and build up funds for when you need them?

See what I mean?

You can't decide on what to do until you know your goal, and you can't sort out your goal unless you know what you actually want. The answer to questions like "*should I put more into pension*" are simple when you know what you're trying to do. It's not rocket science to keep money in hand for a lifetime ambition, nor to work out that if you can't live on 70 percent of your money now and put 30 percent away, you'll have trouble in retirement with no savings and 100 percent of no regular income at all.

What you can do is look at client values (*positive psychology coaching*), their happiness and fulfilment (*flow, happiness*), their goals (*goal setting*). They're all things you may do now and there's no technical finance expertise needed until those things are nailed down.

That's because it's the person that matters. The money is only a tool. Financial advice tends to focus on the tool, but once you have a hammer, everything starts to look like a nail.

What people actually want is to build a life, and what sort of building can you do when your only tool is a hammer?

What life do they want? Would they like to be happy, fulfilled, feel they're working towards something that has real meaning for them? That's what the Dalai Lama thinks and what surprises him about money[2]. It's what features in Seligman's work on happiness[3], that

---

[2] [website] http://www.collective–evolution.com/2014/05/25/someone-asked-the-dalai-lama-what-surprises-him-most-his-response-was-mind-altering/
[3] [website] http://www.amazon.co.uk/Authentic-Happiness-Psychology-Potential-Fulfilment/dp/1857883292

**PART 3: Identifying the competitive edges in the market**

relationships, spending on others[4], values, activities that engage us[5], having a meaningful life[6] are important. That beyond having basics like shelter and food, money makes little or no contribution to happiness[7]. And we know that materialism is linked to being unhappy[8].

## So how can this work in reality?

Remember, financial advisors tell people *"money is important"*, with the corollary *"maximise your money"*. If the client needs specific financial products, fine. When they can go to an advisor and say, "I *want to do X, I need Y in Z years"* – it makes the advisor's job easier. It takes less time and that cuts the fees!

Our aim: To help the client have more tools to realise what they want to build!

The mind set: You're more important than the money, so start with you. Define 'best' in terms of you, not in terms of the money.

An approach: With a client who insists they don't really know what they want, but figures life would be much better if they had lots of money, I typically say: *"Imagine you're 10 or 15 years older, have become famous and are being interviewed on a TV program by your favourite interviewer. What do you tell them about you, the achievements you are proudest of, memories you recall the most fondly? What is it that you've become famous for?"*

Clients sometimes have trouble with this, giving themselves permission to dream, to think about the person they want to be, what matters to them. But with help, they realise what they want their life to look like. Usually it's things like being respected in their job, being a great parent, founding a charity – it rarely involves money and if it does it's usually to have money to give to other people. That's the important stuff, the money doesn't really matter except as a tool to achieve something worthwhile.

---

[4] [website] http://dunn.psych.ubc.ca/files/2010/12/Spending-Money-on-Others-Promotes-Happiness.pdf
[5] [website] http://www.amazon.co.uk/Flow-Psychology-Happiness-Classic-Achieve/dp/0712657592
[6] [website] http://www.amazon.co.uk/Mans-Search-Meaning-classic-Holocaust/dp/1844132390
[7] [website] http://www.dailymail.co.uk/sciencetech/article-1309649/Key-happiness-Start-50k-year-salary-say-American-scientists.html
[8] [website] http://www.amazon.co.uk/High-Price-Materialism-Tim-Kasser/dp/026261197X

So why worry about the money – the person and their life are the important bit. Once the person has a clear idea of what they want to build with their life, they can think about the tools to build it, which might or might not involve money.

And, if it involves money, fine, how much? How can you set a goal that you can't see? But often the financial idea is just to 'maximise your return'. At what risk? Tell me, would you pass up the life you really want, that you can get with the money in a bank, because betting on a horserace might give you a better return? Until you know what you want and what money you need to do it, you can't decide what to do with the money you have now and what risks are worth taking.

# How coaching is increasingly essential to the development of organisational strategy

*Sue Young*

**P**EOPLE HAVE ALWAYS BEEN IMPORTANT TO EFFECTIVE STRATEGY.

## People make strategy work

Despite being a follower of the predominantly intellectual ideas and debates around strategy, people and organisations, in my experience, can easily miss the main point. The overall direction may be clear, but the 'how' or the 'strategies' intended to meet organisational objectives need to be devolved, as well as clearly connected and communicated, to all those who are working in the different levels and areas of an organisation.

A really important contribution is made to the development of organisational strategy when coaching managers are approached in a way to get the best contribution from their people. Integral to this is getting people to appreciate how to get the best out of each other.

My coaching work increasingly involves use of a coaching approach in a wider and more important context than simply separate one to one work with people on their 'personal' agenda and development.

## COACHING HELPS PEOPLE WORK

My practice increasingly involves drawing on my coaching capabilities on multiple issues with multiple teams. I work from the individuals outwards – helping them take more personal ownership and initiating strategic thinking, and enabling others to do the same. It is not just the overall 'plan' or 'system' being imposed on people from above.

My use of the coaching approach in these situations is getting strong encouragement from leadership teams in particular. For the traditional or previous approach to strategy, writing it and then doing it, is just not that simple in modern organisations.

For example:

- **Engaging teams:** In picking up responsibility for developing strategies – create space for collective brainstorming of ideas and identifying priorities for development.

- **Building rapport and common understanding of different specialisms and functional areas within the team/unit:** The standard to work towards is that anyone in the team/unit can talk to others about that area at a headline level.

- **Building common understanding of roles and responsibilities:** Where there is consistency in the team/unit in expectations and understanding of what the prime purpose and accountabilities of everybody's roles are.

- **Clear on organisation contribution:** Everybody has a clear understanding of their organisational position and how that relates and contributes to the overall direction.

- **Appreciation of different contributions:** Relationship development and appreciation of different contributions are identified as a high priority in achieving task objectives.

- **Regular reviews of strategies:** Effective processes for review of what is working well, areas for improvement and key learning points to be taken forward.

All these examples can figure highly in coaching conversations, typically when a new leader is taking on a new team or in the context of an organisational change.


## THE CHALLENGES INVOLVED IN 'STRATEGY'

Seventy percent of all organisational change strategies (Kotter 1996) fall over during implementation. The traditional approach to strategy development is very much both top down and hierarchical with most of the thinking being held at the top level. This is the context we often start working with in organisations, both with individuals and teams.

'Strategy' is one of those massively overused words in organisational structures. Some people throw it around in an attempt to give themselves more credibility, without understanding it. Many business books have been written about it. Many management and coaching gurus pronounce about it. It's one of the main functions at all levels of leadership in organisations.


### Typical flaws with traditional strategy development process

The traditional approach to strategy development is a 'top down' process... with a series of pronouncements being made... followed by ...a... gap! This jerky process can last over months, sometimes years. Into this vacuum floods uncertainty. This can stimulate a climate of anxiety, distrust; a lack of transparency, disempowerment and, ultimately, huge demotivation and disengagement. Typical 'gaps' as experienced by my clients include:

- **The thinking and reasons for choice of strategy are not explained** in terms that people understand or can relate to.

- **There is limited sense–making or interpretation review by local management teams** in the context of overarching organisational strategic directives.

- **The thinking misses out on a great deal of information** that is readily available from people – both on internal processes and the external environment.

- **Lack of explicit clarity about what is fixed, and what needs adding** – and the areas where there is a need or room to develop local strategies.

## Who knows best and who has the information?

In today's dynamic, fast–changing world there is a need for information to flow rapidly to and from the decision makers – and those are not only the people at the top of the organisation. People at the top are the most removed from the front line realities. It is this hard reality that is driving demand for improved leadership and strategic capabilities at all levels of the organisation. Thinking and decision making need to be devolved to those who have the most information to make the best judgment call about what is required. This requires a different 'mind set', which is still outside of many managers' comfort zones.

## SO HOW DOES THE THEORETICAL WORLD DEFINE 'STRATEGY'?

Johnson and Scholes[1] (Exploring Corporate Strategy) define strategy as follows:

> *"Strategy is the **direction** and **scope** of an organisation over the **long–term**: which achieves **advantage** for the organisation through its configuration of **resources** within a challenging **environment**, to meet the needs of **markets** and to fulfill stakeholder **expectations"**.*

There are many definitions of 'strategy' – not unlike 'coaching'! The above is an example that incorporates generally held principles of good practice in the field. This overall general definition can be applied, not just at the top level of an organisation but, at all levels and in all areas where objectives are set aligned to the overall organisational requirement.

---

[1] [website] http://www.amazon.co.uk/exec/obidos/ASIN/0273651129/tutor2u00

**PART 3: Identifying the competitive edges in the market**

Certain elements may be a given. For example, a new senior manager usually inherits a predetermined direction in answer to the question 'what business are we in?'

Strategy in simple terms is planning the 'how' of achieving an overall objective. Different functions and units have to arrive at their own direction and strategy, which is aligned and fits within the overall organisational objectives and strategy.

## THE ROLE OF COACHING IN STRATEGY DEVELOPMENT

Modern approaches to strategy development recognise that this is a 'continuous and evolving' process rather than a one–off exercise. Feedback is continuously monitored and active review is part of how organisations learn and adjust their approach as they go.

### In terms of process, what does coaching as an approach have to offer?

Karen Wise's blog "What is coaching? 10 definitions[2]" (2010) draws on a number of definitions of coaching, a few examples of which are as follows:

1.  "Unlocking a person's potential to maximize their own performance. It is helping them to learn, rather than teaching them." (Whitmore 2003).

2.  "A collaborative, solution focused, result–orientated and systematic process in which the coach facilitates the enhancement of work performance, life experience, self–directed learning and personal growth of the coachee." (Grant 1999, basic definition also referred to by the Association for Coaching, 2005).

3.  "A professional partnership between a qualified coach and an individual or team that support the achievement of extra–ordinary results, based on goals set by the individual or team." (ICF, 2005).

    Also see Jeremy Ridge's "How we can define coaching – 'Do It For Yourself' (DIY)".

---

[2] [website] https://karenwise.wordpress.com/2010/05/20/what–is–coaching–10–definitions/

I see a coaching approach, as defined above linked to good work on strategy development characterised by:

- A willingness to listen and learn from others experience.

- Thinking together and exploring the various perspectives.

- Weighing up the options with their pros and cons.

- Asking good questions.

- Goal oriented.

- Learning and helping others to learn.

- Working collaboratively with others.

- Retaining a clear focus on the overall goal.

- Not losing sight of the bigger context, and where we fit in – a 'systemic' approach in the jargon.

- A clear focus on development and improvement, not only in results but in ways of working.

- Adapting to the requirements of end users.

- Actively developing quality 'partnering' relationships, both within the immediate team, and with a range of external parties.

Most coaches will recognise these as regular themes cropping up in coaching conversations.

There's also a willingness in the most effective teams working on strategy to explore and challenge assumptions and to have the more 'difficult' conversations where some of the parties could see themselves as 'losing out' for the sake of something bigger that they can see the need for and how best they can contribute.

**PART 3: Identifying the competitive edges in the market**

Again, working directly on conflict situations is a theme that often comes into coaching conversations. Taking this into the bigger organisational context can reveal the bigger and hidden forces at the root of what could otherwise be deemed as a highly personal situation.

A recent client of mine shared one of her major strategic issues to be a key partnering relationship with an external organisational. She had become 'stuck' in her personal responses to what had become aggressive and unhelpful behaviour from her colleague. We discussed her approach and came up with various approaches. She came down on one as her preferred option. She was amazed when she shifted towards taking an open and more genuinely curious approach, with the result that her colleague opened up on some of the real organisational pressures she was under. After a hostile start they then went on to develop a good working relationship, which was of mutual long–term benefit to the two organisations. The preparation that helped my client shift was the insights and fresh perspectives she gained from the coaching, and then taking on a coaching approach herself toward how she went on to develop that key working relationship.

## WHAT I FIND COACHING CAN BRING – IMPORTANT OUTPUTS!

### 1. Individual coaching for *just* personal development comes later

Coaching increasingly provides a safe space for managers to think out of the box and explore their options, without feeling inhibited by considering others. Not to say that considering others is completely absent; that will come later. However, on the individual level strategic thinking needs to be done sooner.

### 2. Coaching skills – good questioning, genuinely listening, a more truly open attitude, with a learning 'mindset' – are more widely and directly relevant

Both to the nature of conversations most enabling strategic thinking at the individual and collective levels. GROW, probably the most widely referenced model of coaching, is in essence a problem solving framework that the coach draws on to support the thinking process of clients. However, just like strategy, the process is only part of how coaching operates in reality.

### 3. Quality exploration and broadening of thinking

Person to person relationships that nurture quality exploration and broaden thinking is the fertile soil that generates fresh and more innovative thinking. Creating a 'safe space' where people are treated with respect, where they are encouraged to say what they think, and to bring their perspectives is vital. Good strategic thinking collectively, and ultimately effective action, depends on this.

### 4. Questioning assumptions and a readiness to re–evaluate the real current needs requires up–front investment by managers at all levels

Just as in coaching, the active engagement and 'buy–in' of people to the process is essential to the development of sound strategy. Without that quality of engagement the strategy will fall down.

### 5. Getting positive agreement about the understanding needed

Working with people together, rather than just separately – e.g. team coaching, can often support leadership in having the exchange and conversations that can really help 'break through' on some of the entrenched and assumptive ways of thinking and working held by individuals and the team.

In our coaching with managers the questions we ask our clients can direct them towards taking a more strategic approach in their thinking. In my experience, effective capable managers in fast moving, pressurised organisations can easily default to reactive mode, particularly when they are juggling such a great deal. The space and climate that coaches provide, both for individuals and teams, can lead to a step up in quality of strategic perspectives and thinking. In my coaching I actively encourage my clients to take a coaching approach in how they engage their teams in strategy development, which is best done as a collective process.

**PART 3: Identifying the competitive edges in the market**

Finally, I see the most capable leaders bringing intuitively a coaching approach to the ways they engage their people and teams in strategic planning and in their reviews of implementation. Use these people as role models!

## WHAT NEXT

In bringing a coaching approach as an integral part of strategy development, challenges still remain – dominant hierarchical habits die hard. For example, he artificial divide between task and people still dominates how many organisations approach strategy development. That artificial divide underpins a lot of poor organisational performance.

Regrettably the cultural bias of many organisations and individuals is to focus on an over–simplified naive short term task emphasis in defining objectives.

The opportunity must be seen to be the longer term reward and payback from taking a coaching approach to developing strategy, which is huge.

I leave you with some questions:

- How have you managed as executive coaches to really engage in supporting your clients in strategic development?

- What sort of relationship have you needed to enable the clients to focus on the long–term rewards and pay–back from taking a coaching approach?

- How has your coaching approach evolved with the needs of the organisation?

# CHAPTER 9

# IDENTIFYING THE COMPETITIVE EDGES – THE COACHING MARKET

## "It's a bit messy" reports Eamon O'Brien on the coaching market

*Eamon O'Brien*

**W**hen I was asked recently to describe the coaching market, after a bit of reflection, I thought, "Well, it's a bit messy." The reason why I'm an executive coach is because I believe that people can be quite unusually brilliant. I care about people and teams being the best that they can be. I also believe that if you think out loud about the stuff that needs to be thought about… things happen.

My own personal vision for coaching is that every executive and business leader has a thinking partner. Why thinking partner? I chose thinking partner so as to not get lost in the word 'coach' being preceded by a huge variety of different words such as executive coach, sports coach, fitness coach, life coach, career coach, self–help coach, medical coach, national express coach. The market of coaching has exploded. I wonder that, like most markets, will it end up consolidating into a fewer different types of coaching that are accepted by the market place? I guess for that to happen, coaching must get to the stage that it is a recognized profession with a basic knowledge and a process of accreditation, so that the people who purchase coaching can be confident in the standards of coaching that they are paying for.

What is the coaching market? I first came across 'executive coaching' in the early 1990s. I was working in an organization and I loved it. In that environment, to have someone make me feel listened to for two hours at a time was an amazing and an eye–opening experience. I loved it. I enjoyed listening and helping my team to work things out for themselves. I guess that I actively started to bring a coaching approach to how I led others and that's what got me into executive coaching in the first place.

Now, as a former marketer, I'm a little horrified to notice that I have absolutely no idea how many executive or other type of coaches go to make up my market. I guess I could probably describe the segment that I operate in, but I'm not sure that I could describe how all the other segments fit together to make up the whole market.

And what about from a customer's viewpoint? Well, there it gets a bit messy. From a customer viewpoint, I wonder if the world of coaching appears a little messy with the range of coaching bodies from APECS, ICF, EMCC, AC, AoEC. I'm sure I've missed out many more and I apologize for that. And I wonder if it is now important for coaches and coaching bodies to become custodians of coaching, and so collaborate to bring the coaching bodies closer together.

If I had a magic wand, I would wave it and say, "*Wouldn't it be great if we, as coaches, accepted that we are custodians of coaching and have the duty to leave it in a better place and all coaching bodies collaborated to create the united community of coaching?*" Just imagine that adopting a custodian collaboration community approach led to a recognition that anyone accredited to say APECS, ICF, EMCC, AC, etc. were all in fact accredited coaches for the **Association of Coaches for the United Kingdom and Ireland.** I wonder if that could happen, wouldn't the coaching market be a little bit less messy?

# How the perception of age influences the credibility of the professional coaching space

*Yvonne Thackray, Charlotte Rydlund and Nicholas Wai*

**W**e focus on the perception of age within the executive coach field and by clients. The investigation begins with published reports (Sherpa, ICF Report, Ridler Report) in which the concept of age indirectly factors into, and serves as proxy for, coach experience, background, expectations and credibility.

The key questions to be explored are:

1.  What can be shared across the ages that can help us learn and grow as coaches and develop as an industry?

2.  How can we better align ourselves as coaches to what is demanded from clients?

3.  What is the future of professionalism in coaching (in terms of skills training, adhering to code(s) of conduct, accumulating a certain level of experience in coaching, business leadership and industry sectors, 'white hair', coaching knowledge) as the average age of coaches becomes younger and more diverse?

4.  How do we build a sustainable coaching talent pipeline in order to increase accessibility to other spaces and ensure the future of coaching?

Geographically, the coaching industry is more mature in Europe, North America and Oceania (ICF 2013 Report). It also continues to emerge and grow in South America. There are many training schools and a number of universities providing coaching programs from executive to life coaching and everything in between. In fact there is a surplus of coaches and an uncontrolled plethora of training programs. Every coach's style will vary based on expertise and background, alongside the ever–increasing change in demands for specialities.

There is confusion in the marketplace, which is one of the key issues highlighted by the ICF Report 2013, *"buyers do not actively source coaches"* (ICF, 2013). Furthermore, the majority of coaches who work in organisations are sole practitioners or small groups of coaches of similar age. How can the coaching community help the purchasers of coaching source the right coach for the right client?

Age is categorically used as a differentiator to demonstrate changes in the industry; according to the Sherpa report (2014) external coaches are often more experienced, with more than five years of coaching experience, and 55 percent are above the age of 55 years old compared to 42 percent of internal coaches. In addition, fewer external coaches use documented coaching processes (42 percent) compared to internal coaches (70 percent).

The Sherpa report also found that younger coaches have different preferences for how to measure the benefits of coaching, as well as which assessments to use in a coaching engagement; coaches under 45 prefer 'Impact on Business' while those over 45 prefer the 360 feedback tool to measure progress. Do these reports facilitate the sourcing of the right coach for the client?

In the published reports *experience* was commonly highlighted as being key. Importantly, *"who coaches had experience working with"* (ICF, 2013) and whether the coach has *"sufficient credibility and gravitas for [the] sponsor to put them forward to meet [the] senior coachee"* (Ridler, 2013). It is stressed that what counts are skills in listening, questioning, empathy and lateral thinking – skills that lead to actions and results. These are all learnable skills, which interested and dedicated coaches can pick up regardless of age.

- So how does learning coaching skills, regardless of age, coincide with the need for experience? and

- How do these coaching competencies translate into measurable benefits that clients want?

The key influential reports used for this discussion focus primarily on the short term and historical data to drive the current trends and needs in the industry. However, the medium–and–long–term vision of both the coaching industry and what clients will seek needs more attention. Taking the time and space to build a sustainable coaching talent pipeline, which includes knowledge, experience and credibility, again regardless of age, through a form of consolidation will ensure quality of service whilst retaining creativity and growth.

# Approaching CPD as continuing PERSONAL professional development (CPPD)

## *Sue Young*

**M**ost **recognised approaches** to CPD in established professional bodies is recorded in hours. This includes participating in events such as seminars, courses, undertaking qualifications and other 'classroom' derived learning activities. It is reduced it to a description of activities, often a 'tick the box' exercise, that is input or content driven, rather than outcome driven.

This can be a very proper approach when the relationship between input and the output is clearly understood.

In coaching, outcomes are more open than can be simply predicted. The outcome for the client, or coachee, is often highly personal to them and their circumstances. For example, leadership is often highly personal where the person is the main instrument in how the leadership is exercised. Coaching is highly relational where the dynamics, as they play out between coach and client, are central to the quality of the client's experience and thinking.

How coaches develop their approach and 'model of practice' is also unique to them as individuals. In recognition of this reality, we need to bring the word 'personal' into CPD; so on–going development is known as 'continuing personal and professional development'.

## HOW CAN WE BEST KEEP OUR LEARNING PERSONAL AND PRAGMATIC AS AN INSTRUMENT OF LEARNING FOR OUR CLIENTS?

My personal research always shows that the methods that come out the most highly rated are learning from client work and learning from interaction with peers. Certainly that resonated for me. In fact the most powerful contributions to my learning as a coach have combined these two factors.

Take an example of CPPD from working in a peer group over the last four years on a project to share and develop best practice for team coaches. A huge amount of learning came from thinking with others about the nature of team coaching and the 'what' that we were each doing in our team coaching. There was a great deal added to the outcome that was down to the diversity of experience in the group and the range of perspectives shared, together with real listening and willingness to commit to all agreeing what was best practice. Undoubtedly this quality of peer exchange was probably also the biggest contributory factor in the results we achieved. This massively added to my confidence and articulation around my team coaching practice.

The experience felt uncomfortable in places for this peer team but the resulting review and discussion was of great learning value on a number of levels. It was through a combination of the experience and then reviewing it with peers that we drew out major, and very personal learning points, for each member of the team. We became aware of, and questioned, our own biases and assumptions. The outcome of that learning for the team has been the recognition of the value of testing our practice with other established practitioners. For me personally it heightened my awareness of my own assumptions and ego driven tendencies and how they can get in the way.

For me, this experience is a good example of CPPD in practice. It hits several important aspects of CPPD in coaching:

- Learning about self,

- Self–regulation, and

- Working directly with peers that created a more common approach to a complex professional task.

Similarly, my experience is that with a conducive environment, where the right level of light structure and tone is struck, trust is built and open informal exchange, as though between peers, is created. It is a rich form of development for experienced people, generally. I have experienced this with my own coachees.

In working with our executive coaching clients the same principles apply. We are working with them as peers, even where we are catalysts for their – personal learning process. This can get deeply personal, in both content covered, as well as the atmosphere during the coaching process.

Coaching is particularly powerful for capable and successful leaders who are working in increasingly fast paced and complex organisations. In my personal practice, an area I have been progressively helping my clients to experiment with, finding simple ways to incorporate more 'thinking' space into their daily ways of working helps these clients accomplish in their particular contexts.

As with all learning this is a very individual led process. It has to work for very different personalities and working styles, who have different natural preferences. Consequently I will suggest different approaches accordingly; and work hard to find the sort of creative approach that makes sense for them, personally, in what they are looking for from coaching.

I have to demonstrate to them that I can personally appreciate what they are dealing with, and find ways to introduce ways that the other person personally relates to easily.

What works for one person rarely works for another. It becomes quite personal for me, too! I often consider I need to work with someone as the coach as though I am also working personally 'peer to peer' with them. This is the best way to operate in a way that relates more closely and effectively to people's reality.

**PART 3: Identifying the competitive edges in the market**

For example, one of my recent clients works as a senior manager in a global business, where the pace of change is highly demanding as one change leads into another, with a major re–structuring of the core business currently moving into a phase of implementation. The climate is one of huge uncertainty.

At the start of our coaching, he identified that one of his priority areas was to "*step back and create personal space for myself.*" Two areas of focused objectives were; to find time for strategic thinking to create a two–year vision, and to observe himself more in interaction with others. I had to appreciate his preferred approaches for finding space. He was travelling a lot internationally at the time and used a number of devices – iPad, mobile and laptop – a real road warrior! At the time he was very 'hyper', gushing out a great deal of information very fast, behaving stressed. So getting him to slow down his pace was the first part of him finding mental 'space'. I introduced him to the idea of a journaling app that could live on his iPad where he could just 'download' or capture his thoughts, particularly when he had time on is hands such as when he was waiting in airport lounges. I had primed him in particular to focus on his identified priority of noticing more explicitly his interactions with others – what impact he wanted to have, what he did, observing others' responses, and then reviewing what worked well and not so well as he had hoped. What would he do differently next time?

I had not spoken to him for about three months when we had a recent session. He told me, as well as sounded, he was now so much more relaxed and confident, reporting himself as 'calmer'. He reported being a lot more consciously aware and was taking his 'thinking time' out more confidently. What came across to me was that, although the challenges of his role are still huge, he knows more where he's at with it. He sees it going in the right overall direction. He knows the issues requiring attention. He knows that there are going to be setbacks, but is comfortable with handling them as they occur.

What I have taken from my work is the value of continuing to refine my approach in helping my clients through this more personal, peer–to–peer approach and stimulating reflection into their daily ways of working as leaders.

**PART 3: Identifying the competitive edges in the market**

For me, CPPD is at the heart of what we bring to leaders as well as central to our practice. Peer interaction is a very powerful form of development for experienced coaches, both with our clients as professional peers and fellow coaches. Taking the time to consider what have been our most powerful experiences as coaches, and what we have taken from that into our practice, is a better starting point for me, rather than the more mechanistic and removed approach frequently taken to CPPD.

# Culture driven from the centre: Comparing two coaching bodies

*Yvonne Thackray*

**C**oaching culture is a hot topic for professional bodies in 2015. The majority of the research has been carried out in organisations who have bought into the 'coaching culture', especially where there is – it would seem – a strong internal coaching department. An important and growing trend in the sustainability for coaching overall.

Coaching culture though is like a layer of film that has been rapidly spread over an uneven surface. As soon as there is a slight change in temperature, the film starts to crease, rapidly folding into itself until it has shrunk and lands on a spot that definitely wasn't where it started. It is a word, trendy some might even say, that has been bolted on with only light consideration of the existing coaching knowledge. Importantly, how can anyone (not just the experts) observe that this really exists and is not simply this organisational cycle's catch phrase? This is especially important as coaching is a hot topic amongst organisations to attract and retain the right employees.

## So, what is culture?

Culture is a word that can mean everything and nothing at the same time because it is used in many different contexts, situations and disciplines. It's a bit like 'creativity'! You would think that after completing a masters in anthropology I would know better! I'm happy to say that some of my learning has paid off and that I came away with a better understanding and description. So let me start first with a definition. Culture is the study of human society and how society works i.e. relationships among social roles (e.g. husband and wife, parent and child), social institutions (e.g. religion, economy, politics) and how people express a view of themselves and their world through symbols and values. Culture is about what people say, what people do, the social environment, and its impact on their feelings, attitudes, behaviours, etc. Now we can see what cross–cultural means in this context, the comparison of cultures, typically international in scope.

## When did culture become part of the business lexicon?

Four bestseller books publicised and popularised the concept of corporate culture because organisations, like a small–scale society, exist under certain rules and policies established by the government or industries. Moreover, they can be observed:

1. William Ouchi (1981) *Theory Z.*

2. Richard Pascale and Anthony Athos (1981) *The Art of Japanese Management.*

3. Terence Deal and Allan Kennedy (1982) *Corporate Cultures.*

4. Thomas Peters and Robert Walterman (1982) *In Search of Excellence.*

Culture was now something that could be shared via words to describe the complexities of what's happening inside an organization. Not long after, the term knowledge management became popular in business.

## WHAT IS COACHING CULTURE?

A quick google search shows that the term was first mentioned in 1994 by Barry in *How to be a Good Coach,* without describing what it is.

The second time it was used was in 1999 by King and Eaton in *Coaching for Results*: "*A good coach can also be instrumental in spreading a 'coaching culture' throughout the organisation. That is, having coached the individual manager to hone their skills in a more effective way, that same manager can be coached in how to coach others.*" (pg 147)

Today we have a few more interpretations:

> "*An organizational setting in which not only formal coaching occurs, but also, most or a large segment of individuals in the organization **practice coaching behaviors** as a means of relating to, supporting and influencing each other.*"
> *– E. Wayne Hart, Ph. D.*

> "*A coaching culture exists in an organization when **a coaching approach is a key aspect** of how the leaders, managers, and staff engage and develop all their people and engage their stakeholders, in ways that create increased individual, team, and organizational performance and shared value for all stakeholders.*" *– Peter Hawkins*

> "***Coaching is a predominant style*** *of managing and working together, and where a commitment to grow the organisation is embedded in a parallel commitment to grow the people in the organisation.*" *– Clutterback and Megginson*

I've highlighted what I consider to be the ***key facets*** describing a coaching culture that focuses on the skills and competencies required to make it happen. From the descriptions it's also clearly a numbers game! Time is another important factor, and a coaching culture is not something that happens in isolation, there are also other influences (related and non–related) at play.

However, even with these early attempts of imagining what a coaching culture is, I'm no closer to understanding what it is. This is because the manifestations of coaching behaviours, approach or style, will always vary depending on the individual's state, the situation, the content, the location, the time and that's just for starters. What about definitions? What about how its observed, and how can you identify which are the results of coaching? I think what is being broadly hypothesized is the possibilities of coaching's impacts when it's scaled up from an individual or a small group of individuals to the whole organisation. Everything else that falls in between is less obvious. This raises the question: *Is coaching a means to an end, or an end to a means?*

## LOOKING INSIDE—OUT

Instead of looking outside, and observing how they are managing the coaching culture alongside their company's organisational culture, I thought I'd begin by looking inside coaching and what coaching culture means for professional bodies. How is 'coaching culture' being driven from the centre – wherever that might lie – top down, bottom up, somewhere in between?

Without a clear consensus or agreement of what is 'coaching culture'. The authors mentioned above refer to descriptions such as the coaching style, the coaching approach and the coaching behaviour. I thought a useful starting point that best represents these descriptions is the accreditation/credentialing process carried out by the professional coaching bodies. After all, if any organisations are going to role model what's coaching culture or coaching cultures, a professional coaching body would be the first place to gather such information.

The two professional bodies I'm going to compare[1] are the ICF and APECS, bodies whom I have engaged with since becoming a professional coach. At the ICF, I was one of the founding members and company secretary for the Hong Kong chapter that follows a franchise model. At APECS, I was a member of the accreditation team and project manager for one of the biggest event, the APECS symposium.

---

[1] Quick comment on my comparative approach (2015): I've taken the words directly from their website and, where appropriate and based on my experiences, added my interpretations/opinions of how it influenced my behaviour.

PART 3: Identifying the competitive edges in the market

I share my top three comparisons between the two bodies (for a more detailed review you can freely download the table from the-goodcoach.com website[2]):

## 1. Minimum requirements for being labelled a professional coach – where's the starting line?

**ICF**: To call oneself a professional (certified) coach one needs to have, *"a clear demonstration of coaches' experience as a direct result of coach–specific training approved hours of coaching and emphasize currency of client–coaching hours to ensure that coaches who earn ICF Credentials are currently practicing."*

**APECS**: To call oneself a professional executive coach, an executive coach needs to demonstrate that executive coaching forms at a minimum: 40 percent of their practice over five years, at least five years of organisational/executive experience and a master's degree (or equivalent): *"In making an Application to have your expertise recognised you are required to reflect on your Executive Coaching practice. You will be asked to identify specifically how you meet the APECS Professional Standards."*

## 2. Credentialing/accrediting for professional standards based on the coach's experience (input vs. output)

**ICF**: Focuses on the skills and competencies necessary to be a certified coach (associate, professional, master's) against the eleven core coaching competencies and codes of ethics. Demonstration that a certified coach has met the minimum requirements shall be validated after successfully completing the coach knowledge assessment, and a performance evaluation (audio recording and written transcript) by ICF assessors with little/no feedback from the coach and coachee.

**APECS**: Based on meeting the minimum requirements in which the market i.e. the clients have validated the coaches practice, the applicants are asked to articulate the detailed rationale, philosophy and pattern of their practice against the seven pillars of framework

---

[2] [website] http://the–goodcoach.com/tgcblog/2015/9/2/culture–driven–from–the–centre–comparing–two–coaching–bodies.html

which includes supervision, CPPD, APECS ethical guidelines and professional liability insurance. They share this articulation in their application during the accreditation dialogue, with trained APECS accreditors (APECS peers) who share their views and opinions.

### 3. Appreciation of culture and identity – A nod to diversity and inclusivity

ICF: Skills and competencies are considered universal.

APECS: An appreciation of how the executive coach works effectively within different cultures and how it influences their identity as a professional coach is explored in the application form, the accreditation dialogue and CPPD.

## On further reflection

Compiling this table together, it became clearer to me that there's a difference between reading and living in something that encourages quality dialogues. Without a doubt, each professional coaching organisation (of which there are many) has its strengths and limitations. Each have entered into a market whilst representing different stages of learning and development of the coaching maturation cycle. So they work, in my opinion, across a continuum in which they are the current bookends.

## To CONCLUDE

For now, I believe when most people talk about coaching culture it is a hypothesis of what could possibly happen when coaching (which is to be defined and agreed amongst all the bodies) becomes part of or even embedded as part of organisational life. To date there are insufficient practitioner case studies to validate the realness of this term. However, with the advent and emergence of team coaching and the growing in strength and number of internal coaches, we may begin to understand more of how coaching is really demonstrating its impact, which can be observed and felt as a part of the adoption of that organisation's culture.

It's definitely something any association should really commission by carrying out some robust studies on what it is for coaches and their organisation.

I leave you with some questions:

- When does coaching culture mean to you?

- How do we emphasise the diversity and inclusivity in coaching culture?

- How do you observe coaching culture?

# Fresh thinking, and even honesty, is needed about professionalism in coaching

*Jeremy Ridge*

**I** **thought professionalism was** meant to be good and could be relied on. It seems some fresh thinking is really needed. As it seems, there are a number of different meanings given to the idea representing a number of conflicting interests. Greater honesty about these interests would help. It's an ethical thing!

## WHY IT IS IMPORTANT TO ME

I came into coaching when someone said to me, "*Jeremy, did you know what you do is now called coaching!*" I replied, "*Well I am well used to calling what I do by all sorts of things – driven by what the client prefers to call it.*"

That was some ten years ago, now.

At the time, it became very clear that there was a rush to draw the coaching flag up the pole of general attention. I thought it would be good to establish some real authority, professionalism as I saw it, as to what this coaching thing is about.

Where is the authority to follow?

**PART 3: Identifying the competitive edges in the market**

However, I have found that all that glitters is not gold, as they say!

The issue lies in the widely different meanings people bring to what they really mean by this term 'professional'. It seems we are **still** to establish what would be the best, and most authoritative, meaning for the use of the term – in the best interests of all.

I would like to lay out the different approaches to the term professional, as a way of giving some form to where important work still needs to be done – at least before I feel fully comfortable about my use of this term 'professional'!

## WHY IS 'PROFESSIONAL', AS A TERM, SO IMPORTANT?

To start with, dictionary meanings are also quite open in meaning:

1. Worthy of or appropriate to a professional person; competent, skilful, or assured.

2. Engaged in a specified activity as one's main paid occupation rather than as an amateur.

3. A person engaged or qualified in a profession.

The attraction of using the term is that it short cuts a great deal of time and resource in checking out whether people get what they are looking for.

- The central issue about the use of the term professional is the implied 'contract' created, and whether it is then delivered. (Contract originates as a legal term – but also can refer to mutual expectations more.)

- Users can benefit, as well as 'suppliers'. It is a great idea that has been widely, and increasingly, used across society in many instances.

- It also helps people know what they need to do to be able to deliver the service involved and remain 'professional', and even legal.

- It can even, in some instances, provide assurance against challenge or complaint about services.

- The issue of checks and balances where there are significant risks of self–interest are increasingly important.

And they are all still a major part of the issue when the term professional is loosely applied in coaching.

## My expectations of the use of the term – in brief

The meaning, typically taken from its use, is that the **professional** knows what they are doing.

- They get it right all the time (not occasionally, like amateurs), and

- They can be fully trusted to deliver a service as required, as specified.

- They know what they don't know, and don't stray into this. They know where their boundaries lie for what they do.

This is a very exacting standard, and contract. The term contract makes it clear that there are potential penalties for breaking this contract.

## LOOKING AT THE DIFFERENT 'STANDARDS' USED IN ADOPTING THE TERM PROFESSIONAL

Surveying how it's being applied in our field, there seem to be different *standards* involved in the use of the term professional – which is ironic, as standards are what the whole thing is about! I would expect more honest attention to this standards issue.

Looking at the sources of authority in the field at present, three large categories come first to mind. Two we know well – and the third is more in its early, but important, early stages, and is likely to be the force that really drives progress.

## Category one: The self–appointed, 'supplier', sources of authority

The risk here is conflicts of interest, where the self–interest of the suppliers does not work to the best advantage of the user. The user has little opportunity to input into the supply of the services.

- **Individuals – with self–appointed authority as a professional coach** – May just decide to announce themselves a professional coach – typically on the basis that as they 'earn their living' through what they do, they must know what they are doing.

- **Communities – of 'like–minded' individuals – again on a self–appointed basis.**

As Gray 2010[1] puts in about the journey towards the professionalization of coaching:

> "If coaching is to become a profession it must adopt criteria such as the development of an agreed and unified body of knowledge, professional standards and qualifications, and codes of ethics and behaviour. ... While some of these are already completed or in development, the continuation of a multiplicity (and growing) number of coaching associations suggests that the pathway of coaching to professionalization may be at best bumpy, and at worst derailed."

- This has happened in coaching where numerous bodies have created themselves, or appointed themselves as experts in coaching. They create a basis for **'registering' people** – but on terms they have given authority to by themselves.

- This can be seen also by **'training organisations'.** Anyone can offer a quick two day course, with the award of accreditation. I was raised in a recent paper by Maltbia et al (2014) that the lack of empirical validity of the core competences, the conflict of interest between certifying coach training schools, and the accrediting of their members, threaten their credibility[2].

---

[1] [website] http://www.tandfonline.com/doi/abs/10.1080/17521882.2010.550896
[2] Rajashi Ghosh, Terrence E. Maltbia and Victoria J. Marsick. "Executive and Organizational Coaching: A Review of Insights Drawn From Literature to Inform HRD Practice," in *Advances in Developing Human Resources*. (2014) pp. 1-23.

- It can also be seen in other **'knowledge oriented'** communities which may see their perspective adding an edge to their members in the field. For example, psychology and psychotherapy/counselling have both adopted the term 'coaching' in relation to their mainstream professional position by starting 'coaching divisions'.

The lack of agreement for where authority lies across this major diversity of claims speaks even more to the real risk of conflict of narrow interest. It is remarkable how little serious collaboration of substance there is yet across all these bodies.

In medicine, as an example of a more mature area for 'professionalism' that may be worthy of role–modelling, a recent review saw more issues ahead in considerable detail. Haffert and Castellani (2010) identified ten key aspects of medical work (altruism, autonomy, commercialism, personal morality, interpersonal competence, lifestyle, professional dominance, social justice, social contract and technical competence) and then arranged these within different clusters to identify seven types of professionalism: Nostalgic/ entrepreneurial/ academic/ lifestyle/ empirical/ unreflective/ activist.

> *"Traditional definitions of professionalism, within both medicine and sociology, have identified professional dominance as key to medicine's professional status.... Nonetheless, a top–down hierarchical model of work (as reflected in the professional dominance model) no longer seems to capture these complexities – even as the underlying complexity of medical work, the uncertainties of knowledge and its application to patient care, and the tremendous variabilities that exist with the patient population continue to demand some measure of individual expertise and discretionary decision making. ... How organized medicine responds to the problems of internal integration (e.g., increasing subspecialization) and to the challenges of external adaptation (e.g., the buyer's revolt) will have a great deal to say about the nature and sustainability of medical professionalism in the future. Traditional conceptions of what it means to be a professional – as a stand–alone entity–are neither systematically realistic nor ultimately sustainable. Like it or not, we remain awash in a sea of complexities[3]."*

---

[3] [website] http://www.personal.kent.edu/~bcastel3/6_increasing%20complexities%20of%20prof.pdf

**PART 3: Identifying the competitive edges in the market**

## Category 2: 'Independently' appointed nation/state or international authority

This category brings some independence to the checks and balances. However, the disadvantage is that there will be a lack of knowledge for what is involved in practice, and an excessive over reliance on exacting procedure, rather than inclusion of the substance that matters.

The UK 'chartered' designation is an example here. The professional body granted the use of this (UK) controlled term actually cedes authority for its works to the state.

> "A Royal Charter[4] is a way of incorporating a body, that is turning it from a collection of individuals into a single legal entity... incorporation by Charter should be in the public interest. This consideration is important, since once incorporated by Royal Charter a body surrenders significant aspects of the control of its internal affairs to the Privy Council. ... This effectively means a significant degree of Government regulation of the affairs of the body, and the Privy Council will therefore wish to be satisfied that such regulation accords with public policy."

ISO 17024 is a great process for accreditation – but does not include the knowledge and understanding that is needed in the process.

> "ISO/IEC 17024:2012 contains principles and requirements for a body certifying persons against specific requirements, and includes the development and maintenance of a certification scheme for persons[5]."

The danger is that just because it is possible to create an exacting system for a process it can be put about as having 'authority'.

---

[4] [website] http://privycouncil.independent.gov.uk/royal–charters/chartered–bodies/
[5] [website] http://www.iso.org/iso/catalogue_detail?csnumber=52993

## Category 3: End 'user' authority

We are now increasingly seeing the start of other forms of authority more involved in deciding how coaching should work. Especially with 'executive coaching' – as those involved can be more assertive and knowledgeable. This is also being led by developments in medicine.

**Internal coaching:** In executive coaching, large organisations in particular have created 'internal coaching' by using their own staff to provide coaching of other staff. These organisations are even fashioning their own internal structures for accreditation, and other internal mechanisms for developing their internal coaching – that key to professional status. This is even increasingly independent of current 'self–appointed' bodies.

After all, in executive coaching the use of what is called the 'chemistry' session is typical. The end user decides who has the most 'professional' capabilities by making their own selection of the coach for them. The demonstration of having to use the term 'chemistry' – borrowed from other areas is symptomatic of the issue. This would appear to signal a big blind spot that still exists in the field about what really matters. It still relies on whom the end user 'senses' (somehow) that they can work better with to achieve their goals.

**The expert/professional patient:** Perhaps one of the most recent innovations is the idea in the medical profession about bringing the 'patient' as the user more directly into the frame. In this way of thinking the patient is considered an expert about their particular condition. An article in the BMJ "'Expert Patient' – Dream or Nightmare?" is quick to highlight the opportunities and risks, but opens up the challenge to the medical profession[6].

Unfortunately, this can still seem to challenge traditional notions of trained/learned knowledge based authority. The methodologies for enabling 'professional/expert patients', as well as coaches, is less in evidence.

We keep on referring to how the coachee sets the agenda, and also sets the process, as it suits their needs/learning structures.

---

[6] Joanne Shaw. "'Expert Patient' – Dream or Nightmare," in BMJ. (2004)

**PART 3: Identifying the competitive edges in the market**

The process of contracting is key to ensuring expectations are managed professionally. However, in coaching there is often discovery during the process, rather than everything being known at the start – so contracting takes in a new meaning than the simple 'original general objective'.

These are clear signs that users have taken up the need to bring their own expertise into the mix.

## FITTING YOUR PRACTICE INTO THESE APPROACHES TO PROFESSIONALISM

1. **Coachee professionalism is key:** When I consider my own practice, I can see clearly that it is centrally based on the need to work with the expertise of the coachee. However, there is still some difficulty finding frameworks and standards for how 'professionally' knowledgeable the other person is about their learning opportunities. Terms like andragogy refer to this – but it is still poorly developed and accepted.

2. **Team based professionalism:** Eventually there will be an evolution of the idea becoming common elsewhere, that a 'team' of different experts/professionals may need to be involved because the issues/opportunities at hand are too wide ranging to fit into one profession's box – let alone one professional's box.

3. **The rush to oversimplification:** Perhaps the greatest risk remains the rush to over simplification of how coaching works.
   This generates a push towards conformity with something that is seriously lacking in rigour.

I constantly find fellow established practitioners who want to share the detail of their practice, as they experience how it works, but find too few opportunities to attract them to do so.

Tell me, how do you demonstrate your professionalism with your clients?

PART 3: Identifying the competitive edges in the market

PART **4**

*Extending the frontiers of knowledge through each practitioner's practice*

# CHAPTER 10

# MOVING FORWARD, WHAT NEXT

## How to raise the standards of coaching in 9.5 important ways!

*Yvonne Thackray*

The good coach attracts other like–minded coaches (full/part time/casual – delete as appropriate) who have a vested interest in looking beyond the current state of the market. We participate in group discussion. We reached out to peers, bloggers, and tgc readers to ask them to share what they have noticed in their market that influences how they practice in the field; we're grateful for all the delicious snippets of knowledge they share with us. This allowed me to reflect on and connect the broader field and consequently offer valid evidence which supports what resulted in the 2015 list of the "9.5 important ways to raise the standards of coaching."

In a nutshell, our way ahead is to individually share case studies of our professional practice and stories of our personal development. It is only through these important contributions that we can really broaden and deepen our understanding of how we are giving personal attention through coaching that helps to raise a human's potential. What we do is more than just the theory or models. We need to be more confident in ourselves and share the real benefits of coaching. What follows are the 9.5 reasons for why this is important (a few may even consider these as strategic issues of the coaching sector!).

## 1. Coaching as a field will continue to grow. It will become even more grounded when it is seen as a means to an end rather than an end to a means.

Coaching is part of human evolution. It will continue to grow and slowly mature into its full potential of 'getting the best out of each human'. Understanding how and where coaching can be best applied to get optimal returns is important. Case studies are slowly beginning to emerge into the broader community. In particular, segments of practice for e.g. on–boarding, transitioning to senior levels of responsibility, returning from extended leave i.e. maternity leave and leadership. Here's an example of positive evidence:

> *"Changes in staff attitude surveys that can be related back to coaching interventions can be powerful – GlaxoSmithKline (GSK) has generated convincing positive evidence of coaching impact through their global staff survey by comparing leadership impacts in the teams of those coached with those not coached[1]."*

**The way ahead: We need to encourage more case studies to be shared and exchanged that document the benefits and limitations of how coaching contributes towards 'getting the best out of each person'.**

## 2. There is a need to both increase the amount of coaching being done and raise awareness of the benefits of coaching.

Coaching is part of a portfolio career:

- Some will work full time in coaching that includes training and supervision.

- Some will be offering to coach in addition to their usual technical role.

- Some will be providing coaching in addition to or as an integral part of their role as manager and/or leader.

- Many others will be doing coaching without realising that it is coaching.

---

[1] Doug Montgomery (2015) 'The practicalities of measuring the ROI of coaching: A reflection'

**PART 4: Expanding the frontiers of knowledge through each practitioner's practice**

The mainstream coaching market, within the current narrow definition of coaching, is perceived to be a tough and competitive market. There seem to be far more qualified coaches and more demand for (and possibly availability of) coaches coming from a senior corporate background who have moved into coaching. They bring their vast experiences with them and a style (a more directive approach) based on how they've experienced varying levels of positive impact from their coaching, shaped by their operational experience within particular contexts and conditions.

A growing conundrum for professional bodies and 'qualified' coaches is when, or who is, defining the client and/or market, and in what ways are they actually making coaching work? Are the current self–assessed qualifications enough to differentiate and decide who fits into the role(s) of a professional coach, and whom should be excluded? Possibly not. Fresh graduates from various programs (academic through to training schools), after some work experience, are seeking work in this field, and looking to work with or alongside other experienced coaches.

**The way ahead: We need to pay attention for the talent in coaching – what is the pipeline?**

### 2.5 Don't be surprised when your target market hasn't heard of coaching and start from the remedial end!

Although many people and organisations haven't heard of coaching, the idea of coaching is being spread from reports and those who work, or have worked, in multi–national corporations and have offices in different parts of the country and world (for example Germany, India, France, Hong Kong, China, US).

> *"Less than 0.00006% Professionals work in coaching. This means that there is potentially 15,400 clients\*[2] per coach."*

\*Clients – Active working population in the world (excluding unemployed, low–skilled occupations and non–routine manual jobs).

Opportunities to introduce coaching skills and attributes regarded as an increasingly important part of daily management and leadership.

---

[2] [website] http://www.ilo.org/wcmsp5/groups/public/-dgreports/-dcomm/-publ/documents/publication/wcms_337069.pdf

**PART 4: Expanding the frontiers of knowledge through each practitioner's practice**

This has resulted in an increase in demand for coaching skills training for managers which provides that part of the formal learning process in leadership development programmes. They should typically involve 'on the job' projects, either that individuals identify themselves or projects that a team of 'learners' work on and share back. This should include not only the business outcomes but learning points. This is a growing trend.

**The way ahead: Coaching isn't sacred. There are plenty of opportunities for engaging in delivering coaching across the whole organisation at all levels (front line through to the CEO). It's knowing when coaching serves the purpose.**

### 3. Listen to the market. Sponsors of coaching evaluate the outputs delivered from coaching – it's too variable!

Companies, in particular large corporates, are sophisticated users of coaching. They are questioning the limitations of self–appointed qualifications and accreditations. The competency models used for training coaches is limited in delivering consistently reliable outputs, and this has resulted in one of the big four accounting firms, PwC[3], leading their own way to develop *"a set of global coaching standards, using the UK firm's practices as a benchmark for the rest of the world."* While Deloitte[4] ditto are *"Bringing together member firms with mature coaching cultures in other countries, with the UK firm, to drive consistency and best practice using Deloitte University in EMEA"*. They are no longer endorsing any professional body. Or the Learning and OD manager from the Royal College of Nursing reporting that *"the ILM provides a possible alternative route to accreditation, one that is less demanding and more appropriate in scale than EMCC[5]."*

**The way ahead: Sponsors are developing and building best practice of evaluating how coaching works best in their organisation. They have the data. We need to pay attention as they'll dictate the market in the future.**

---

[3] Ridler & Co. Case Study."The Development of Internal coaching in the Big Four Accounting Firms", (Mann, 2014) p 17
[4] ditto
[5] Internal Coaching Group (2015) "What is the role of APECS in supporting and promoting Best Practice in Internal Coaching", from *2014 APECS Symposium.* (2014)

**PART 4: Expanding the frontiers of knowledge through each practitioner's practice**

4.  Internal coaching, mainly applied as part of their strategic risk management, is on the rise in effective organisations. It takes time, effort, careful planning and adequate resources.

The more mature companies who have received external coaching and moved beyond the scope of it being simply a purchasing decision, and particularly after the 2008 financial crisis, are taking coaching in–house. Organisations developing their internal cadre of coaching have demonstrated this to be a cost–conscious solution, as well as helping to retain longer the talent and motivation of various employees who are driven to expand their role laterally. There are many strategies for building an internal coaching group (see 1), the most popular being coaches who typically do individual coaching sessions as an addition to their 'day job' and frequently outside regular working hours.

In the current market (see 3) internal coaching can be regarded as a threat to external coaches. The reality though is that it raises the profile standards and practice of coaching because they understand the environment their clients work in. They can strategically find ways to pilot coaching interventions and demonstrate the benefits to the organisation in their own language. In effect, internal coaching can scale the practice of coaching within bounded conditions and its nuances. The needs of the organisation that seeks diversity, which involves an appropriate level of independence and specialism that matches the individual, and who chooses to participate in or is assigned to coaching, will most likely drive the balance of internal and external executive coaches.

**The way ahead: Internal coaching has an amazing contribution to take coaching forward. Can we create a forum, a 'pow wow', for exchanging coaching stories and practices with each other?**

5.  Articulating the benefits received as a result of coaching that impacts the needs of organisations is not a straightforward process.

Appropriating the accounting performance measure of ROI may be more of a marketing hyperbole that comes from coaches (mainly external) that are seeking to justify their work quickly to sponsors. The limitations of correctly executing ROI is the difficulty in isolating those factors that contribute to the impacts from coaching. A capacity to articulate what it is that has positively resulted in tangible shifts from behavioural changes.

Like any consultant/freelance, it always takes more time to build relationships and reputation with the sponsor to delivering coaching itself. When that opportunity arises, and repeatedly, the sponsor is explicitly delegating to the coaches how their coaching can benefit the individual with personal attention, placebo or not, within their strategy. Established Internal coaching functions report[6] that whilst, *"Robust coaching evaluation processes are in place... none is relying on data from evaluations to justify continued investment in coaching as there exists an underlying belief in all firms that the investment in internal coaching provides excellent value."*

**The way ahead: Evaluations of the impacts from coaching need to be shared and validated by the sponsors (not purchasers) in the language of the client. It is important to get across how these evaluations relate the positives for the individual, team, function, and the organization. This is because they typically know how the ripple effect of the impacts (behavioural) relate to performance. The question is more; how or in what ways can these stories be shared that demonstrates and evidences the validity of practice for the individual coach?**

### 6.  A lack of consensus building of what is coaching.

Coaching is neither a legally regulated nor a controlled term that is bequeathed to a profession, hence the continual confusion of what any coach actually does in the marketplace. For example, coaching assignments have been used to outplace leaders. It has been used to help obliquely the 'unhappy/high potential' few who stay and/or get promoted to cope with all the burden and pressure that falls on their shoulders as 'high potential coaching/ middle management coaching/ leadership coaching/ C–suite coaching'. Coaching can thus be packaged as a form of developing potential as managers move into more senior positions that are typically the merger of a number of positions. It is becoming an acceptable part of the learning & development portfolio

---

[6] Ridler & Co. Case Study."The Development of Internal coaching in the Big Four Accounting Firms", (Mann, 2014) p 14

that is increasingly becoming more popular in large organisations that have senior management sponsorship.

**The way ahead: Contradictions exist in how full human potential can be reached and in what condition. Let's clarify what the purposes of coaching are and what outcomes can be expected that lets the public and clients know that they can trust a coaching professional. From there, perhaps then we can start building a definition for coaching.**

## 7. A scarcity of a body of knowledge to demonstrate and evaluate the conditions for, and impacts from, coaching.

Since the International Coaching Research Forum held in Dublin 2007, and according to an interview with Lew Stern[7]:

> "[From the 100 topics proposed] from 2008 to 2012, more than 100 studies total in more than 80 journals where they were published. In those peer–reviewed journals, there were only basically 100 studies in five years having to do with what goes on
>
> in coaching, and a little over 40 about outcomes and not quite 30 about coaching in organizations. There were about 20 articles about coaching versus other helping practices and how they differ."

Where does knowledge come from in a new field like coaching? From the coaches themselves. The experiences of how practitioners create and sustain themselves in their market, and how they create the conditions for coaching is the first place for researchers to investigate (perhaps even using participant observation as an approach). The researchers may then understand more of how the bricolage of tools (coach training) are being applied in the various situations and contexts.

Perhaps as coaches, and through our professional life, we're too used to the notion of the expert having all the answers and have less confidence in ourselves. A delicate balance obviously has to be drawn between being confident and overconfident (guru–like) and really

---

[7] [website] Lew Stern Interview: Research on Professional Coaching
(http://libraryofprofessionalcoaching.com/wp–app/wp–content/uploads/2014/06/Lew–Stern–Inteview.pdf)

**PART 4: Expanding the frontiers of knowledge through each practitioner's practice**

consider and understand how what we do intuitively can be explored and grounded in more details and facts.

**The way ahead: Understanding the cause and effect of coaching is not a perfect science. However, it shouldn't stop us in applying the approaches more to understand more of how we do what we do and at the same time continually increase our self–awareness.**

### 8.  Understanding how coaching is brokered.

Winning organisational contracts typically requires independent executive coaches to work with a number of different associations – coaching consultancies through to management consultants (small, medium and large). It's even less clear what opportunities are available for independent contractors working directly with SMEs, and even MNCs, compared to solopreneurs/freelancers.

And this leads to an important question; in order to safeguard the field, what type of coaching contracts/agreements alongside the selection process (similar qualifications, accreditation, assessment centres, interviews) are being used? What is becoming more noticeable is a move towards seeking more centralised control in the use of external coaches, rather than senior people going directly to their own preferred individual coach (although this still happens at the top)!

**The way ahead: Understanding the various ways and approaches for coaching contracts could lead to the best practice guidelines for all parties involved (that can also be appropriately underwritten).**

### 9.  Coaching supervision needs to move towards fitness to practice. It should focus on professional development, of which personal development is an essential part of a coach's development. Perhaps CPPD is better placed to encourage fitness to practice.

Coaching supervision, like coaching, lacks any formal definition. Most training programs/academic courses adapt frameworks from other therapeutic backgrounds to focus on developing the mental (including emotional) health of the individual. Borrowing from academia, a supervisor is typically an individual (lecturer/professor) who is a specialist within a particular discipline (single/cross) whose role is to guide and set the standards for students to carry out their research and then present their results to the best advantage. The question we as coaches need to ask is: "*What type of supervision is required for healthy individuals that coaches should be working with that meets, at a minimum, fitness to practice professionally?*"

While supervision is working on defining what this should be; a more practical and useful approach is to take advantage of something like 'Continuing Personal and Professional Development' (CPPD) where a small group of peers (minimum three to five people) come together and use the coaching approach to creating a learning environment where they can talk about the challenges of coaching, for starters:

- From building a practice through to encountering unique challenges that arise in coaching and finding alternative (and most likely trial and tested) ways to manage it.

- Share personal developmental stories that have helped them nudge forward their practice overall.

- Trial new approaches/technology and understand their strengths and limitations.

- Compare one's practice and approach and learn from others, where appropriate.

- Discuss ethical issues and dilemmas.

- Challenge definitions and understanding what the real boundaries in coaching are.

**The way ahead: Create a learning environment for continuing personal and professional development amongst a small group of peers, and share some of the themes and stories with the broader community to also learn from. This way we are building towards and contributing to the practitioner field of knowledge together.**

## To summarise

As stated right at the start, to keep nudging the field forward we each need to individually share case studies of our professional practice and stories of our personal development. It is only through these important contributions that we can really broaden and deepen our understanding of *how* we are giving personal attention through coaching. It's this quality of attention that is helping towards raising a human's potential.

The question is: How do we continually create the engagement?

- What do you think? Do you agree or disagree?

- What would you like to say or contribute towards raising the standard of coaching?

# Coaching on an agenda that involves risk

*Kim Stephenson*

**H**ow much do you hear about the VUCA environment (volatility, uncertainty, complexity, ambiguity)? If you're coaching in the real world (which is VUCA and distinct from coaching in theory), it's handy to be clear about those terms and consequently, to know where you can help and where you can't.

Coaching practice needs to recognise the way the world is – or coaching can turn into economics, sounding lovely in theory, but leading to financial meltdown in reality.

However, I see masses of practice based articles that mention these terms, often written by people who – sometimes in the same article – talk about how people shouldn't be too risk averse, or should 'calculate risk'.

Since I specialise in leadership around financial decisions it's easier to demonstrate what I mean with financial examples, both because there are lots of numbers and measures of risk and because I have lots of examples to choose from experience.

**PART 4: Expanding the frontiers of knowledge through each practitioner's practice**

## UNCERTAINTY AND RISK

### A 'gamble'

Take for example a casino. You know the odds, the payoff if you win, the stakes (what you'll lose), you know when the gamble finishes and when you'll be paid (or have lost your stake). You know all the potential outcomes and could calculate a complete decision tree showing the odds and return of each potential series of outcomes. You also know things won't change in the middle (they won't switch packs of cards or roulette wheels on you in the middle of the game). So even from the beginning the risk is totally calculable. We call it a gamble and "risky" but it is (in insurance terms, because you can set a premium for it) a true risk. That is to say it's mathematically precise. It might be technically difficult to calculate but it's not complex, it's simple. It's also unambiguous.

### A 'calculated risk'

Take the investment of capital into the purchasing of a plant. You don't know the odds of it winning or even what winning would look like. You don't know what you'll win if you do (whatever winning is). You may have no idea what the stakes are (you could have leveraged debt). You don't end the bet (even with an exit strategy) or know when the payoff will come (if it does). You can't know, let alone calculate, all the potential outcomes. Consequently, you cannot construct a decision tree, which, even if you could, would be growing while you created it, if for example, somebody comes along with new technology and puts you out of business – that wouldn't happen in a casino.

So an investment of this kind is not calculable in the same sense as the gamble. We call it a calculated risk but it's not calculable and not a risk (in insurance terms, you'd call it uncertainty and refuse to insure it). It is not just difficult, it's impossible and it's complex. It's uncertainty, not risk. Even the feedback you get is ambiguous (did you go bust or make a profit because of your skill or by luck: there's no way to tell for sure).

## Implications:

I get asked about investment in those situations, to coach people about what they see as and would call risk. But they're not risks, they're uncertainties. When I ask about how the client will cut through all the complexity and ambiguity of the potential future situations to try to put some numbers on potential outcomes, they start to realise that being 'risk averse', or not being mathematically savvy enough to calculate risk isn't really the issue.

What they don't ask for help with, until I prompt them to, are decisions that look easy, but are actually difficult. These include complex situations involving uncertainty, where everything is guesswork and maths is largely useless. That's where I can really help, by asking the right questions.

### AMBIGUITY, CHAOS AND COMPLEXITY

I've already mentioned some of this, but let's take another example.

A client is expanding into a new area, something they've done before (it could be a product area, a geographical area, anything, the principle is the same). The assumption is often that a mentor is what is needed, somebody who has been there before. So it's seen simply as a case of applying experience and calculating the risk.

Of course, it isn't a risk, but is experience valuable? Perhaps the sort of extensive, high–level experience that the Boards of the Bank of England, the Treasury and the Federal Reserve had in 2007 that relaxed financial regulation and enabled the 2008 financial meltdown!

Sarcastic Kim! But there's a point to that. Decisions in life can be simple; kill or be killed, fight or flight etc. On the other hand, most of life is non–linear, in that the total result can be more, less or bear no apparent resemblance to the sum of the parts. Chaos means that the precise starting conditions may have a huge effect on the outcomes (the 'butterfly effect') so experience may be very misleading because apparently similar starting conditions lead to wildly different outcomes (the repeat strategy leads to massive profits first time round, yet leads to bankruptcy the next time).

Complexity means that there can be 'emergence' – things happen as a result of interactions that you can't predict from analysing all the parts. Overall, human life can be seen as a complex, self–organising system on the edge of chaos – which is a fancy way of saying that it's unpredictable and impossible to understand in detail. Business is the result of the interrelation of all the human lives and choices within it – therefore business is even more complex and non–linear than any one of those lives.

Consequently, we cannot calculate all the possible options for action because we have absolutely no way to calculate even the whole range of potential outcomes. We do not know how all the parts would fit together in all the different combinations possible and we have no idea how they would influence one another.

## Implications:

The assumption is that experience of and in an industry, a process, a management level is vital. It's often handy, but it isn't a guarantee. When clients ask what experience I've got of CEO functioning or widget manufacture, it might be a fair point to assume I can't help. Maybe what the client actually needs is a guide to the way things are usually done – not how they can be done well, but how they are done conventionally. However, if a client is facing a real decision, then that sort of experience might be a disadvantage, as it could blind them to the actual ambiguity (and paucity) of data and the complexity of the situation.

Again, where the coach can help is in asking the right questions, in getting the client to think about what assumptions they are making about the world being simple and predictable, in allowing the client to realise the data aren't unambiguous and that the decision process is not one of just repeating what has been done in "*similar situations*" in the past – chaos theory says that similarity doesn't mean sameness, on the contrary it might mean total difference.

## VOLATILITY

People usually use the word volatility in the combustion sense, something that can flare up quickly and is changeable.

So it is. Yet in finance it's got an allied meaning. A 'volatile stock' is one that tends to move sharply up or down. There are measures of the sharpness of the movement relative to the market as a whole, an index of a portion of the market, and so on. Those measures (such as Beta, Sharpe Ratio, Smart Beta etc.) are part of the hunger for predictability in an uncertain world.

So in finance, when there's talk about investors' risk appetite, complaints that people are risk averse, and regulations about matching investment portfolios to customer risk profiles, they'd love to be talking about risk – where they could apply some numbers. Sadly, they can't talk about risk because it's not risk, it's uncertainty. So they call it risk, as if to limit and capture the uncertainty, because that's a nice fiction that makes people believe the numbers are meaningful. Which leaves the problem of inventing some numbers to be meaningful.

You remember from your statistics homework the standard deviation; the square root of the deviance, which is a measure of dispersion. In other words, a measurement of the amount of movement around the average, which is a fair description of volatility.

What financial people do is to substitute volatility for risk. They calculate, using statistics based on distributions, standard deviations etc. and look at how much the shares tend to move around compared to the norm within the market. And they call that the risk.

Which is great. Except:

1. The stock market is not normally distributed (it's platykurtic, which means fat–tailed).

2. The data are not independent of context (prices one day depend on the prior days and influence the following days).

3. The stats don't work for the distribution we've got. They only apply to independent data anyway.

PART 4: Expanding the frontiers of knowledge through each practitioner's practice

The events of 2008 demonstrated that this is a complex problem. It's uncertainty. It's not calculable. The data are ambiguous. The outcomes are not linearly dependent on the inputs and, while the prices are volatile, you can't accurately measure their volatility, certainly not by using maths that isn't designed for the data you've got, that you can't interpret unambiguously and whose volatility is complex and uncertain.

## Implications

A good coach could have asked the tough questions, like, "*What are you assuming in this situation?*", "*How are you deriving your estimates of risk and volatility?*", "*Given how ambiguous the data are, how much of your own money have you gambled on your interpretation and only your interpretation being right?*"

## IN CONCLUSION

There's a lot that a coach can do by asking questions. They can help people think through the options more thoroughly. They can help to test people's assumptions and recognise that living in a VUCA world isn't just a phrase to say "*Yes, I know about that*" and then carry on regardless. It's not helpful to acknowledge we live in that world and then go back to talking about risk, assuming data are reliable and unambiguous, that experience always has positive value, that the world is simple and interpretable in a linear fashion and that any word such as volatility always means the same thing irrespective of context and can be assigned values that are consistently meaningful.

Coaching can mean pushing the client very hard. And a lot of clients really don't like that. We all tend to say, "*I welcome constructive feedback*", but how many of us, hand on heart, really do like it when instead of the friend (or coach) that we're counting on to say, "*Wow, you're a genius*" says instead, "*How have you got these numbers; have you got any basis for this assumption; do you realise how many dependencies you've got that assume events occur in the order and for the reasons you expect?*"

It's tough to do. It's tough to hear. However, I think it's what – at the executive level at least – coaches should be doing.

**PART 4: Expanding the frontiers of knowledge through each practitioner's practice**

# East meets West – how different philosophies can combine and inform coaching

*R. Ramamurthy Krishna*

**I** **have often seen** how a lot of Eastern philosophy seems to have no formal research data. However, if you look at the concepts that Eastern philosophy has integrated, and then go back looking for scientific evidence from Western philosophy, I think there's a pretty good integration.

And if we keep working on that integration, then I think there is some strong Eastern philosophy thinking which Western philosophy thinking can, like the yin and yang, meet up to really inform what coaching could be about.

There are many significant philosophies in this idea of 'East' – for example, China, Japan, Hong Kong, India, Sri Lanka and many more... To make a start, I believe that ideas which come from Indian philosophy can be useful here.

## THREE TYPES OF EXISTENCE FROM INDIAN PHILOSOPHY

I would start with three types of existence that exist within people, which comes from a typical Indian philosophy which talks about the *Sattva*, *Rajas* and the *Tamas*. These states, or energies, exist in everyone, all of the time.

## THREE TYPES OF EXISTENCE

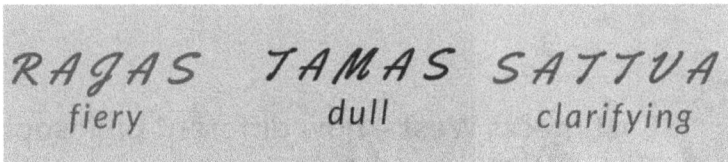

RAJAS     TAMAS    SATTVA
fiery              dull              clarifying

### Key processes in the three types of existence:

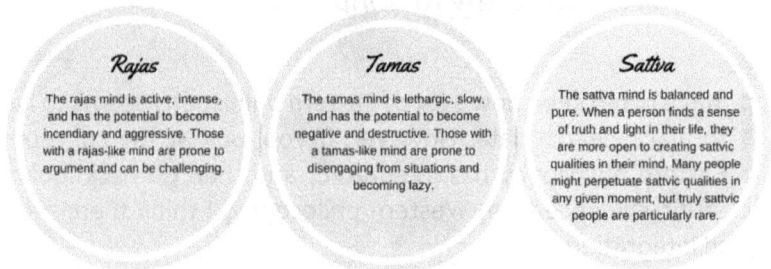

**Rajas**

The rajas mind is active, intense, and has the potential to become incendiary and aggressive. Those with a rajas-like mind are prone to argument and can be challenging.

**Tamas**

The tamas mind is lethargic, slow, and has the potential to become negative and destructive. Those with a tamas-like mind are prone to disengaging from situations and becoming lazy.

**Sattva**

The sattva mind is balanced and pure. When a person finds a sense of truth and light in their life, they are more open to creating sattvic qualities in their mind. Many people might perpetuate sattvic qualities in any given moment, but truly sattvic people are particularly rare.

Indian philosophy does not clarify these as stages. "*Yes, it can be a stage of life, but it actually categorizes more of a personality type.*" Rather, it classifies people as belonging to three broad boxes.

### Immediate connection with fundamentals of neuroscience

People can often go through a process that follows the three types of existence. This is where philosophy and neuroscience research has a lot of integration.

We begin with words that can be taken from different philosophies which help to bring together a common ground and understanding.

For example, we know that language as a function can free itself from the cortex when it starts growing around the age of 24 to 30. It is at that age that you would be dominated by the Rajas – yet they are still not polished, and so you cannot enjoy everything life has to offer.

We know that the prefrontal cortex also has a part to play in the mental function of learning. Here you have access to your experiences, those that come from memory, your internal experiences, the top–down processing and the bottom–up processing that altogether drives the perception. These then become much more methodical and broader in the Tamas.

With this development, your thinking starts to undergo a transformation. It becomes, for example, more willing to really contribute to the society.

Does this happen because people give up? No. It happens because people have enjoyed, are happy, and now they think, "*Okay, I've seen it all.*" That's the growth of the brain function in which you actually shift your experience and start looking at the self–directed people in society, as I say, as against experiences–directed people in society.

So the experience of neuroplasticity arrives from both Rajas and Tamas, especially when you are talking about higher levels. When you do talk about higher levels you are talking about the inner call, you're talking about self–realization, you are looking at islands of self–motivation and stuff like that. So that is how I see these two disciplines integrating together.

## PROGRESS TOWARDS 'INDIVIDUATING'

One aspect of Eastern philosophy says 'to realize', to the extent that I know. As I accumulate social experience and contemplate the purpose of life, we are realizing our 'humanity'. Human beings have largely matured. For this realization to become 'complete', we go through a process of reincarnation, or rebirth, again, and again, and again, until a time you are able to reach the Sattva mind set.

For me, that is individuating. You actually start looking at the experiences. You start looking at what is positive, pure, pleasurable and divine, which is Sattva as against Rajas – Rajas being more about a controlling mind set. There are also people who are very human, and full of Tamas, which can be negative, impure, painful and dominating.

And in terms of being able to move from:

- Negative thinking to positive thinking,

- Impure to pure,

- Analysing to Self–Reflection,

- 'I–Me–Myself' to 'We–Us–Ourselves'

As you move to Sattva, it becomes more positive, purer, serene and more serving. You move from, I, me, myself to be ourselves and the world.

So that is individuating for me. That change of mind set is, I think, a big task for coaches to see as being both worthy and more relevant.

## COMBINING MODES OF EXISTENCE WITH PROCESSES

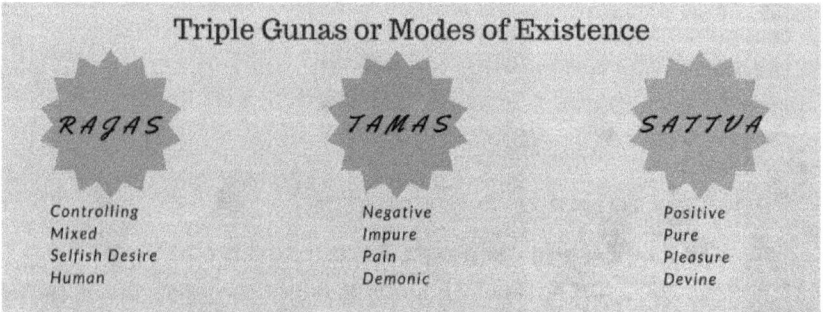

Triple Gunas or Modes of Existence

| RAJAS | TAMAS | SATTVA |
|---|---|---|
| Controlling | Negative | Positive |
| Mixed | Impure | Pure |
| Selfish Desire | Pain | Pleasure |
| Human | Demonic | Devine |

I see that my purpose is driven by Sattva. The individual starts to realize "*I want to be positive*", "*I am purer*", "*I'm not driven by pleasure*". This seems to be the purpose and goal of individuation.

Individuating does not happen (and may be, should not happen) when individuals are driven by Tamas. One needs to first enjoy the pleasure before one can give it up! That would probably make the life transformation more complete!

Another way of saying this is if people realize that their purpose of life is broader and not simply just about existing. Connecting it to Western philosophy, we might discuss the hygiene factors, because you're not yet in the growth factor.

We need to enjoy pleasure and pain before we give it up. As we move up, we move from Tamas, and we are able to be more accepting of the pleasures and the pain. We may even draw learning experiences from what pleasure and pain teach us.

### Example one – consider the story of Lord Buddha.

He was a royal by birth. As a prince, who was still young and going through early experiences, he was often hidden from all the pains of the world. He was not allowed to see any pain. But when the prince did get an opportunity to see people suffering that pain actually created 'insight' for him about life. (We might consider insight as a neuroscientific explanation of the Aha moment). It made the prince move toward the Satvva state of mind. However, those people that are yielding Rajas, they use that energy to control the mind. Therefore they seek penance, deep penance, and they try to get through all the distraction that would remove you from this penance.

Remember the purpose of life is Sattva and so one must always be cautious of distraction. And the purpose of Satvva is very clear:

*"The world is in us. We create the world. There is enough for everyone."* When you reach the state of Satvva, you 'soar' high!

And, when we move to Sattva, you will actually realize the 'pure state'.

**PART 4: Expanding the frontiers of knowledge through each practitioner's practice**

### Example two – A recent example from cricket – India against Bangladesh! (Cricket is a very important aspect of our culture!)

At the very last ball to be bowled, the skipper of India gets himself ready. The other team has to get two runs to win; one run to tie. He is absolutely focused, and very cool. He signals the bowler to bowl the ball outside the leg stump. The batsman misses the ball and he, as the wicket keeper, collects the ball that goes through to him. As the player at the other end has to run, he then runs down to hit the stumps with the ball before the other player can reach safety; the captain gets the victory, right?

The energy he shows – after this, is that he is not jumping up and down with excitement, saying that, "*We have done it!*" He is simply part of the crowd. He says, "*We may be done, but let's wait for the final verdict to come.*" Even when the final score board says that the last one is out, he still doesn't jump in the air. That's clearly Sattva energy. For the Bangladeshi who had a much stronger desire to simply win aimed for the big victory, they went for the big hits – and missed. When all they wanted was singles, not boundaries from big hits.

Now, if you see this from Western philosophy, then we're talking about the executive function which is now fully–loaded with all types of negative neurotransmitters. These negative transmitters shut you down from thinking, which is what happens as you grow from Tamas to Rajas.

#### APPLYING TO COACHING

So as a coach, if you are able to work with a person, the inner conversation that you will have shall be driven by what type of energy? If your client is driven by desire, or by a pure, positive energy, what type of conversation should you have in response to this?

As I'm talking to you, your inner dialogue could be saying that I need to maintain the best impression of the mind. My inner dialogue proposes to me that I need to contribute my best to the coaching world.

Some of you might refer to what I'm talking about to mindfulness, for example. When we are talking about mindfulness, we're talking about mindfulness meditation that comes from the East, from China and Sri Lanka. This mindfulness is all about being aware of the inner dialogue that is going on inside of you and through you. Please note, we are not saying that you control this inner dialogue.

And so, if I know my inner dialogue and that's the job of a coach to show them (the clients) the inner dialogue that's going on, it then may be possible to try to reframe the inner dialogue.

You can actually go higher. But if your inner dialogue is just going to be 'unconscious' because you are too busy dealing with the outer world then this "*Unconscious*" state shall continue to dominate and probable continue to be in Tamas.

The role of the coach is to say that, "*Look, you can change your inner dialogue. And if you look, you already have been enjoying all the pure, demonic, pain, impure, negative thoughts that you enjoy. You have moved to controlling your pain, you then control selfish desire. Now, if you actually give up, and then require, which is to a large extent, the sovereign leadership counsel that you pick up, you are moving from a transactional to a transformational to a sovereign you.*"

What I've shared is my approach, my way of connecting important philosophies that inform my coaching. You may choose other ways of thinking, such as: Christianity, Buddhism, Hinduism or Islam. Each and every one of us is in some way ultimately serving the world. For me, it is the Sattva energy that comes from the inner dialogue. If you're continuously negative, you're not going to reach the purpose of your life. We must move from a 'doing' state, to a 'being' state. That's the true way, which is what I call "*living this way*".

## WHERE DO WE GO NEXT WITH THESE IDEAS?

I know how these ideas work for me in helping me work between Eastern and Western philosophies. There is still a great amount of practical detail that has to be worked out within these broad ideas. It is important to have this view of bringing all these philosophies further together.

I am hoping to share more examples of how this works in practice. For example, it even applies to making sense of diet – something which may or may not be very important in any coaching agenda. It may be a hidden factor/indicator of some issue which has surfaced, but has yet to be appreciated, even at this level.

| RAJAS | TAMAS | SATTVA |
|---|---|---|
| Foods that give us motivation and keeps us attached to our ego and creates desires | Foods that make our mind sluggish and promote diseases | Foods that promote purity of mind and intelligence |
| Coffee/Black tea | Red meat | Milk |
| Chicken | Alcohol | Herbal tea |
| Eggs | Fast food | Ghee |
| Onion/Garlic | Fried food | Whole grains |
| Dark lentils | Frozen food | Fresh juicy fruits |
| Citrus fruits | Canned/Stale food | Fresh vegetables |
| Very spicy foods | Refined Sugars | Honey |
| Chocolate | Tobacco | Nuts |
| Salt | Soda | Mung beans |
| | | |
| Eating too fast | Over eating | Peace while eating |

Referenced from connectsciencetodivinity.blogspot.com

# Blogging about my coaching practice: A powerful boost and reconnection to my aspirations

## Sue Young

**thought, having done** blogging with the good coach (tgc) for a while, it felt like a good time to stop and take stock. What I have found with my blogging is that it's taken my reflection and explicit articulation of what I do in my practice to a new and more aware, proactive level. As such it's has been a very powerful personal and professional experience.

## 1. LIMITATIONS OF TRADITIONAL STRUCTURES FOR DEVELOPMENT AS AN EXPERIENCED PRACTITIONER

**Limitations of Traditional 'CPD':** Like many experienced coaching practitioners I am a member of several professional bodies (not just coaching) and keep records of my CPD for compliance purposes. However I do not capture in those formal records the highly–personal, continuous informal learning that happens in my day–to–day practice, particularly around interaction with colleagues and clients.

In surveying what the professional bodies and coaching bodies write on the subject of CPD I can only find very general level commentary. Most of the writings in the field feel very removed from the day–to–day 'messy' reality of operating in the organisational worlds we work in. They miss the typical themes and issues that emerge in professional client work. There is little written by practitioners for practitioners and little about learning by coaches from their practice.

- **Even supervision is limited in a similar manner:** Taking care not to do something wrong – by whichever standards of a body concerned – is not the same as what I am doing and learning that works so well.

- **Self–managed learning:** I keep an on–going personal journal, which I find an invaluable reflection tool for myself. Saying that, expressing and articulating for something that is going to be read by others externally is a very different process.

- **'Traditional publishing':** I have written articles for professional publications and professional conference papers – but this also requires conforming to the style and perspective of other audiences.

- **Client Proposals:** Even client proposals can require a great deal of practice information. However, yet again, this has to be written for what the particular client is looking for.

## 2. REVIEWING HOW I HAVE FOUND THE BLOGGING PROCESS

**Keeping a regular discipline to it:** I've committed to write a blog once a month. Although demanding, particularly when I have to fit it in around what, at times, has been a very heavy client workload, it has never felt onerous.

**Finding my own themes:** Again this has been very different to other professional writing I do, which tend to be much more planned and focused. Although I have in mind at any point two or three themes that draw my attention as being of personal interest and worthy of exploration and expressing, it has been a very natural and emergent process.

**Evolution of themes:** I observe that my earlier blogs are around more general themes I have been passionate about over the long term, reflecting the general beliefs and values that underpin my overall coaching approach and philosophy. As I have progressed in my blogging, I notice the blog themes becoming more related directly to my personal practice and exploratory of the real issues and dilemmas that arise.

### 3. REVIEWING THE BLOGGING THEMES/FOCUS THAT HAS EMERGED PROGRESSIVELY

**First stage of blogging – long–term key 'theoretical' lenses:**
Re–connecting to some underpinning long–term key 'theoretical' lenses and underlying values that inform my coaching.

The real thing my MSc academic study time did for me was to allow me to survey the broader field of formal knowledge about people in organisations. This gave me both the confidence and an increased ability to step back and objectively evaluate models and theories and see more objectively, both what they added and their limitations.

**The principles of adult learning in coaching was a natural for my first blog:** Learning from experience has always been a strong area of personal interest that has informed my approach, both as a facilitator and coach. In my facilitation and coaching I have always been inclined towards encouraging people to reflect on, personally connect to, and share their experience with others as core to a deeper and more personalised learning process.

The discovery of adult learning during my MSc was a true affirmation of my natural approach, with those key principles of how we learn primarily from our experience, and how social interaction is central and clearly identified as a key learning enabler. One of my strengths is using my natural presence and style to create a safe confidence building space that encourages people to explore and be more self–disclosing – creating an environment conducive to learning. This underpins my coaching approach, as I encourage clients to become more capable and effective 'strategic learners' going forwards.

**Strategy and experiential learning, both at organisational and individual levels:** I guess these are the two big theoretical lenses that most inform my coaching approach and are the subjects of my first two blogs – strategy and experiential learning, both at organisational and individual levels. These two are inextricably linked, as the strategy development process is a structured and collective form of learning where regular feedback and review is central.

With an early career background in business strategy I've always found the real divide that exists in most organisations between the 'hard' area of strategy and 'soft' area of people in most organisations completely artificial. I don't see strategy as solely a 'top down' approach but rather a process to which individuals and teams at all organisational levels need to contribute.

**Middle stage of my blogging – taking principles of how we really learn into CPD – both for our clients and ourselves as practitioners:** In leadership and coaching – both highly relational and situational driven contexts, thinking and practice about real CPD in these contexts is not written about much. In my research, interestingly, only two fields came up as sources of much research and writing – the education and health sectors. In organisational and business fields there is not much research on CPD readily available.

The skills of 'reflective practice' or 'reflection in action' are becoming more fundamental for effective leadership in a fast moving and increasingly complex, interrelated world. In my coaching I often help clients incorporate ways of working and ways to allow space for the essential thinking required, both individually and collectively, to bring about organisational change. I review this explicitly in a couple of blogs, both from client and coach perspectives, and it is an on–going area of interest and development in my coaching approach.

**Later stage: this falls into two areas**

a. **Reviewing a coaching approach as an enabler of organisational change beyond the traditional one to one context:** My blogs go on to explore how a coaching style and approach are becoming more widely used, although many of these have been around in a smaller way for many years. For example, action learning, peer coaching and team coaching. Where organisational change truly happens is at the individual and team levels. Approaches that coaching uses are key enablers of jump shifts in the perceptions and behaviours required for organisational change.

b. **Current themes emerging directly from my practice:** These are typical themes emerging from coaching practice with topical leadership and organisational relevance. The themes selected so far in my blogs include the true leadership contribution of middle managers, managing upwards, resilience and incorporating more thinking and reflection as a manager, particularly when under high time and workload pressures.

At this stage in my blogging I wanted to explore in more detail my practice and use case examples as material, drawing on what was happening in the present more specifically, both for my clients and for myself in my selection and experience of coaching interventions.

## 4. WHAT HAVE I FOUND TO BE THE BENEFITS OF BLOGGING?

**Stepping back I can see the evolution and patterns of my blogs and how they represent** a more coherent, articulation expression of my practice approach, than I would otherwise have been able to see so clearly. It feels like a release of built up experience, thoughts and feelings that I'm articulating for the first time in such a coherent way.

Through the process of thinking, researching the field and expressing myself I have found what is a grounding and confidence–building experience that better enables me to be clear about both what I bring and what I am about as a professional practitioner.

**It re–connects me to with why I got into this line of work in the first place**. It's easy to be busy, flexing myself to meet the priorities and preferences biases of the client. The most important part of that is probably what I don't say.

Blogging is helping me be truer to myself and share my perspectives more coherently in conversation with clients on issues that are important for them to take account of in order to make more informed choices. It's sharpened my intent and given me more areas to focus on and investigate in my practice. I am developing more of a researcher/practitioner mind set where I am noticing and responding to the subtle detail of the interactions and their impact more explicitly and openly. I am more confidently alert to the risks of falling into being collusive with what may be flawed and limited thinking into which the client may be drifting without awareness.

**It's helped me earth, raise my awareness and self–supervise my coaching practice and how I work:**

- Reviewing case examples – what I did and why I did it.

- I'm more consciously making choices in the moment.

- Self–supervising more explicitly and stepping up in terms of my personal reflections and review what I bring into supervision with others.

- It's helped me realise more explicitly how my whole career/life experience connects to and informs what I do. Just the process of reviewing my blogs here has made some of these patterns more visible and explicit to me.

- It's raised my awareness of my own potential bias and therefore developed my confidence and ability to step outside myself. It has pushed me to be more genuinely open to and interested in others perspectives.

## The community of tgc – seeing that my expression is part of something bigger that I value

- It's practitioner focused. In this way it is more closely related to my interests and what I do than any other forum/publication I've come across.

- Authors are experienced practitioners from a wide range of backgrounds and cultures with different perspectives to bring.

- It allows me to explore real issues, previously only discussed informally with a few close peers, as they would be deemed to be too sensitive to raise in other contexts.

- The philosophy, approach and interest of tgc is not only at the individual level, but part of the wider organisational, industry and social context. It's part of the bigger picture of organisational and social change.

- tgc sets an inclusive tone that welcomes diversity whilst recognising and raising the tough issues that coaching maybe needs to take more of a coherent position on. It also deliberately takes an independent whole–industry perspective. The nature of its structure and ownership allow for this, as it is not compromised due to vested interests or positions. As a result it is open to putting forward or representing and encouraging thoughts and ideas around the tough issues facing the coaching world (industry or profession, or both...?).

- Due to all that tgc is, I feel no restrictions on what I can explore or express, providing I can evidence my views by relating to my personal practice.

- Gaining feedback from tgc's 'blogitors' has really helped me communicate what I want to get across in a more coherent and explicit way. When writing I find I can get too close and not see the wood for the trees – and this is done in a 'light touch' way, aimed at helping me enhance and stay true to what I want to get across. A true coaching approach!

## Finally I'm finding I am really enjoying writing as a form of self–expression

- The process of expression forces me to get in touch with what I really think.

- The creative process of evolving ideas and their expression.

- Researching the field to check out what other sources of research and alternative perspectives have to bring.

In summary I really enjoy my blogging with tgc. I am finding it a powerful developmental process – both personally and professionally.

I'm really interested to hear from other bloggers about their blogging journeys. As it's such an individual process I expect there to be some diverse and different experiences of blogging. It will be fascinating to see what patterns emerge, particularly around the learning experience of blogging.

So, a call to fellow tgc bloggers to share your experiences of blogging and how you notice the subtle ways it evolves for and with you!

# Using a research approach to learn from coaching experience? My learning about (coaching) readiness as an example

*Jeremy Ridge*

**M**y **own experience** has been a powerful source of learning about coaching. However, I also benefitted from a rigorous 'research' approach to really gain a sense of my experience. I think more value could be made of this sort of approach.

The term 'reflection' is often used as a way to learn further from experience; I think it is possible to go further with the sort of rigour that research can introduce to this process of reflection.

I will start with some perspectives I have found on the issues involved in learning about coaching. It is a complex subject.

I will also consider approaches to research, which can vary widely; especially when researching the nature of human experience.

I also offer an example from my practice records of how I used a more research approach. I have chosen an example from one key aspect – my understanding of (coaching) readiness (as it is often termed, currently.) This also helped me see how coaching outputs can be recognised more clearly at the immediate time of the coaching process.

PART 4: Expanding the frontiers of knowledge through each practitioner's practice

## THE SORT OF CHALLENGES THERE ARE FOR LEARNING IN COACHING

The emergence of coaching has brought with it a desire to work out, and agree, exactly what it is. Research is often a means of finding this sort of agreement, especially when results can be reproduced independently, by others, for example.

Organisations have sprung up recently with an attempt to provide this 'agreed picture' of what is involved in coaching. This has resulted in various approaches to credentialing, or accreditation, and then the additional processes of training that can follow – all conforming idealistically to various 'defined models'. The origin and validity of these models can often seem still more invention than a researched process – by some of the appropriate standards of research that is! These 'models' can be very open to widely differing interpretation, in practice.

What I have always found ironic is how coaching began because of the potential inefficiencies of much training in many subjects in which the same  message is shared to a large audience – and thus there is a lack of attention needed to be given to different individual learning needs based on their specific knowledge relevant to the issues. Coaching is now often besieged by the requirement for more of this training! Yet training may not always be the most efficient form of learning.

## HOW DO PEOPLE LEARN – THE IMPORTANCE OF EXPERIENCE

An example from 'executive coaching' can well illustrate some of the research into how people learn – as reported by the 'learners' themselves. This research, the 70/20/10 findings I share below, introduces some important appreciation of how experience was important to the way that executives/managers themselves reported they learned. After all, helping managers learn is the central focus of executive coaching.

Importantly, formal organisations can often provide access to important data on adult learning than the more open social systems we live within; and which can also be seen as a form of (social) organisation.

## How we learn – the 70/20/10 rule

The 70/20/10 model introduces some key perspectives on research into how managers learn.

Morgan McCall and his colleagues working at the Center for Creative Leadership (CCL) are usually credited with originating the 70:20:10 ratio[1].

Based on a survey asking nearly two–hundred executives to self–report how they believed they learned, McCall, Lombardo and Eichinger's surmised that:

Lessons learned by successful and effective managers are roughly:

- 70 percent from challenging assignments.

- 20 percent from developmental relationships.

- 10 percent from coursework and training.

> *This is rather like saying – in coaching I learn most*
> *from working with my clients!*

It is very difficult to model real people in any research, or training model. (I have worked with some very good actors, however. But the real intimacy of the context is never quite there.)

This leads to the issue about the complex nature of the knowledge required to know what I am doing in any coaching.

## The importance of knowledge for informing learning

Learning leads us towards inquiry into the nature of knowledge, and how it can inform learning.

An example of this, which I find highlights a simple and dramatic perspective about just what is involved, has been best expressed as far back as 1853! Auguste Comte is largely accepted as having tried to bring these links about science and the study of more complex worlds such

---

[1] Michael Lombardo and Robert Eichinger. *The Career Architect Development Planner* (1st ed.). Minneapolis: Lominger. (1996)

as our 'social' world together, such as introducing the idea of 'sociology'. He also has a reputation of bringing these big questions into real focus for consideration back at that time. For example, his writings started another huge form of enquiry by bringing, what is often referred to as 'positivism', an approach that enables research to be important as a basis for real knowledge.

### Comte's 3 stages of forming human knowledge and understanding[2]:

*"From the study of the development of human intelligence, in all directions, and through all times, the discovery arises of a great fundamental law, to which it is necessarily subject, and which has a solid foundation of proof, both in the facts of our organization and in our historical experience.*

***The law is this: that each of our leading conceptions — each branch of our knowledge — passes successively through three different theoretical conditions: the theological, or fictitious; the metaphysical, or abstract; and the scientific, or positive.***

*In other words, the human mind, by its nature, employs in its progress three methods of philosophizing, the character of which is essentially different, and even radically opposed: namely, the theological method, the metaphysical, and the positive. Hence arise three philosophies, or general systems of conceptions on the aggregate of phenomena, each of which excludes the others. The first is the necessary point of departure of the human understanding, and the third is its fixed and definitive state. The second is merely a state of transition."*

I also often use the term 'generalisations' as another term for the metaphysical/abstract. And this often explains the difficulties I find with so many of the frameworks and models around the coaching world.

Study of these generalisations (– such as even Comte's generalisations!)

---

[2] Auguste Comte, *Cours de philosophie positive*. (1/6) kindle; Harriet Martineau and condensed to form *The Positive Philosophy of Auguste Comte* (1853)

can indeed help to progress learning. But this may be a very personal matter – which frameworks appeal to each of us in making more sense of any data – may depend on just what any person's particular experience consists of.

Comte's generalisations helped me organise a lot of my experience and make sense of it. Whether it creates sense of itself is a different matter. The experience has to be there for the framework to bring sense and meaning.

For example, I get some form of learning when I come across ways that others have sometimes explained things, in a way that allows me to make sense of the data/perspectives my experience has been accumulating, but which haven't been linked together before.

## HOW CAN RESEARCH FORM A BASIS FOR KNOWLEDGE AND LEARNING IN COACHING?

Sometimes matters are still too complex for traditional methods of research, especially as a basis for valid knowledge of the best standard. Coaching is still in this zone. Events between even two people, in a private room, in coaching, can defy traditional approaches to research and in establishing what happened and why in a way that is reproducible by others.

One of the difficulties about the most rigorous forms of research is how it may be limited to what can be measured, in a way that will lead to numbers and statistics – the currently popular basis for real measurement in science. However there is a reality that can be important, but which can't be measured, yet, by conventional research. Experience, then, may be the only approach to research that is *really* possible.

Research takes many forms, and many more forms are evolving to overcome those limitations. There is also the matter of quantitative and qualitative approaches to research, as it is currently seen (e.g. http://chronicle.umbmentoring.org/on-methods-whats-the-difference-between-qualitative-and-qualitative-approaches).

PART 4: Expanding the frontiers of knowledge through each practitioner's practice

What I'd like to share is a number of typical and important features of research that have been useful to my learning:

a. **The assumption of cause and effect:**
What is critical is considering the possibility of finding out what is going on from the information that can be available. This then enables the testing, and learning, about what is the sequence of causes and events in any interaction.

Much debate continues about this as many events are still so complex that we lack any robust methodology to identify exactly what is happening. Interactions between two people, such as in coaching, are an example of this complexity.

b. **Experience as a form of 'data':**
Experience is a source of information, or data, that can inform this complexity. However, human experience can be subject to quite limited perception, as well as massive complexity. It is a challenge to recognise our possible internal biases that may be due to limitations in our perception.

Each person is a completely different set of variables, or underlying influences, that can come to bear on any interaction. Then you add in the rituals and processes of 'social behaviour' – where the data you get from another person can be difficult to judge – we are all fantastic actors – it is what we have learned and been taught after all.

c. **Using behaviour as the data about events:**
Typically we are also limited to behaviour as a form of data. This may also be a very inexact understanding of the detailed causes and events taking place. However, my experience began to find there are predictable patterns for how behaviour in coaching can make an important difference.

d. **The coach's behaviour in a cause/effect sequence with the coachee's behaviour:**
The challenge is to know one's own behaviour, as well as appreciate how it may be perceived rather than intended.

e. **Even though difficult, I have found it useful to make a start with some basics of research[3]:**

- Keeping records on the experience process, data analysis and variability encountered.

- Keeping records in a systematic way.

- Involving colleagues, and participants, where possible, in design and data analysis.

- Being upfront about my own assumptions, underlying beliefs and values that I may be introducing.

## RESEARCHING 'READINESS' FROM MY EXPERIENCE:

I have chosen readiness as an example as it is at the heart of the cause/effect question. Taking one of my definitions of Coaching as:

*"What can a coach do to create the conditions that enable a coachee to find more and more effective ways to explore their own learning."*

This sets out, in research language, my hypothesis of what I'm choosing to test, observe and adapt accordingly during these types of interactions.

And this is outlined as a pattern of the typical sequence of behaviours that I was finding (see Table on following page).

The key issue is to learn what behaviours may have a pattern in creating more effective conditions.

I have adopted this more currently popular term – readiness – because of the way it is often used to portray the potential for appropriate conditions. However, in many current coaching publications readiness is often defined as a condition independent of the coach and what they do.

---

[3] [website] zimmer.csufresno.edu/~donnah/**Research%20Paradigms**.ppt

**PART 4: Expanding the frontiers of knowledge through each practitioner's practice**

Table of the typical sequence of behaviours I found:

| 1. Early seconds: | **Watch to establish initial comfort** ... some general introductions |
|---|---|
| 2. First minute: | **Start with a fairly neutral/safe subject** ... get people comfortable with expressing their open thoughts |
| 3. Initial minutes: | **Show listening that gets noticed – play back their words** ... learn to use, and acknowledge their words and meanings |
| 4. Still initial stages: | **Testing where the energy is** ... tell tale signs of where their real energy is lurking |
| 5. Establish trust: | **Watch for signals of confidence in this process** ... Earning trust |
| 6. Bring Myself in: | **Offer my own perspective...** at a right level |
| 7. Move to an agenda: | **Agreeing the dimensions of dialogue** ... depending on the learning – self efficacy of the person concerned – learning capability and awareness around this |
| 8. Set the programme: | **How to work through the agenda** ... which way/to what extent of what they are up for |
| (In practice, this may entail some form of checking out of their style preference for example – open or structured ...etc. ... using 360 or other profiling instruments – these have to be very carefully used as well) | |
| 9. Continuous checking: | **Even going back** ... occasionally to other preparation as before |
| 10. Conclusion: | **Discuss and agree the positive outcome** ... to establish as appropriate for this cycle |

### Notes of patterns that emerged from my research that impacted my coaching behaviours

My learning was taking me down a road that what the coach does can have a dramatic influence on readiness. In particular, I was growing a view that readiness was something that could be influenced, but I was still trying to put together the 'evidence' among the patterns of cause and effect of what was involved. I have selected some of the notes I have in my own learning journey, at a stage which was exploring this disconnect about appreciating how to 'impact – stimulate – create' readiness.

## LEARNING FROM OTHER PEOPLES' RESEARCH.

I realised I was changing my behaviour – but was not sure why – or what was causing these changes at different parts along the whole cause effect chain involved. More formal research summarised extensively by Carkhuff[4], in particular, provided me with a missing framework. It provided a powerful understanding of how readiness goes through particular sequences in the other person. This framework, see Table on following page, uses the term *"self exploration"* as another term for my 'readiness'.

Readiness, (or self–exploration, as used here) is an essential basis for considering the output, or results, of any coaching, rather than too much focus on coaching inputs. It is important to know in every moment what progress is or what valuable outputs are.

The Carkhuff framework summarises five stages of how readiness builds. And critically how it builds in response to helper/coach behaviour. The critical behaviours by the coach are:

- Respect,

- Empathy,

- Genuineness,

- Self–disclosure,

- Specificity,

- Immediacy, and

- Confrontation.

The framework is especially important for identifying the significant impact of some of these forms of behaviour (Respect/Empathy/ Genuineness/Self–disclosure) during typical earlier stages of any coaching process. When, and only when, confidence is established,

---

[4] [website] http://carkhuff.com/body–of–work/

**PART 4: Expanding the frontiers of knowledge through each practitioner's practice**

through these behaviours by the coach, can the more action oriented coach behaviours then become appropriate (Specificity/Immediacy and Confrontation).

A summary of the OUTPUT framework[5] to use in working with readiness:

---

### HELPEE SELF–EXPLORATION IN INTERPERSONAL PROCESSES: A SCALE FOR MEASUREMENT

**Level 1 No signs**

The other person does not discuss personally relevant material. They avoid any indication of self–descriptions or self–exploration or direct expression of feelings that would lead them to reveal themselves in the dialogue.

**Level 2 Little sign**

The other person may respond with discussion to the introduction or personally relevant material in a mechanical manner and without the demonstration of feelings. They simply discusses the material without exploring the significance or the meaning of the material or attempting further exploration of their feeling in response to any effort to uncover related feelings or material.

**Level 3 Some sign**

The other person starts to voluntarily introduce personally relevant material but still in a cautious and mechanical manner and without the demonstration of feeling. This material is given without spontaneity or emotional proximity, and without any indication of willingness to inward probing to discover new feeling and experiences in relation to it.

**Level 4 Starting**

The other person introduces personally relevant discussions with spontaneity and emotional proximity but without indication of establishing focus toward inward probing to discover new feelings and experiences. The voice quality and other characteristics are very much "with" the feelings and other personal materials that are being verbalized.

**Level 5 Spontaneous**

The other person actively and spontaneously engages in sharing openly their own inward probing to discover new feelings and experiences, and their interpretations, about themselves and their world. In summary, the second person is fully and actively focusing upon and exploring themselves and their world.

---

[5] ditto

This research is important as it helps to establish a 'diagnostic' framework for what coach behaviour is most important at any time.

It is also important to recognise that 'readiness' to effectively work with another person only really starts at level 3. There is a great deal that can, and needs to, be done to get to this level – before progressing to straight forward 'problem solving' mode. And this can vary with each person; as well as vary within the same person from moment to moment.

Readiness can be strongly influenced by the behaviour of the coach.

## CONCLUSIONS

I have outlined how I have found various ideas associated with the idea of research to make more sense of my experience, which has enhanced my own learning about coaching. In particular, the way of making sense of outputs, or important progress, in the coaching and in the immediate moment – not just as a result of actions after the coaching.

This short commentary still opens up many further questions. But, for me, it has been an important basis for continuing to develop my Practice in Coaching:

1.  **On generalisations!** To the reader, here, the terms are obviously similar to 'generalisations' because there is a lack of definition for them to be easily reproduced exactly by others. However the real value is the meaning they have for myself, which is extensive and detailed in my own awareness.

2.  **Intuition:** I suspect we all do this more than we often 'report'. It is like learning to ride a bicycle. A great deal is 'intuitive' – but it is there to be reported should we practice reporting more. This can then accelerate the learning.

3.  **Other research:** There is a great deal of other relevant research material that can be related to these ideas. Research in all of the social sciences has grown massively in recent decades. However we still need to work on integrating these – for example the research of mainstream psychology and how it does or doesn't link with psychotherapy/counselling.

PART 4: Expanding the frontiers of knowledge through each practitioner's practice

4. **Terms that mean something in particular to each coach:** I often find coaches build their own terminology that means something special for them as they build their understanding of events in coaching. This is important. The emphasis on finding 'one model' that says it all for everyone may be a long time coming.

5. **There is obviously much more to be explored** behind the outlines in this piece. This blog is more an outline of an agenda, rather than as much as could be further researched behind the summary of ideas here.

Exploring further ways to fulfil coaching's potential is important for me. It is my experience of the wider field, as well as my coaching practice, which continues to suggest where these opportunities are most important, as expressed here.

If you also consider there is more that can be done, then how about sharing some of your 'research', and outline your own experience of practice in coaching?

# Blogging as a form of practitioner research – meaningful, personal and professional development in coaching

*Yvonne Thackray*

Encouraging coaches to blog about their practice both broadens and deepens the quality of content that is currently shared. Writing requires us to expend energy describing and giving attention to all that is happening and going on during a coaching session. Talking in the moment allows us to recreate and focus on what's important to the other. It makes use of all the cues (consciously or unconsciously observed) that are normally harder to articulate and write intimately about. It requires conscious thinking, sense–making and re–engaging with a skill that we use less frequently. Importantly, this *really* starts when we are able to express what's actually happening in our own words, in order to bring out that ambition of being the best coach we each can be!

The good coach intends to bring together the personal, commercial and academic reasons for blogging because:

- We want to engage with other like–minded professionals who practice coaching (formally and informally). They are the leading edge practitioners who are continually developing new knowledge in our field (the commercial/the market).

- Altogether we can demonstrate a level of rigor and apply the more attainable and positive strengths of learning that can be found in more traditional institutions as forms of practitioner research (academic).

- And, importantly, we can make it an enjoyable, even fun, learning and developmental experience for and amongst the diverse practitioners (social/community)!

*"Oh my gosh! There are benefits??? I would say blogging is like going to the dentist, like washing your bed lines, and like getting on the scale. All necessary for good health and hygiene but bloody uncomfortable!!!"*

## BACKGROUND

The purpose for blogging is shifting in the current technological landscape. At the start, it was a marketing/advertising piece for companies to encourage potential clients/customers and a gateway into their real services. For individuals, it was a personal way to share and log what's happening and what's important to them. It has morphed into both a means of self–help and a critical review of everyday items through to the most esoteric subjects that attract an audience.

For both commercial and academic blogging, it increases the blogger and/or organisation to greater public scrutiny and criticism whilst enhancing their status.

Fast forwarding to 2016, it seems that every type of organisation is dabbling in or focusing their efforts on writing some form of blog because it's another way that they can use to connect, when the conditions have been met, and engage in a two–way dialogue that provides access to audiences beyond the normal groups the organisations tend to focus on.

**For commercial organisations,** blogging is part of their strategy to connect directly with the customers and learn what's working or not working. In essence, the customers are being directly engaged to participate in the design process and standard engagement of the product process. According to Mark Shaefer from *{Grow} (Social Media Explained)* – the top 5 categories for what's defined as 'the best big company blogs in the world[1]':

- Quality of content (is it interesting, creative, well–written, human?).

- Consistency of publishing.

- Engagement with audience.

- Social sharing activity.

- Alignment with corporate objectives.

**For academic organisations,** blogging is described as 'conversational scholarship'. It is an alternative means to find a more engaging style of writing to connect with a wider and more diverse audience[2].

Following Debra Lupton's and Eszter Hargittai's research on academic blogging[3],[4], there are five key reasons for academics to blog:

- It is argued that the practice forces academics to think about their research and writing in new ways, bearing in mind the multiplicity of potential audiences and the ways readers can respond to the material presented (Kitchin 2014, Kitchin et al. 2013).

- Some bloggers use their writing as a way of developing ideas and seeking engagement with others before they formalise their ideas into a more traditional academic piece (Adema 2013, Carrigan 2013, Daniels 2013, Estes 2012, Gregg 2006, Maitzen 2012).

- This use of social media for developing scholarly writing and ideas has been described as being an 'open source academic' (Carrigan 2013).

---

[1] [website] http://www.businessesgrow.com/2015/01/12/best–company–blogs/

[2] Melissa Gregg. "Feeling ordinary: blogging as conversational scholarship." In:*Continuum*, 20 (2), (2006) pp 147–160.

[3] [website] https://simplysociology.wordpress.com/2014/01/13/research-on-academic-blogging-what-does-it-reveal/

[4] [website] http://crookedtimber.org/2004/11/18/the-academic-contributions-of-blogging/

**PART 4: Expanding the frontiers of knowledge through each practitioner's practice**

- The mechanisms for exchange and feedback on some blogs are akin to the formal review process at some journals, and, to the extent these mechanisms differ, one is not necessarily superior to the other.

- Blog posts are now often cited in more traditional academic forums; some scholarly journals are incorporating blogs, multimedia or open access repositories as part of their online presence. Meanwhile, academic presses are experimenting with new digital modes of publication, including shorter online book formats with faster than usual turn–around times between acceptance of the manuscript and publication.

> *"Blogs that allow comments make it possible for others to discuss the posted material... Not only is the original post available to all subsequent readers but so are the reactions of others. Sure, there are all sorts of limitations present. It may be that the most appropriate people are not reading the post and so those who would be able to offer the most helpful and relevant critique are not present in the discussion. But this is often likely true in the journal refereeing process as well."*

— Eszter Hargittai (2004)

## THE GOOD COACH'S APPROACH TO BLOGGING

Blogging can provide the means to offer the blogger–practitioner an honest and humble sharing of what's important to them. This is because the blog can also be very experiential and personal to the writer. In this way it differs from other forms of published material such as articles, journals, reports, papers etc.

- It's a space for the blogger–practitioner to reflect, ground, integrate and share aspects, opinions and views of their practice.

- Blogging offers insights to the reader of the blogger–practitioner that might stimulate their thoughts, compare their own approach with, or learn more of the practice and increase their understanding of working with healthy individuals.

It also fills a gap as it attempts to readdress the balance between technical (scientific) and practitioner knowledge. Eraut (1994) suggests that "*the dominant conception of learning is our culture – so dominant that children have been socialised into it by the age of 7 or 8 – is that learning involves the explicit acquisition of externalised codified knowledge[5]. [And when] people are so accustomed to using the word 'knowledge' to refer only to 'book knowledge' which is publically available in codified form, that they have developed only limited awareness of the nature and extent of their personal knowledge[6].*"

This means that without realising it, we unconsciously hold technical knowledge, what Eraut refers to as externalised codified knowledge, as having a higher status than practitioner knowledge because it is implicit and less understood.

Accessing this implicit knowledge holds the premise that during the process of coaching, learning takes place. What works in one context may not work in another context. Therefore further learning needs to take place because each recipient behaves differently. Observing what happens during coaching is never the same for the individuals participating in the coaching. The individual see it from within the action – that moment by moment behavioural responses (verbally and non–verbally) – during the coaching conversation.

Bridging and raising the status of practitioner knowledge begins with practitioners sharing their experiences in their own words – both what works for them and their limitations. Together they build both the knowledge base and rigor of reporting through blogging. Furthermore this,

- Allows the blogger–practitioner to develop further rigor in their practice and contribute towards the practitioner knowledge base and towards standards of practice, and

- Gives the reader another way to connect to the blogger–practitioner and get to know them: this does require the writer to carefully balance their professional and personal persona on the digital platform.

---

[5] Michael Eraut. *Developing Professional Knowledge and Competence* (Routledge, 1994) pg 35
[6] ditto *pg 29*

**PART 4: Expanding the frontiers of knowledge through each practitioner's practice**

This doesn't mean that 'trolling' or 'backlash' doesn't happen because others will have a differing opinion. This becomes about managing inappropriate comments (i.e. directly attacking the individual) vs. negative comments or critiques that are based on the arguments presented in the blog and that create a safe space for positive interactions and engagement to take place.

We also asked our practitioner-bloggers what they saw as their top three benefits of blogging, and we share some of their responses below:

—----------

*1. I feel passionate about bringing the effectiveness of coaching practice forwards. It has enabled me to say things that have, for some strange reason, been avoided elsewhere but which are central to the practice of coaching.*
*2. It's enabled me to relax about being academically comprehensive in putting a point up.*
*3. It's enabled me to give voice what was previously intuitive. The nature of the perspective, not just the external facing. It's important to share views.*

—----------

*1. For my style of blogging it is an opportunity to combine it as a time for reflection of what's happened so far and applying to something that relates back to coaching. It's a reflective space to help others. Reflections that apply to their context, and for me to try to find relevance.*
*2. It's getting that distance and taking that time to externalise from the day to day to write something in a blog format. It forces me to organise my thoughts.*
*3. Sharing and knowing that it might inspire someone else. It's got to be actionable by the reader, not simply academic.*

—----------

*1. Taking time out to reflect on themes currently relevant to my practice and that I have a keen interest in. Also the process of tuning in to what I want to say and working through the creative process of crafting its expression.*

*2. Stimulating a more focussed observing. Noticing a 'researcher and writer' mindset. This adds to my sense of being a more detached professional and it gives me a sense of satisfaction from feeling part of and contributing to something bigger than just my own personal practice.*

*3. Enjoyment of expression and finding my voice. Obtaining feedback.*

———----------

*__One__ is putting my thoughts in order. I often have ideas about things that appear pretty self–evident to me, but don't always put them into a coherent pattern that other people (might) understand as distinct from them living a full and independent life in my head. __Two__ is having some constructive feedback. It's easy either to assume that one's conception of an issue is black or white. You're wrong or you're right. The truth is often a shade of grey. So bouncing the ideas off somebody else can help clarify where the ideas of real value are and where the argument is weak. One finds out more about what particular shade of grey it is rather than thinking 'I'm an unappreciated genius' or 'I'm an idiot'. __Three__ is having an editor. It's easy, as in two, to see everything as good or bad and thus to miss elements that are actually essential and need emphasis, similarly, it's easy to fall in love with a prose style or a felicitous expression (like that) and lose impact.*

———----------

*1. The discipline of thinking with rigour.*
*2. The search for some clarity in communication.*
*3. The thrill of getting something out there.*

*Things I find difficult with blogs:*
*4. They are everywhere.*
*5. Inability to discern between advertorial and insight.*

**PART 4: Expanding the frontiers of knowledge through each practitioner's practice**

—----------

1. *Consolidate my learning and insights.*
2. *Sharing and contributing to the community.*
3. *Personal brand building.*

—----------

1. *Sitting down to write something spurs my creativity. I ask myself 'What do I think is interesting these days?'*
2. *It also leads me to develop the ideas further for myself, and ....*
3. *For any others who choose to engage with me on the topic. While I have only barely dipped my toe in the water of blogging so far, I look forward to having more interaction with others in the future.*

—----------

1. *The very act of writing down my thoughts on coaching, and other topics that I am passionate about, is good fun. I enjoy both the output and the journey that the writing represents. Both are useful, and often the posted blog is not the final destination of the thinking.*
2. *I like the idea that I can share my thoughts with others and get interesting and useful feedback from them.*
3. *For a long time I did not think I had a lot to say, so if you like, blogging is a forum in which I am finding my voice. It may be a form of self actualisation, and becoming visible in the world. That may sound very grand, but I am writing as much for myself as any reader. These are my thoughts. I've synthesised that and I own them. The reader can choose whether to agree or not, to comment or not. My choice is to blog and it is really good to have a choice.*

—----------

We're part of a community that's adopting available technology and adapting common approaches to sharing, exchanging and engaging in coaching practitioner knowledge. In our way, and in our own words, the real benefits of blogging further include increasing both our confidence and articulation of why we do what we do – are you interested in participating?

**PART 4: Expanding the frontiers of knowledge through each practitioner's practice**

Finally, here are some other thoughts to consider:

- Being validated amongst your peers and key influencers in your network, and being able to draw relevant disciples to your practice – how might that support you and the field of coaching in raising the standard of practice and available practitioner knowledge?

- Imagine writing between six and twelve blogs, where each blog varies between 1000 and 2000 words, over one or two years on the good coach – you'll have written the equivalent of a master's dissertation! Or perhaps even a short book of your professional practice. Firstly congratulations! And secondly, how might you celebrate that?

PART 4: Expanding the frontiers of knowledge through each practitioner's practice

## Epilogue

Our approach is not to rush to a 'final solution'; rather we're more interested in finding those patterns that may eventually lead to similarities that have evolved from the realities of the diverse practice that already exists. We hope that after reading our book - whether it's in your private space sitting in your favourite seat, or discussing with peers as part of a exploration or reading group, or simply with others around you – it has motivated you to start your own practitioner research through blogging.

As you've witnessed there isn't one way to do this, and so tailor your blogs to begin with what's most important to you right now in your practice, and begin exploring how you like to make sense of your coaching approach. And then, enjoy sharing your leading edges with the wider community with the support of the good coach. To begin stimulating some ideas check out the *Blogger's Guidelines* that is available to read both on the website: http://the-goodcoach.com/the-guidelines and towards the end of *Translating Coaching Codes of Practice,* or even connect with one of the blogitors at the good coach (email: blogs@the-goodcoach.com) to begin a conversation about what you'd like to take as your first step.

What we do know is this – the real knowledge lives where the leading edges of everyday practitioner practices. We just have to keep finding ways to get to it. Share with us how we can do it better.

# CONTRIBUTOR'S BIOGRAPHY

Organized alphabetically

————-----

**Aurora Aritao** is an executive coach and leadership development consultant, focused on social-emotional intelligence, positive psychology and adaptive leadership. She brings fifteen years of corporate experience to her coaching: leading global, multi-functional teams while defining, launching and growing award-winning technology solutions at companies like Microsoft and Vodafone Group. She is trained in clinical organisational psychology from INSEAD (EMCCC), which deepens her understanding of human behaviour in organisations. Her interests in change leadership, motivation, stress and emotional resilience, group/systems dynamics, diversity and individual/team productivity influence her coaching interventions. Also a certified Brain-based Coach, she facilitates workshops for the NeuroLeadership Institute.

Email: aurora.aritao@insead.edu
LinkedIn: https://hk.linkedin.com/in/auroraaritao

————-----

**Charlotte Rydlund (MBA)** is an international Fortune 500 executive turned technology entrepreneur who has been coaching and mentoring others for more than 10 years. With a passion to empower others to succeed and grow, her coaching focus has always been on enabling career transition and driving change. Trained in Executive Coaching at Columbia University, she is actively applying her coaching experience in building her venture funded business, and her multi-national team.

Email: c.rydlund@pacta.io
Website: www.pacta.io

————-----

—----------

**Doug Montgomery (PhD, APECS, ICF PCC)** is an executive coach, coach training facilitator, mentor coach and ILM coaching and mentoring tutor. Over twenty-eight years in pharmaceutical R&D at GlaxoSmithKline, he developed his leadership skills in increasingly senior roles. Doug's coach training started while at GSK and led to becoming a Director of Coaching at GSK's Coaching Centre of Excellence. After leaving GSK he set up Elmbank Coaching to fulfil his passion for coaching and supporting the personal and professional development of others, developing coaches and training leaders who want to adopt a coaching approach in their work and life.

Email: doug@elmbank-coaching.co.uk
Website: www.elmbank-coaching.co.uk

—----------

**Eamon O'Brien …**
- Believes people and teams can be quite unusually brilliant.
- Supports and challenges clients to develop their careers, be engaged and take meaning from their work, and so achieve results.
- Brings creativity, honesty, humour and energy to work. He holds a M.Sc. in People and Organisational Development, a Post Graduate Certificate in Coaching and is an APECS Accredited Coach.
- Qualified as a pharmacist and spent fifteen years in marketing and sales within the pharmaceutical industry. He developed a flair for working with individuals and teams to develop ways to improve their performance and that of their brands.

Email: eamon@crandc.co.uk
Website: www.crandc.co.uk

—----------

———-----------

**Isobel Gray (BA, MA)** has worked for over fifteen years as a coach and facilitator. Her real area of interest is around the relationship between the individual and the organisation, and the things that help and hinder the best outcomes for both. The catalyst to her writing poetry was the spontaneous flow of thoughts and feelings following the sudden death through cancer of her beloved cat about five years ago, and she has continued to write poetry on a range of themes - nature, people, relationships and organisational life. *"I find poetry as a form of expression an earthing and liberating creative process."*
Email: isobeligray@gmail.com

———-----------

**Jeremy Ridge (Dr.) (BSc Econ, MSc Applied Psychology, PhD)** has been in practice through a number of stages in providing attention to people and their development. Jeremy began with research into Organisational Behaviour (PhD); and then developed a Business/ Practice designing and leading 'Development Centres' as a key mechanism for organisational change and development, with a range of large international organisations. This work naturally lead to a wider interest in the field. Jeremy has also worked with a number of professional bodies in executive positions, for example Chair of APECS (Association of Executive Coaching and Supervision).

Email: jeremyridge@mac.com
LinkedIn: https://uk.linkedin.com/in/jeremyjohnridge

———-----------

----------

**Kim Stephenson (CPsychol, ACII, DipPFS)** is a practicing coach, psychologist, author and public speaker. From over a decade in finance, he became interested in people's thoughts, feelings and decisions about money. This led to a portfolio of mainstream business psychology, neuroscience, coaching, writing and speaking, and a particular focus on financial decisions made by individuals, teams and organisations. He's worked with many professions as board member or consultant (notably accountants, auditors, psychologists and financial advisors) and is a regular contributor to the media. He's authored two books on personal finance and is currently working to improve standards of financial education.

Email: kim@stephenson-consulting.co.uk
Website: www.tamingthepound.com

----------

**Laura Bradshaw-Heap (MSc, MA)** is a freelance curator, arts practitioner and researcher. She works within in the contemporary craft discipline. Contemporary jewellery can be a research led or a practice based genre, depending on the individual's focuses and interests. Check out her most recent collaborative project: https://www.rubbishtogold.com

Website: https://laurabradshawheap.wordpress.com
Twitter: LBradshawHeap
Instagram: https://www.instagram.com/laurabradshawheap/
Academia: https://ucl.academia.edu/LauraBradshawHeap
LinkedIn: https://uk.linkedin.com/in/laura-bradshaw-heap-36896214

----------

—----------

**Laurent Terseur (M2, Bi-lingual APECS, ICF ACC)** is an executive coach and a systemic team coach and facilitator. A former corporate treasurer and then a banking senior executive, he has over two decades experience in multi-cultural, highly competitive environments including Deutsche Bank, JP Morgan and Barclays. Laurent works with clients spanning across various industries and cultures, on change and leadership influence, impact and performance through increased collective intelligence. His practice integrates insights from cognitive neurosciences and systemic coaching and is informed by his extensive track record in building highly collaborative and effective teams and his multi-faceted understanding of matrix organisations.

Email: laurent.terseur@gmail.com
LinkedIn: https://fr.linkedin.com/in/laurent-terseur-8916561

—----------

**Lilian Abrams (Ph.D., MBA, APECS)** is an organizational psychologist with more than twenty years of Fortune 50 consulting experience, in all manner of organization and leadership development areas and applied research. She has been a Senior Consultant for Towers Perrin, Watson Wyatt, Nabisco, and Kaiser Permanente, and an accredited executive coach for many client organizations, including ADP, BASF, BMS, KPMG, Unilever, Warby-Parker, Sanofi, New York Presbyterian Hospital, and the FAA. As New Jersey Organization Development (NJOD) Learning Community's Education Team Chair, she facilitates learning to bridge the gap between academia and practice. She teaches, publishes, and serves, always seeking to learn and bring the right learning to the right people at the right time.

Email: labrams@abramsandassociatesllc.com
Website: www.abramsandassociatesllc.com

—----------

—----------

**Liz Pick** has been an executive coach for twenty-three years and has a special interest in the impact of wellbeing in the workplace. Her approach to coaching allows both organisations and employees to achieve sustainable improvements in productivity, by addressing the link between performance and wellbeing. By integrating  clients' need to achieve objectives with personal priorities, her clients develop resilience and wellbeing alongside competencies in their roles. Her approach has proved particularly successful in high–pressure environments and her blogs encourage coaches to question the way the address client wellbeing in their professional practice.

Email: liz.pick@performanceandwellbeing.com
Website: www.performaneandwellbeing.com

—----------

**Dr. Lucille Maddalena** is an Executive Coach, Leadership Trainer, and Consultant in Organization Development. Best known for her work supporting Senior Executives during career and business transitions, she guides the alignment of team goals with expectations by bridging interpersonal communication with practical business management. As a key part of global leadership initiatives, she has created coaching models for clients, functioning as Master Coach to identify and manage Leadership Coaches at regional sites. She has guided over 6,000 corporate executives at Fortune 100 firms to successfully advance in their careers during times of organization change.

Email: lucille@mtmcoach.com
Website: www.mtmcoach.com

—----------

———-------

**Lynne Hindmarch (MSc, MA, APECS)** is a business psychologist who works as an executive coach and coaching supervisor. Her practice also includes team building, career counselling and assessment for selection. She has over twenty years' experience of psychometric profiling, and is qualified in a wide range of assessments, which she uses to help clients increase their self-awareness. She has published articles on self doubt, self-efficacy and the use of psycometrics in coaching. Her background is in counselling, higher education, training and development in organisations, and consultancy. She is on the committee of The Psychometrics Forum.

Email: lhindmarch@obc.org.uk
Website: www.obc.org.uk

———-------

**Martina Weinberger (MBA, APECS)** is a partner at Toguna Leadership – a boutique consultancy specialising on designing and delivering bespoke leadership development interventions for the professional services world. Martina's background is in strategy consulting and marketing, she is an APECS accredited executive coach and holds an MBA from INSEAD. *"I love my work best, when I support companies and leaders in achieving their (business) objectives whilst at the same time creating kinder, more sustainable environments for themselves and others around them. Contributing towards purpose and happiness is what makes me get up in the morning."*

Email: martina.weinberger@togunaleadership.com
Website: www.togunaleadership.com

———-------

—----------

**Morton Patterson** (BA Hons, NLP Prac) is a practicing coach, business consultant and facilitator. He has over fifteen years' experience in business consulting and facilitation, and a background in IT as a former Ernst & Young advisor. Morton is gifted in his calm open manner and ability to support clients with practical strategies to grow and develop their business. He specialises in helping business owners in the UK and internationally to understand the value of their services and to package and price them confidently.

Email: morton@mortonpatterson.com
Website: http://www.mortonpatterson.com

—----------

**Nicholas Wai (ACC, MOrgCoaching, MBA)** is a corporate coach and facilitator based in Hong Kong. He has more than ten years of international corporate experience, a master qualification in organisational coaching from the University of Sydney and a MBA from London Business School, as well as an Associate Certified Coach credential from the International Coach Federation. Nicholas works with a range of clients including multi-national and local organizations, small business owners and individuals in enhancing individual and team effectiveness, as well as trains and mentor coaches the next generation of coaches in China.

Email: nick@the-goodcoach
Website: www.the-goodcoach.com

—----------

—-----------

**R Ramamurthy Krishna** brings thirty years of multi industry, multinational culture experience. A Global Professional in Human Resources, A Professional Certified Coach from International Coach Federation. He is the only Indian to be admitted to Association of Professional Executive Coaching and Supervision, United Kingdom. Krishna bring a rare flavour of neuroscience to leadership having been certified by Neuroleadership institute, Australia. An active blogger, author and speaker. He is also one of the few persons in Chennai to run his own Executive Coaching School and presently engages himself as Practicing Cognitive Transformationsist and Perspective Partner with Potential Genesis HR Services LLP.

Email: rrk@potentialgenesis.com
Website: www.potentialgenesis.com

—-----------

**Sue Young, (MSc CMC IC, MAC, APECS)** has worked for over 20 years in the UK and Europe with senior and middle levels of management as an OD Consultant, Executive Coach and Leadership Team Coach in a range of private, public sector and not-for-profit organisations. She enables greater leadership at all levels in an organisation, engaging people in organisational and cultural change. She has developed specialisms in working with High Potential individuals and groups from traditionally social disadvantaged backgrounds, helping them realise their leadership potential, and in developing coaching skills and attributes for Health professionals, and organisations' specialist internal coaches.

Email: sue.young@innovapartnership.co.uk
Website: www.innovapartnership.co.uk

—-----------

——----------

**Yvonne Thackray (MSc, MEng, APECS)** is a practicing coach, researcher, author-blogger and editor. Yvonne has almost a decade of experience in coaching coaches and other international clients, as well as supporting other professional bodies whether as a board member, volunteer, or accreditor. She founded *the good coach* and currently serves as its CEO working alongside the operational team and periodically meets with the supervisory group to check that the good coach's approach to ownership is in-line with best practices for achieving real independence. All together they are continually building towards a representative knowledge base as shared by everyday practitioners.

Email: yvonne@the-goodcoach.com
Website: www.the-goodcoach.com

——----------

# GUIDELINES TO BLOGGING

**W**e **see blogging** as a form of practitioner research, and a meaningful approach to personal and professional development in coaching. (For more details read "*Blogging as a form of practitioner research*")

Encouraging coaches to blog about their practice takes on and expands on, how blogs are currently being shared. We hope that after reading the blogs, this has inspired you to share too.

Sharing your coaching experience is a courageous act in itself. Writing expends more energy because it requires conscious thinking and sense making of what is actually happening during the process of coaching.

Importantly, blogs are individual expressions that start with one's own word in order to bring out the ambition of being the best each coach can be.

Reach out to us and let us know what you would like to blog about, or even send your blog to the blogitoral team, who will be your first point of contact (email: blogs@the-goodcoach.com).

- We will read your blogs carefully and with respect, and offer any 'light' touch support that you might require (which may be none or a little) before we all agree to publish.

- We may also suggest edits for clarity as part of the publishing process.

- We have no set rules for blog length - it's open to you to write as much (~2000 words) or as little (~500 words) as you wish.

- Once we've published your blog, you'll be informed when someone posts a comment.

- We moderate all the comments as they come in, but if you're ever worried about this, just contact us.

## TIPS FOR WRITING A BLOG

- **Context**: Coaching is a big subject ... still developing ... and everyone does it from their own way – which is why we need to recognise this and appreciate it more

- **Sharing our knowledge:** Blogging here is about sharing your own experiences, and practice, in doing coaching

- **Share your knowledge:** We invite you to share your experience for how you live it, and make sense of it

So ....

### 1. What headline(s) do you want to talk about?

Be guided to something you feel positive and strongly about what you have been doing – in what coaching is about as you see it. (Remember a lot of people are finding they have been doing what is now called coaching for quite a time, or they just see it called something else!) And where you would feel good to have had a go at explaining it in ways others could appreciate.

### 2. Why do you think that matters?

This isn't a race or a comparison exercise. It's about you and what is important to you. That is what matters – in whatever aspect it comes to you.

This is about talking about yourself – not others!

### 3. What part(s) of your experience and practice were this headline involved in?

Be detailed and expansive about how you saw what was going on, how you were involved, and how you saw things working, as well as reports from the others involved.

At the same time please be general/impersonal about the actual examples. We don't need to know the content details – for reasons of confidentiality – about the practice you are talking about.

## 4. Linking to the wider languages/disciplines

Making sense may involve expressing yourself, in your own words, and also offering some linkages to some of the current popular words you have come across to use in referring to what you are talking about.

We are still building common language/agreed terms and there is still important diversity in how people feel it is best to refer to this multifaceted area of coaching practice.

## 5. What are some possible further steps / questions that could be useful for others to consider for themselves in what you have been talking about

Blogs are short summaries – not long detailed research reports, so there is a license to say more and say it more freely.

We are celebrating your experiences in a blog, rather than fitting in with what someone else says was the right thing to do.

It's about what you believe works for you in working with coaching with others.

## FINALLY...

- **Have fun whilst you write** – start anywhere and just write, and if there is an image/video clip/quote that helps make your point add it. There is always time to go back and edit. For now, just go with the flow of writing.

- **Be comfortable with your style** – it's not about conformity, it's about diversity and the freedom to express your experiences of coaching in your own style and approach.

- **More than just writing** – explore all the creative ways that you'd like to share your knowledge whether as a passage of writing, a paragraph of text with some bullet points, or as a poem. Enjoy the experience, and you're readers will too.

- **We've got you** – if you don't feel like your blog reads well, whether it's around the flow of the blog or being grammatically correct, don't worry. We are here to provide that 'light' touch and support.

## Our position around copyright

Following the UK Copyright Law (who are members of the Berne Convention for the Protection of Literary and Artistic Works) any leading practitioner (author) who publishes their blog through the good coach (automatically) owns the copyright of their specific piece of work. The author, to their best of their abilities, has checked that any referenced materials are fair use, appropriately referenced, fact-checked, and where necessary seeked the necessary permission for use.

Under the Creative Commons Attribution 4.0 International license the author (licensors) gives the good coach permission to distribute, remix, tweak and build upon your work, even commercially, as long as the good coach credits you for the original creation.

# BIBLIOGRAPHY & REFERENCES

Allen Tough. *The Adult's Learning Projects.* (Toronto: OISE, 1971)

Amy J.C. Cuddy, Matthew Kohut and John Neffinger. "Connect, Then Lead." In: *Harvard Business Review.* (2013)

Andrew Buckley. "The mental health boundary in relationship to coaching and other activities". In: *International Journal of Evidence Based Coaching and Mentoring Special Issue.* Summer. (2007)

Anita Williams Wooley, Ishani Aggarwal and Thomas W. Malone. "Collective Intelligence in Teams and Organizations", in *Collective Intelligence Handbook.* Can be found at: http://cci.mit.edu/CIchapterlinks.html (MIT Press, 2016)

Anita Williams Wooley. "Evidence for a collective intelligence factor in the performance of human groups", in *SCIENCE magazine.* Vol. 330 (2010)

Auguste Comte, *Cours de philosophie positive.* (1/6) kindle; Harriet Martineau and condensed to form *The Positive Philosophy of Auguste Comte* (1853)

"CIPD Research Report: Creating an Engaged Workforce", from: *CIPD.* (January 2010)

"CIPD Employee Outlook survey", from *CIPD.* (Autumn 2014)

"CIPD Employee Outlook survey", from *CIPD.* (Summer 2014)

David Dinwoodie, William Posmore, Laura Quinn, and Ron Rabin. "Navigating Change: A Leader's Role." In: *CCL White Paper* (2015)

David Kolb. *Experiential Learning: Experience As The Source Of Learning And Development.* (Pearson Education Ltd., 1984)

David MacLeod and Nita Clarke. "Engaging for Success: enhancing performance through employee engagement. A report to government." (2012)

David Rock. "Managing with the Brain in Mind." In: *Strategy+Business.* (2009)

David Rock and Christine Cox. "SCARF® in 2012: updating the social neuroscience of collaborating with others." In: *NeuroLeadership Journal.* (2012)

Deryck Stec. "The personification of an object and the emergence of coaching," in *Journal of Management History*, 18(3), (2012) 331-358.

Deryck Stec. "Using history to comprehend the currency of a passionate profession," in *Journal of Management History*, 18(4), (2012)

Evian Gordon. *Integrative Neuroscience: Bringing together biological, psychological and clinical models of the human brain.* (Singapore: Harwood Academic Publishers, 2000)

George T. Doran. "There's a SMART Way to Write Management Goals and Objectives", in *Management Review.* (AMA Forum, November 1981) 35-36

Gerd Gigerenzer. *Risk Savvy: How to make good decisions.* (2015)

Gerry Johnson and Kevin Scholes. *Exploring Corporate Strategy.* 6th Edition. (Pearson Education Ltd., 2002)

Gillie Bolton. *Reflective Practice: Writing and Professional Development.* (SAGE Publications Ltd., 2011)

Heide Estes. "Blogging and academic identity." In: *Literature Compass*, 9 (12), (2012) 974-982.

Herminia Ibarra. *Act Like a Leader, Think Like a Leader.* (Harvard Business Review Press, 2016)

Hilary Lindsay. "Adaptability: The Secret to Lifelong Learning." (PARN, 2014)

Hilary Rose and Steven Rose. *Genes, Cells and Brains: The Promethean Promises of the New Biology.* (Verso Publishing, 2014)

International Coach Federation. "Executive Summary: 2013 ICF Organizational Coaching Study." (ICF, 2013)

Internal Coaching Group. "What is the role of APECS in supporting and promoting Best Practice in Internal Coaching APECS 4th Annual Symposium." Retrieved from: www.apecssymposium.org (2015)

Ivan Illich, John McKnight and Irving Kenneth Zola. *Disabling Professions.* (Marion Boyars Publishers Ltd., 2011)

Jack Mezirow. *Transformative Dimensions of Adult Learning.* (Jossey Bass Inc., 1991)

Janneke Adema. "Practise what you preach: Engaging in humanities research through critical praxis." In: *International Journal of Cultural Studies*, 16 (5), (2013) 491-505.

Jeffrey Pfeffer. *Power: Why Some People Have it - and others don't.* (Harper Collins, 2010)

Joanne Shaw. "'Expert Patient' - Dream or Nightmare," in *BMJ.* (2004)

John R. Katzenbach and Douglas K. Smith. "The discipline of a team", in *Harvard Business review.* (1993)

John Kotter. *Leading Change.* (Harvard Business Review Press, 1996)

Judith Underhill & Sue Young. "How CPPD can make a difference", from *2014 APECS Symposium.* Retrieved from: www.apecssymposium.org (2014)

Kate Nash. *Secrets & Big News: Enabling people to be themselves at work.* (Kate Nash Associates, 2014)

Kim Stephenson and Ann B. Hutchins. *Finance is Personal: Making your money for you in college and beyond.* (Praeger, 2015)

Lilian Abrams "ROI: Collecting Evidence of Our Success APECS 4th Annual Symposium." Retrieved from: www.apecssymposium.org (2015)

Malcolm Shepherd Knowles. *The modern practice of adult education: From pedagogy to andragogy.* (Cambridge Book Company, 1980)

Malcolm Knowles. *The adult learner: A neglected species.* (Houston: Gulf Publishing Company, 1973)

Marshall Goldsmith. *What got you here won't get you there.* (Profile Books Ltd., 2008)

Martin Seligman. *Authentic Happiness: Using the New Positive Psychology to Realise your Potential for Lasting Fulfilment.* (ATRIA, 2003)

Matthew Lieberman. *Social: Why Our Brains are Wired to Connect.* US. (Oxford University Press, 2013)

Matthew Lieberman and Naomi Eisenberger. "The pains and pleasures of social life: a social cognitive neuroscience approach." In: *NL Journal.* (2008)

Melissa Gregg. "Feeling ordinary: blogging as conversational scholarship." In: *Continuum*, 20 (2), (2006) 147-160.

Michael Eraut. *Developing Professional Knowledge and Competence* (1994)

Michael Lombardo and Robert Eichinger. *The Career Architect Development Planner.* (1st ed.). (Minneapolis: Lominger, 1996)

Michael Segalla. "How Europeans do layoff." In: *Harvard Business Review.* (2009)

Mihaly Csikszentmihalyi. *Flow: The Psychology of Happiness: The Classic work on how to achieve happiness.* (Rider, 2002)

Neil Rackham. *Spin®Selling* (McGraw-Hill, 1988)

Patrick Williams. "The Potential Perils of Personal Issues in Coaching. The Continuing Debate: Therapy or Coaching? What Every Coach Must Know!" In: *International Journal Of Coaching In Organizations.* (2003) 21-30.

Peter Block. *The Empowered Manager.* (Jossey Bass Inc., 1987)

Peter Bluckert. "The Similarities And Differences Between Coaching And Therapy." In: *Coach the Coach.* Issue 2. (Fenman, 2004)

Peter Hawkins. *Leadership Team Coaching: Developing Collective Transformational Leadership.* 2nd Edition. (Kogan Page, 2011)

Peter Scales. *Continuing Professional Development in the Lifelong learning sector.* (Open University Press, 2011)

Peter Sioterdijk. *You must change your life.* (Polity Press, 2013)

Rajashi Ghosh, Terrence E. Maltbia and Victoria J. Marsick. "Executive and Organizational Coaching: A Review of Insights Drawn From Literature to Inform HRD Practice," in *Advances in Developing Human Resources.* (2014) pp. 1-23.

Richard Pascale and Anthony Athos. *The Art of Japanese Management.* (Penguin Books Ltd., 1983)

Ridler Report. "Trends in the Use of Executive Coaching in collaboration with EMCC UK." (2013)

Ridler & Co Case Study. "The Development of Internal coaching in the Big Four Accounting Firms." (Mann, 2014)

Rob Kitchin. "Engaging publics: writing as praxis." In: *Cultural Geographies*, 21 (1), (2014) 153-157.

Rob Kitchin, Denis Linehan, Cian O'Callaghan, and Philip Lawton. "Public geographies through social media." In: *Dialogues in Human Geography*, 3 (1), (2013) 56-72

Robert B. Cialdini. *Influence: The Psychology of Persuasion.* (Harper Business. 2007)

Rohan Maitzen. "Scholarship 2.0: blogging and/as academic practice." In: *Journal of Victorian Culture*, (2012) 1-7.

Scott Keller and Colin Price. *Beyond Performance: How Great Organisations Build Ultimate Competitive Advantage.* (McKinsey & Company, 2011)

Sherpa. "Executive Coaching Survey '14: Evidence & Interaction" (Sherpa Executive Coaching, 2014)

Stephen Covey. *The 7 Habits of Highly Effective People*. (Simon and Schuster UK Ltd., 2004)

Sue Thompson and Thompson Neil. *The Critically Reflective Practitioner.* (PALGRAVE MACMILLIAN, 2008)

Tatania Bachkirova and Elaine Cox. "A Bridge Over Troubled Water: Bringing Together Coaching And Counselling." In: *The International Journal Of Mentoring And Coaching.* 2(1) July. (2004)

Terence Deal and Allan Kennedy. *Corporate Cultures.* (Perseus Book Publishing, LCC, 1982)

Thomas Peters and Robert Walterman. *In Search of Excellence: Lessons from America's Best-Run Companies.* (Harper & Row Publishers, Inc. 1982)

Tim Kasser. *The High Prices of Materialism*. (MIT Press, 2003)

Viktor E. Frankl. *Man's Search for Meaning: The classic tribute to hope from the Holocaust.* (Rider, 2004)

William Davies. *The Happiness Industry: How the Government and Big Business Sold Us Well-Being.* (Verso Books, 2015)

William James. "Chapter 11: Attention," in *The Principles of Psychology.* (Henry Holt and Company, 1890)

William H. Young (ed.) "Continuing Professional Education in Transition," in *Continuing Professional Education in Transition: Visions for the Professions and New Strategies for Lifelong Learning.* (1998)

William Ouchi. *Theory Z.* (Avon Books, 1981)

# ONLINE REFERENCES

Alan Chapman (1995-2014) "Kirkpatrick's learning and training evaluation theory"
http://www.businessballs.com/kirkpatricklearningevaluationmodel.htm

American Psychological Association, "The Road to Resilience"
http://www.apa.org/helpcenter/road-resilience.aspx

Association for Professional Executive Coaching and Supervision
www.apecs.org

Brightside, "What is reflective practice?"
http://www.brightknowledge.org/knowledge-bank/medicine-and-
healthcare/spotlight-on-medicine/what-is-reflective-practice

Carers Trust. "Key facts about carers." (2010)
http://www.carers.org/key-facts-about-carers

CBS "Couple wins $1.1M; Gives almost all of it away" (2010)
http://www.cbsnews.com/news/couple-wins-11m-gives-almost-all-of-it-away/

Charles Tidwell. "Non-Verbal Communication Modes"
http://www.andrews.edu/~tidwell/bsad560/NonVerbal.html

David E. Gray. "Journeys towards the professionalization of coaching:
dilemmas, dialogues and decisions along the global pathway." (2010)
http://www.tandfonline.com/doi/abs/10.1080/17521882.2010.550896

David C. McClelland and David H. Burnham. "Power is the Great Motivator." (2003)
https://hbr.org/2003/01/power-is-the-great-motivator

Deborah Lupton. "Research on academic blogging: what does it reveal." (2014)
https://simplysociology.wordpress.com/2014/01/13/research-on-
academic-blogging-what-does-it-reveal/

Deloitte. "New Research from Deloitte suggests that Organizations needs to tap into existing passionate workers for sustained performance improvement." (2014) http://www.prnewswire.com/news-releases/new-research-from-deloitte-suggests-that-organizations-need-to-tap-into-existing-passionate-workers-for-sustained-performance-improvement-278499361.html

Disability Rights UK. "Doing Seniority Differently." (2012) http://www.disabilityrightsuk.org/doing-seniority-differently-summary

Donnah Hardina. "Research paradigms." (2008) zimmer.csufresno.edu/~donnah/Research%20Paradigms.ppt

Doug Montgomery. "The practicalities of measuring the ROI of coaching: A reflection." (2015) http://the-goodcoach.com/tgcblog/2015/11/9/the-practicalities-of-measuring-the-roi-of-coaching-a-reflection-by-doug-montgomery-guest

Elizabeth W. Dunn, Lara B.Aknin and Michael I. Norton. "Spending Money on Others Promotes Happiness." (2008) https://www.researchgate.net/publication/5494996_Spending_Money_on_Others_Promotes_Happiness

Eric Barker. "A neuroscience researcher reveals 4 rituals that will make you happier."(2015) http://www.businessinsider.com/a-neuroscience-researcher-reveals-4-rituals-that-will-make-you-a-happier-person-20159?IR=T

Ernst & Young. "Ernst & Young's maternity coaching improves retention of talented women." (2013) https://www.gov.uk/government/uploads/system/uploads/attachment_data/file/204611/1370512_Materniity_Coaching_case_Study_1_DRAFT.pdf

Eszter Hargittai. "The academic contributions of blogging?" (2004) http://crookedtimber.org/2004/11/18/the-academic-contributions-of-blogging/

Fiona Macrae. "Key to happiness? Start with £50k a year salary, say American-scientists" (Daily Mail, 2010) http://www.dailymail.co.uk/sciencetech/article-1309649/Key-happiness-Start-50k-year-salary-say-American-scientists.html

Frederic W. Hafferty and Brian Castellani. "The Increasing Complexities of Professionalism." (2010)
http://www.personal.kent.edu/~bcastel3/6_increasing%20complexities%20of%20prof.pdf

Grace Lewis. "One in five line managers 'ineffective', according to employees." (2015)
http://www.cipd.co.uk/pm/peoplemanagement/b/weblog/archive/2015/02/20/one-in-five-line-managers-ineffective-according-to-employees.aspx

Helen Wright. "Line manager roles are key to a great workplace." (2015)
http://www.personneltoday.com/hr/line-managers-roles-are-key-to-a-great-workplace/

International Labour Organisations. "Full report: World Employment and Social Outlook: Trends 2015." (2015)
http://www.ilo.org/global/research/global-reports/weso/2015/WCMS_337069/lang--en/index.htm

ISO. "ISO/IEC 17024:2012 Conformity assessment – General requirements for bodies operating certifications of persons." (ISO, 2012)
http://www.iso.org/iso/catalogue_detail?csnumber=52993

Jessie Daniels. "From tweet to blog post to peer-reviewed article: how to be a scholar now." (2013)
http://blogs.lse.ac.uk/impactofsocialsciences/2013/09/25/how-to-be-a-scholar-daniels

Joanne Evans, Ian Macrory and Chris Randall. "Measuring National Well-being: Life in the UK, 2015." (Office for National Statistics, 2015)
http://www.ons.gov.uk/ons/dcp171766_398059.pdf

Joe Martino. "Someone asked the Dalai Lama what surprises him most, his response was mind altering." (2014)
http://www.collective-evolution.com/2014/05/25/someone-asked-the-dalai-lama-what-surprises-him-most-his-response-was-mind-altering/

Josh Bersin. "Becoming irrestible: A new model for employee engagement." (2015)
http://dupress.com/articles/employee-engagement-strategies/

Karen Wise. "What is coaching? 10 definitions." (2010)
https://karenwise.wordpress.com/2010/05/20/what-is-coaching-10-definitions/

Lew Stern. ""Interview: Research on Professional Coaching." (LPC, 2014)
http://libraryofprofessionalcoaching.com/wp-app/wp-content/uploads/2014/06/Lew-Stern-Inteview.pdf

L. Lawrence-Wilkes & A. Chapman. "Reflective Practice" (Businessballs, 2014-2015)
http://www.businessballs.com/reflective-practice.htm

Mark Carrigan. "Continuous publishing and being an open-source academic."
http://blogs.lse.ac.uk/impactofsocialsciences/2013/12/23/continuous-publishing-and-being-an-open-source-academic/ (2013)

Mark W. Schaefer. "The 10 best big company blogs in the world." (2015)
http://www.businessesgrow.com/2015/01/12/best-company-blogs/

Merriam-Webster: Dictionary and Thesaurus
http://www.merriam-webster.com

Nicholas Wai. "'Why we do what we do?' ... How to make use of this knowledge to set our new year resolution." (2014)
http://the-goodcoach.com/tgcblog/2014/12/31/why-we-do-what-we-do-how-to-make-use-of-this-knowledge-to-se.html

Nicholas Wai. "Our needs and Our behaviours." (2014)
http://the-goodcoach.com/tgcblog/2014/11/27/our-needs-and-our-behaviours-by-nicholas-wai.html

Oprah Winfrey. "The Simple, Life-Changing Question that Hardly Anyone Can Answer." (2015)
https://www.linkedin.com/pulse/simple-life-changing-question-hardly-anyone-can-answer-oprah-winfrey

Privy Council Office, Charter bodies
http://privycouncil.independent.gov.uk/royal-charters/chartered-bodies/

RADAR. "Doing Seniority Differently: A study of high fliers living with ill-health, injury or disability (Final Report)." (2010)
http://www.disabilityrightsuk.org/sites/default/files/pdf/doingsenioritydifferently.pdf

Robert R. Carkhuff. "Science in the Service of Humankind: An Annotated Body of Work."
http://carkhuff.com/body-of-work/

Robert McKinney, Michele McMahon and Peter Walsh. "Danger in the Middle: Why Midlevel Managers aren't ready to lead." (2013)
http://www.harvardbusiness.org/sites/default/files/PDF/17807_CL_MiddleManagers_White_Paper_March2013.pdf

Steelcase. "Engagement and the Global Workplace." (2016)
http://info.steelcase.com/global-employee-engagement-workplace-report

Steve Crabtree. "Worldwide, 13% of Employees are Engaged at Work." (2013)
http://www.gallup.com/poll/165269/worldwide-employees-engaged-work.aspx

Sue Young. "Helping Middle Managers Step up into their True
Organisational role."(2015)
http://the-goodcoach.com/tgcblog/2015/11/9/helping-middle-managers-
step-up-into-their-true-organisational-leadership-role-by-sue-young

Tom Atlee. The co-intelligence institute website.
http://www.co-intelligence.org.

The Co-Intelligence Institute. "Five Dimensions of Co-Intelligence."
http://www.co-intelligence.org/I-fivedimensions.html

The Columbia Coaching Certification Program, "Coach Foundations"
http://www.tc.columbia.edu/coachingcertification/index.asp?Id=Coach+F
oundations&Info=Coach+Foundations

The Economist. "The Hawthorne effect." (The Economist, 2008)
http://www.economist.com/node/12510632

The Times. "Bosses lack concern for mentally ill staff." (The Times, 31 March 2015)
 http://www.thetimes.co.uk/tto/health/mental-health/article4397453.ece

The Work Foundation. "Health at Work Policy Unit."
http://www.theworkfoundation.com/Research/Workforce-
Effectiveness/Health-Wellbeing/Health-at-work-policy-unit

WHO. "Basic Documents: Forty-eighth edition (Including amendments
adopted up to 31 December 2014)" http://apps.who.int/gb/bd/PDF/bd48/basic-
documents-48th-edition-en.pdf#page=7 (2014)

Wikipedia, Drefus model of skill acquisition.
https://en.wikipedia.org/wiki/Dreyfus_model_of_skill_acquisition

Wikipedia, GROW model.
https://en.wikipedia.org/wiki/GROW_model

Wikipedia, Neil Rackham.
https://en.wikipedia.org/wiki/Neil_Rackham

**NOTES**

**NOTES**

**NOTES**